'Drawing on a wealth of intellectual expertise and practical experience, Professor Jorma Kalela has produced a stimulating book for thinking historians. He challenges us to scrutinize professional practice and to engage in profound and possibly unsettling ways with what it means to be an historian today.'

— Hilda Kean, Director of Public History and Dean, Ruskin College, Oxford

'A timely, accessible and convincingly argued case for more attention to be given to the preparation stage of historical writing, along with a thoughtful and at times provocative discussion of the role of historians and history in the twenty-first century. I found the book to be stimulating, thought-provoking and personally useful for my own research planning.'

— Toby Butler, University of East London

Everyone has a personal connection to the past, independent of historical enquiry. So, what is the role of the historian? *Making History* argues that historians have damagingly dissociated the discipline of history from the everyday nature of history, defining their work only in scholarly terms. Exploring the relationship between history and society, Kalela makes the case for a more participatory historical research culture, in which historians take account of their role in society and the ways in which history-making as a basic social practice is present in their work.

Making History not only asks provocative questions about the role of the historian, it also provides practical guidance for students and historians on planning research projects with greater public impact. This book is vital reading for all historians, lay and professional, and will be an essential text for undergraduate and postgraduate courses on historiography and research methods.

WITHDRAWN

D1145727

Also published by Palgrave Macmillan

Peter Beck   *Presenting History: Past and Present*

Alun Munslow   *The Future of History*

John Tosh   *Why History Matters*

David Cannadine   *Making History Now and Then*

David Cannadine   *What Is History Now?*

Making History

The Historian and Uses of the Past

Jorma Kalela

© Jorma Kalela 2012

All rights reserved. No reproduction, copy or transmission of this publication may be made without written permission.

No portion of this publication may be reproduced, copied or transmitted save with written permission or in accordance with the provisions of the Copyright, Designs and Patents Act 1988, or under the terms of any licence permitting limited copying issued by the Copyright Licensing Agency, Saffron House, 6–10 Kirby Street, London EC1N 8TS.

Any person who does any unauthorized act in relation to this publication may be liable to criminal prosecution and civil claims for damages.

The author has asserted his right to be identified as the author of this work in accordance with the Copyright, Designs and Patents Act 1988.

First published 2012 by
PALGRAVE MACMILLAN

Palgrave Macmillan in the UK is an imprint of Macmillan Publishers Limited, registered in England, company number 785998, of Houndmills, Basingstoke, Hampshire RG21 6XS.

Palgrave Macmillan in the US is a division of St Martin's Press LLC, 175 Fifth Avenue, New York, NY 10010.

Palgrave Macmillan is the global academic imprint of the above companies and has companies and representatives throughout the world.

Palgrave® and Macmillan® are registered trademarks in the United States, the United Kingdom, Europe and other countries.

ISBN 978–0–230–27681–9 hardback
ISBN 978–0–230–27682–6 paperback

This book is printed on paper suitable for recycling and made from fully managed and sustained forest sources. Logging, pulping and manufacturing processes are expected to conform to the environmental regulations of the country of origin.

A catalogue record for this book is available from the British Library.

A catalog record for this book is available from the Library of Congress.

10   9   8   7   6   5   4   3   2   1
21 20 19 18 17 16 15 14 13 12

Printed and bound in Great Britain by
CPI Antony Rowe, Chippenham and Eastbourne

For Kirsti

Contents

6 The Impact of Historical Research 146

The functions of the historical profession – The role of history in society – Impact assessment by funders – The potentials of a participatory historical culture

Preface: Why History?

'Why history?' is a more fruitful question than the conventional 'What is history?' People need knowledge of the past, and everybody uses this cognition in his or her own way. Accounting for the past, or creating histories as American historian David Thelen puts it, is 'as natural a part of life as eating or breathing'.[1] Why then are there historians, too? What justifies the existence of their profession?

The origins of this book go back a long way, to my experiences outside the academic world. At the end of the 1970s, having lectured in history for some thirteen years at the University of Helsinki, I was confronted with an unfamiliar idea about history: the meaning of the past for 'ordinary people' was quite different from what it was for my profession.

The differences between scholarly and lay concepts of signifying the past were revealed to me by an assignment when working (1979–86) as the commissioned historian of the trade union of workers in the Finnish paper and pulp industry (hereafter, Paperiliitto). In a project that lasted seven years I trained more than 200 members of the union to do research in what, I had to acknowledge after some time, in their view was their own history.[2]

The questions that eventually led to this book presented themselves while I was still working at Paperiliitto and, at the same time, instructing members of certain white-collar unions. Why do so many people reject scholarly histories as irrelevant, and often even as patronizing? What is embedded in the obvious differences between lay and professional conceptions of the past? On what counts do lay views of history warrant a revision of scholarly research practices? What is the function of my own profession in society and where lies the justification for our work?

The Tea Party Movement of the 2010s, which cherishes the American Founding Fathers, highlights the challenge that is underrated by the historical profession. Scholars have not had any difficulty in showing the anachronistic nature of current interpretations of what took place two centuries ago, but that has not diminished the appeal of the views advocated. The point is that many non-academic accounts of the past are of a different order from scholarly histories, their rationale is not the knowledge conveyed. This is why academics should, as the American historian Gordon S. Wood affirms, aim 'at understanding what (the Tea Party movement) means' instead of displaying their 'contempt for the attempts of ordinary citizens to find some immediate and emotional meaning in the Revolution'.[3]

What the Tea Party Movement makes clear is that there are multiple uses of the past, and, accordingly, numerous genres of history. Wood's opinion, in turn, presents in practical terms the insight into a narrow way of thinking that gradually emerged in my mind after the Paperiliitto years, during the 1980s and 1990s. One strand of history, the discipline, has been elevated to a privileged position, with the implicit purpose of ruling over other kinds of histories.

To measure the variety of non-academic accounts against disciplinary standards has been for scholars virtually the only way of thinking about them. More importantly still, professionals have ignored the purposes and social function of non-academic histories. The reverse side of this condescending stance on history-making outside the university world has been a parochial, inward-looking scholarly self-awareness with, as will be demonstrated repeatedly in the following pages, many unfortunate, self-defeating tendencies.

What ensued from this criticism was, initially, an effort to identify and discuss the weaknesses in disciplinary ways of thinking about the social and cultural context where historians work. This reassessment of historical research resulted in the predecessor of this volume, a textbook discussing the traditional theoretical and methodological questions in the field. This was published in 2000 and has become a standard text in Finland.[4] The message of the book is that the conventional mode of reflecting on the historian's theoretical and methodological issues has been restricted. Scholars have turned a blind eye to several aspects of research work which are of great practical consequence when a specialist on the past reflects upon the societal aspects of his or her study.

The relationship between historical enquiry and history-in-society dominates the present book too, but with the emphasis on the other end of the equation. What is reasonable to expect from the specialists, and in which ways should they redeem the trust many of their contemporaries place in them? These are questions to which the profession has not paid the attention that is any way near what the future historian has the right to expect during his or her period of training.

The implied angle from which to look at the craft leads also to more fundamental queries. What lies behind the various uses of the past? What is history for, in general? How should professionals react to laypeople who create histories? It turns out that history-making is a much more complicated matter than just the disciplinary practices of which historians willingly talk – not to mention the idea of some postmodernist thinkers according to which history is the historians' invention. History-making is an everyday practice: people continue to make use of their experiences in all sorts of ways.

My hope is that members of any society will accept, as the British historian John Tosh has recently emphasized, history by its nature as the citizens' resource.[5] As regards my fellow historians, my wish is that they take on a more balanced way of thinking and greater self-awareness. The foundation for the new perspective needed has been well encapsulated by the philosopher David Carr, whose position served as the motto for my 2000 book. Carr wondered why his colleagues were blinded by an all-embracing scholarly pattern of thinking, in a way that also resonates with academic historians.[6]

What strikes me...is...that throughout, the focus of philosophical reflection is on history as an established, ongoing discipline with strictly cognitive interest. Questions about 'our' knowledge of the past are really questions about the historian's knowledge of the past.... What is under analysis is exclusively the connection between the historian and his or her object.

This approach thus suggests, without saying it in so many words, that 'our' only real connection to the historical past is the result of historical enquiry, whereas it seems obvious to me that we have a connection to the historical past, as ordinary persons, prior to and independently of adopting a historical cognitive interest.

* * *

The idea of producing a book on the role of history in society was born around ten years ago and has matured during the past seven years in retirement. Arriving at the need to expound the key dimensions of my professional self was perhaps a (current) outsider's reaction to the prevailing academic conditions (not only in Finland) where the very idea of scholarly work keeps on being relegated down on the priority list. At the same time, a citizen worried about the increasing meaninglessness of the idea of responsible use of power (in all western countries) cannot help wondering what role history should play in twenty-first-century societies.

Here I should point out two major shortcomings of this book: first is the omission of reference to recent works written in German. English and German have somewhat dissimilar history-related vocabularies. 'Geschichtskultur' ('history culture', 'culture of history'), for instance, is a central concept in German discussion but has not acquired an established status in English; in this book its equivalent is the rather vague 'history-in-society'. Sorting out these kinds of differences, especially their connections to various patterns of thought and traditions of thinking, would have called for more research and taken more space to explain than I could afford. The second shortcoming is that the book deals with history-making only in the western industrial world. The failure to explore the role of history in other cultures, in the Islamic world, for instance, results simply from my insufficient knowledge.[7]

A number of people have supported me throughout this project. Many helpful discussions, especially with Hilda Kean and Pat Thane, but also with Peter Mandler, Rob Perks, John Tosh and Chris Wickham, introduced me to the world of British historians. Their comments on various parts of the manuscript, my too frequent requests notwithstanding, have been invaluable. As to the substance of my arguments, the most important remarks have been made by Pauli Kettunen, my closest colleague for almost four decades. In addition, Anne Heimo, Markku Hyrkkänen and Jouni-Matti Kuukkanen have been valuable teammates on the Finnish side for many years.

I also owe a debt to Frank Ankersmit, Antoon Van den Braembussche, Ronald Grele and Chris Lorenz for their many stimulating discussions. In Finland there are a great many colleagues, and students at all levels, to whom I am grateful for perceptive and helpful comments. Kate Haines at Palgrave Macmillan and the anonymous reviewers she brought on board I want to thank not only for useful comments but also for valuable encouragement. Glyn Banks has taught me a lot when editing my English, and Elizabeth Stone did an excellent job in forcing me to clarify my arguments.

In a way, the present book is the end result of the research project The Political Aspects of History, financed by the Academy of Finland in 2003–06 and directed by me. The actual production of the treatise has been supported financially and legally by the Finnish Association of Non-fiction Writers.

The book is dedicated, with love, to Kirsti Stenvall. Kirsti made me realize some two decades ago the significance of the generational change then under way in research into society and culture: my prime audience was not those about to retire but those about to enter the scholarly world. The undergraduates listening to my lectures at the University of

Tampere in the autumn of 2010 made me wonder whether a similar change is taking place in today's academic world.

Since the book is written in the spirit of 'history is an argument without end', I welcome all criticism and comments: jorma.kalela@utu.fi.

Helsinki 16 September 2011
Jorma Kalela

1
Introduction: Second Thoughts about History

History is an everyday matter, and everyone really has a personal connection to the past, independent of historical enquiry. But there are, in every society, also historians, and it is reasonable to ask why they are needed. Examining this actuality, the relationship between the two, is what *Making History* is about.

The message of the present book includes many suggestions. One of them is that historians would be well-advised not to take the conventional parameters of their discipline as self-evident, and should pause for reflection every time when confronted with a matter that appears to be, or is presented as, a given. Too many aspects of historical enquiry have been taken for granted. 'History' is an example.

Accounts of the past serve present purposes; histories have innumerable functions and are of countless types. History-making is a multifaceted affair, and by no means the prerogative of historians. The histories created do also influence each other, and my suggestion is that their interaction be called the never-ending *social process of history-making*.

As regards historians' relationship to history-in-society, some of the factors that must be taken into account are scholarly ones while others emanate from the circumstances in which the specialists on the past work. Making historians better aware of the effects of the latter is the task of *Making History*; the book seeks to help them in getting to grips with the societal conditions of their work.

Historians, too, participate in the social process of history-making, they do not look upon it from outside. They are 'parts of history', as my main source of inspiration, the Cambridge historian E. H. Carr, neatly puts it, 'conscious or unconscious spokesmen of the society to which they belong'.[1]

The work of historians is inescapably rooted in the society in which they undertake their research, and they aim beyond the prevailing views of the past in that culture. How historians should, and how they can, cope with involvement in social history-making, are questions the present book is intent on answering.

Approaching history-in-society

The heart of *Making History* is the historian's relation to everyday history-making, a feature of humanness that specialists on the past have virtually bypassed. The prime aim has been to find an alternative way of thinking that combines the idea of history as a discipline with recognition of the purposes that bring about other types of histories. This new kind of self-awareness calls for giving up patterns of thought with poor foundation and discussing issues neglected by the profession, rather than dramatic changes in research practices.

Taking seriously the ways in which people use the past, or in general terms the idea of history, is incompatible with one of the academics' favourite notions. 'Theirs was the real history', as the Princeton scholar Linda Colley describes the opinion of her colleagues, 'the rest was amateur at best; at worst, dross, propaganda, fairy-tales.'[2] To be sure, this stance is not widespread any more, as Colley herself has stated, but still now and then one finds statements indicating that the old attitude is left unexpressed only because it is not now 'politically correct'.

In any case, the notion of history-making as a basic social practice, as the British historian Raphael Samuel has it, is an alien idea for most historians. The accounts of the past which are an integral part of anyone's growing up, and which influence the way they lead their lives, are not thought of in terms of history. Yet these *popular histories*, accounts handed down, for example, in the family, neighbourhood or workplace, are an essential part of the context where the historian does research. Samuel's point is well worth taking seriously: 'if history was thought of as an activity rather than a profession, then the number of its practitioners would be legion'. The Estonian writer and film director Imbi Paju, who has brought to light the repression of people's private memories, is not alone in claiming that 'history is too grave a matter to be left only to the historians and politicians'.[3]

Public histories are an equally crucial part of the historian's context. 'History is the battleground of Europe here and now.' This statement of the Estonian President Toomas Hendrik Ilves in 2008 in the foreword to Imbi Paju's book evokes an age-old situation, that professional historians have not taken seriously enough. Different interpretations of the past are constantly struggling in public against each other. How can a French historian studying Turkish history at the end of the First World War ignore the bill passed by his or her parliament in 2006 making it a crime to deny that Armenians suffered 'genocide' at the hands of the Turks? Politically loaded accounts are, however, only a tiny minority of the infinite number of public histories; various media abound with even the most commonplace references to the past.

Everyday history is a term describing the multifaceted mass of popular and public histories which no historian can escape before starting to work with material in archives. In his study *Silent Submission*, which dealt with the formation of foreign policy in the Baltic countries before their annexation to the Soviet Union, the Estonian historian Magnus Ilmjärv faced a situation familiar to a host of his colleagues. It was not only the popular and public histories of his countrymen on top of scholarly works, but also a multitude of divergent western interpretations, in addition to Soviet ones, which he had to take into account while developing the questions informing his study.[4]

The point of Figure 1 is to show the interplay of public, popular and scholarly histories. It is their interaction that constitutes *the practical context of historians' work*. Every one of them lives surrounded by everyday history, even if they denounce that setting as of marginal importance. The circle denoting *scholarly histories* is proportionally far too large. The idea of the terms *public histories* and *popular histories* is illustrative: the function of these categories, to be discussed further in Chapter 3 below, is to help the historian in elaborating his or her chosen topic. In other words, it is the analysis of the context of the particular

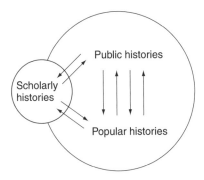

Figure 1   The dynamics of the social process of history-making

study rather than the character of the accounts in question that Figure 1 depicts.[5]

The secondary aim of the present book is to discuss historians' means of getting to grips with their unavoidable involvement in the surrounding society. Intervention in public argument is for quite a few of them a self-evident part of their craft, as is testified by the angry responses on the use of history in connection with the invasion of Iraq that was launched in 2003. Why was British rule in Iraq between the two world wars ignored, for instance? That period would have provided food for thought about historical precedents in many ways, as for example John Tosh has demonstrated. And yet the British media said next to nothing about that period of history. Politicians, in turn, focused on the most frequent analogy used by governments in many countries in support of various policies: the 1930s appeasement towards Nazi Germany. The result was 'closing down any kind of alternative reading of what Saddam might be up to and what ought to be done about him'.[6]

Together with Tosh's *Why History Matters* (2008), the Oxford historian Margaret MacMillan's *The Uses and Abuses of History* (2009) provides a recent example of the argument for more vigorous professional response to the multitude of various public histories.[7] Both of these books are animated by the historians' social responsibilities: they are reactions to the reluctance of professionals to enter into public debates. Many (still the majority?) of MacMillan's and Tosh's colleagues approach contemporary disputes as a context historians should keep away from. The unfortunately common result, when non-intervention is taken for granted, is an uncontrolled involvement in current disputes.

Similar counterproductive practices, often also the result of relying uncritically on received ideals, are revealed in the chapters that follow, and my intention is to suggest remedies. At the same time, the idea is to provoke discussion about the main reason for the many self-defeating routine practices: that is, the failure to take proper notice of the circumstances surrounding the historians' work. The objective is to avoid, for example, creating situations where insufficient attention paid to the context of the research turns the specialist on the past into a virtual piece of driftwood floating on the current circumstances. Remedies are sought by demonstrating and dealing with the various ways in which any account of the past, and especially scholarly works, participate in the never-ending social process of history-making – irrespective of whether this is or is not the creator's intention.

Historians' relation to history-in-society and their ways of coping with involvement in society are integral parts of the overall view, or paradigm, of history as a discipline. This paradigm, the parameters defining historical research, underwent an unmistakable change during the last quarter of the twentieth century. This shift brought to light many issues associated with the two aims pursued in the present book, while some questions on hitherto contentious aspect of historical enquiry even found a resolution, at least for the time being. On the other hand, historians are still clearing up remaining elements of the confusion created by the issues that the transformation brought to the fore. The present volume concentrates, with a view on its two themes, on those dimensions of the change that have been dealt with insufficiently or even brushed aside.

The paradigmatic change in historical research

The perennial question 'what is history?', an age-old topic of philosophical dispute, was turned into a practising historian's predicament. That, in a nutshell, is what happened during the last decades of the twentieth century; and it is this transformation of the parameters of historical research which will be explored in this introductory chapter. There were two simultaneous routes which led to the change. The first was the disruption within the discipline itself that elevated cleaners to a status on a par with kings, and the second the so-called linguistic turn in the study of society and culture, which questioned the familiar tenets of historical research, reality, objectivity and truth.

The changes within the discipline are illustrated by histories, for example, of sexuality, the environment or animal rights. Studies of these kinds of subjects, not deemed previously fit for scholarly interest, became commonplace. At the same time, approaches considered hitherto problematic, if not downright heretical, mushroomed: oral history, history of mentalities, gender history, micro-history, and so on. These features were highlighted by the 'new histories', orientations which were not new but old ones that had been traditionally discriminated against. These actual agents of the disruption made, interestingly, headway without strong opposition in late twentieth century. To allow these trends to enter the mainstream of historical enquiry was equal to questioning the profession's received notions about the actors, themes and approaches of historical research. In short, historians themselves caused an upheaval within their own discipline.

Assigning the 'new histories' legitimate status took place at the same time as academic historians faced the consequences of the linguistic turn, the trouble symbolized by Hayden White's *Metahistory* from 1973, for instance.[8] Quite a few historians, perhaps even the majority, interpreted the ensuing situation as a 'vehement attack by postmodernists on the notion of scientific history, based on the rigorous investigation of primary sources'.[9] This response reflects the origins of the challenge posed by the linguistic turn: it came mostly from outside the profession. Consequently, it is only gradually that historians have begun to reassess their traditional basic tenets.

The experience of 'the postmodernist threat' overshadowed the simultaneous disruption within the discipline: there were only scattered discussions, not a systematic and comprehensive assessment, of the new perspectives on actors, themes and approaches. Nor was the significance of the concurrence of the two analysed. Historians' traditional epistemological conventions changed, as will soon become evident, but in the main this went unnoticed.

Lack of reflection notwithstanding, the resulting upset was yet deep enough to be characterized as a paradigmatic change. And since the transformation was completed in a relatively short time, actually by the turn of the 1990s,[10] it is no exaggeration to speak of a 'scientific revolution' in historical research.[11]

The various dimensions of the paradigmatic change will be discussed in their relevant contexts below. The issues to be dealt with include, among others, the multitude of pasts, the kinds of materials counting as sources, the ways of reading sources, the discourses of reality, the perplexing nature of truth, the nature of historical knowledge, the different meanings of time – not to speak of the great number of ways of understanding history.

While many historians are puzzled by the transformation of their discipline, many of their academic colleagues have hardly noticed any changes. Scholars in fields closely aligned to the study of history tend to harbour anachronistic ideas of the nature of the historian's work – in spite of the likelihood that the paradigmatic change within the discipline of history has its counterpart in their fields too.

From the historian's perspective, the situation created by the changes certainly calls for a rethinking of the traditional division of labour within the academic study of society and culture. The distinctiveness of the historical discipline has never been clear-cut in terms of subjects, materials and methods, but to define its particularity in the early twenty-first century seems to be more difficult than ever. The difference of historical enquiry from related fields of research is close to non-existent after, for example, 'the historic turn in the human sciences'. Memory, too, is an ample symbol of the prevailing circumstances, since studies connected to remembrance abound in practically all academic fields.[12]

The position of memory as a subject of research common to many disciplines indicates, from the historian's viewpoint, significant changes in the cultural context where they perform their work. The present book alludes to many of them but focuses on one aspect of the new cultural landscape, the novel aspects of history-in-society. The point is that everyday history, too, was transformed towards the turn of the twenty-first century thanks to the unparalleled number of people engaged with history.

Elitism toppled?

The new nature of history-in-society was also noticed by scholars. Margaret MacMillan even writes of 'the history craze' with reference to both public and popular histories. She analyses among other things the widespread enthusiasm of non-historians for various history-related events and activities.[13] For the present book, another largely unnoticed, simultaneous aspect of history-making is quite as important: professional historians adopted, in terms of research, a new perspective on non-academic histories. My first book on historians' methodology from 1972 testifies to the preceding situation.[14]

My book was inspired by E. H. Carr's *What is History?* (1961), one of the most influential twentieth-century works on historical enquiry. These two books convey a significant trait of our profession in the 1960s: the role history played in people's daily lives was not then of concern for academic historians. Whatever the reasons for the scant attention of professional historians, it seems probable that reaction against the built-in, long-lasting elitism of mainstream historical research is part of the explanation for the relatively effortless entry of the 'new histories' into the mainstream.

The breakthrough of previously repressed orientations had deep repercussions. Earlier, it had been states, not cleaners or tourists, that were the key players; foreign policies or industrial structures had been the central topics, not gender relations or the rights of animals. Transnational and intercultural themes proliferated, too. Disputes over what should be the principal subjects of history acquired a new tenor as the Warwick historian Paul Smith writes: 'One of the most consistent passions in the historical writing ... has been for giving voices to those seen as hitherto voiceless in the master narratives of history – the poor, women, minorities of every ethnic, social and ideological description.'[15]

The profession, as the Norwegian Grand Old Man of oral history in Scandinavia, the historian Edward Bull Jnr put it, began to 'correct the distortions of history generated by class', to fulfil everybody's right to history.[16]

In other words, historical enquiry underwent a successful insurgence against the elitism and nationalism that had hitherto dominated mainstream research. This was rooted in opposition to ideas like that of high politics and great men as being the 'proper' substance of history. Today, at the beginning of the twenty-first century, all sorts of orientations, ranging from micro- to macro-history, from cultural to multicultural history, from environmental to global history, flourish. All of these 'perspectival paradigms', as the London historian Mary Fulbrook aptly calls them,[17] have legitimate status, and there is no consensus according to which only some of them represent 'real' historical research.[18]

The extent of the paradigmatic change remains, however, open to question. The relation between historical enquiry and history-making as a basic social practice is a case in point, since 'most academics look askance' at popular uses of the past. The ensuing accounts are regarded as 'a diversion from the real job of reconstructing and interpreting the past'. It is the task of the profession to advance archive-based scholarly knowledge that has been reliably reconstructed and explained.[19] Many historians, however, especially younger academics, disclaim this traditional concept of 'proper' history, and refute accusations that their profession inhabits an ivory tower separate from society.

True, a growing number consider that they must be sensitive to issues important to the public at large, but the implications of this have not been thought through or discussed. One even wonders at the nature of the new attitudes, since these historians only seldom ask, as regards public and popular histories, 'why these topics?' Are they seriously interested in the significance their fellow citizens attach to the knowledge of the past? Have they given thought to what lies beneath the surface of the everyday interpretations of the past? Do they recognize that these non-academic accounts are histories in their own right, often with functions which are not necessarily obvious?

Such sceptical questioning is supported by the ambivalent attitude of many professional historians towards heritage. On one hand, it is important to underline that, for example, many events and displays on the subject of British ancestry contradict the findings of historical investigation. In addition, as Margaret MacMillan stresses, the information conveyed is often questionable. 'Much of the past that we get through the heritage business is sanitized', for instance, she writes.

People are shown 'lovely reconstructions, lovely houses, but not pigs running around, or people with rotten teeth, or any number of odors that assault our contemporary senses'. With the use of the term 'business' she also makes an important point, since heritage is an umbrella term covering a multifaceted industry.[20]

On the other hand, not all the activities connected to traditions are merely commercial. Historians have every reason to ask, for example, for what purpose and by whom an artefact has been displayed. More important still, they should take seriously and think about why people do 'travel to historic sites and reconstructions and witness re-enactments'. Those interested in these matters are hardly just unthinking consumers of entertainment.

The point to be emphasized here, as with reference to the Tea Party Movement in the Preface (see p. ix), is that the knowledge conveyed is not the only perspective from which to reflect on everyday history – the function of the various traditions, commemorations and rituals cherished must also be taken into account. Under scrutiny are patterns of behaviour and thought which for many people represent the most cherished aspects of their community. This is why meticulous epistemological analysis alone is not sufficient; one has to give consideration also to the many meanings already embedded in, or that may conceivably be attached to, the historical accounts. In addition, as will be demonstrated in the following chapters, historians should take such considerations into account during the planning stage of their undertaking, while transforming the topic chosen into the subject to be studied.

This leads me to remark on the conceptualization of heritage itself. Pointing out that many American historians write about 'memory' where their European colleagues would refer to 'heritage', and some even to 'tradition', is the introductory part of my argument and notes the implicit common element embedded in all these terms. Irrespective of which term they use, historians tend to assume, or at least give the impression of, coherence among 'the people'. This tendency reveals the most unfortunate blind spot of the historical profession.

Chapter 3, 'The People Addressed', seeks to present two arguments against this prevailing approach. First, those making up the historians' audience are not just passive consumers of the knowledge offered, and, secondly, the heterogeneity of 'the people' must be taken into account. Members of any society mutually construct a multitude of overlapping 'shared histories', and these are, from the historian's angle, more useful than the imprecise and capacious concepts of 'memory', 'heritage' or 'tradition'.

The social context recognized?

The ways historians have renounced their previous elitism show that the paradigmatic change progressed accumulatively: toppling the traditional stance revealed the need to rethink other approaches. Just as tackling one received premise triggered reassessment of related positions, this has also been true of the circumstances surrounding historians' work. The initial element here was the legitimizing of the many different perspectival paradigms, while the knock-on effect was substituting outward-looking patterns of thought for the previous inward-looking approach.

An illustration of the world of the historical profession before the paradigmatic change has been made by the French historian Michel de Certeau: specialists on the past, he stated, pretended to produce histories, de facto, in 'nowhere'. Another Frenchman, the philosopher Paul Ricoeur, used the expression 'a sort of state of socio-cultural weightlessness' to characterize the same tendency to ignore the social setting of the research.[21] However, it is worth emphasizing that the pattern of thought the two Frenchmen criticize was not peculiar to historians alone, as has been demonstrated by Steven Shapin who teaches history of science at Harvard. Mainstream historians were part of a broader school of thought 'that holds scientific knowledge to be transcendent, discovered not made, placeless, timeless, objective, unsullied by the conditions of its creation or the personalities and prejudices of its makers.'[22]

It is no exaggeration to claim that, as late as the beginning of the 1980s, phobia about societal influences was an integral part of the scholarly historian's professional self-awareness. The attitude is illustrated by the criticism of my 1972 book on methodology, which was interpreted as a call to politicize historical research because its argument allows a scholar to have societal objectives. Yet the volume had the same objective as the present one, and it is the opposite of politicization. Historians have to achieve intellectual control over their inescapable two-way involvement in society: their questions are connected to current circumstances, and their findings do have consequences – their intentions notwithstanding.[23]

The small number of problems regarding research practice which were discussed before the paradigmatic change were not connected to the social and cultural conditions in which historical enquiry takes place. The relation of scholarship to history-in-society was an issue about the role of the profession, not of a particular study. The agenda did not include either the individual historian's role as a researcher nor his or her relationship to the surrounding society. The then prevailing situation is characterized by debates among historians. The key issues discussed were philosophical rather than about historical enquiry: the nature of history and the relationship between history and the past, for instance. Nor was there any significant room for historians' peculiar ways of reasoning and arguing; questions of methodology were virtually restricted to using the sources.

At the beginning of the twenty-first century, historical research is done in very different kind of circumstances, and this is also reflected in the new professional self-awareness that has been emerging since the 1990s. The emphasis lies on the individual historian's work, and on his or her choices. Whichever perspectival paradigms are selected, the historian knows that his or her choice at least implies taking a stand on current economic, social, political or cultural debates – not to mention those choices which are overtly intentional in this respect. Historians have at least implicitly, if not manifestly, acknowledged their status as cultural critics – a role which will be gradually unfolded in the following.

This new kind of relationship to society is also reflected in the historian's considerably greater freedom to specify the subject to be studied than in the 1960s, when I started my career as a historian. In those days there was a strong tendency to take the actors, themes and approaches of historical enquiry for granted, and to regard the choice between them as neutral. Today, to belittle the historian's responsibility for defining the parameters of the study is markedly more difficult; it is even not uncommon that a historian is criticized for paying too little attention to his or her social and cultural setting. Still, it is reasonable to argue that the changeover has stopped at a halfway house.

The positive part of the change is that the need for the historian to make an argument for his or her choice of perspectival paradigm is beneficial. Having to explain, for example, 'why I am doing gender history' certainly helps one in defining the significance of one's study in general terms. The insufficiency of the change lies in the limits of the orientation: the mere opting for a perspectival paradigm does not specify the reasons for defining the subject to be studied in a particular way.

There is today a test of strength between several perspectival paradigms, technological or children's history, for instance, but no comparable debate about the individual historian's position. In this sense, individual historians are still left to their own devices. As regards the surrounding society, his or her objectives remain the preserve of historiographical, that is, *ex post* analysis. An *ex ante* scrutiny continues to be the historian's private affair, that is, the historian is not required, at the outset of the research undertaking, to anticipate, to reflect on and display the influences embedded in the probable findings. Lack of impartiality in making choices is there right from the beginning of the research project: no historian, either professional or lay, is able to start with a clean slate. Whatever topic he or she chooses, meanings have already been attached to it, and the subject being delineated already has some kind of position in the social process of history-making. In other words, all historical research is rewriting history. Not to think carefully about the reasons for choosing a topic and developing it into a subject to be studied is tantamount to being a pawn in somebody else's hands. The sensible historian makes a systematic effort to identify the various links of the selected theme and reflects on them. He or she also thinks about the responsibility implied by the decisions made.

Neither is the relevance of the gradually emerging subject by any means self-evident, but depends on the connections the historian decides to emphasize. Here, the historical nature of the subject must be considered: its significance is independent neither of the situation where the study will be undertaken nor of the audience being addressed. One historian wants to demonstrate the consequences some past decision has on a hotly debated current issue; another to show that there are antecedents strikingly at variance with what is lazily assumed to be 'natural' today – and so on. The point is that every historian should take time diligently to unearth 'why I have chosen this topic and why I have elaborated it into this particular subject'.

In addition to the attention called for by the choices made, care is required regarding one's relationship with the values and explanatory schemes embedded in common sense.[24] Far from being 'the fixed standard it always pretends to be, common sense is a historical phenomenon'; it is in motion, as the American colleague Thomas L. Haskell emphasizes. Historians forget that the criteria for judgement authorized by common sense are not timeless at their peril. Current ideas and beliefs, 'what everybody knows', change with time, and for 'historians' not to pay active attention to this incurs the grave risk of imposing the concepts and discourses of their own time on the people they are investigating.

The commonness, the unarticulated status of common sense is another problem it creates; it is only seldom that situations arise which present grounds to expound the assumptions implicitly made. Yet, as Haskell states, 'even the smallest details of everyday experience' may depend for their meaning on 'what everybody knows', On the other hand, the shared histories which were introduced at the end of the previous section (see p. 9) alleviate the historian's problems. These conglomerates of views of the past, mutually constructed by certain groups of people, are useful instruments since it is not reasonable to assume that there exists only a common sense in the singular. 'Shared conceptual frameworks', a key characteristic of common sense, do not vary only from one era to another, but also from one social group to another.[25]

Common sense provides a fruitful perspective also on one of the key notions historians cherish. They emphasize, and with good reason, that they write in ordinary language, but have not reflected on the implications of this. They have not thought about what it means to present their findings in everyday terms, that is, with the help of the ways their audience conceives of reality and expresses its beliefs. In other words, they have not considered what follows from relying on the discourses prevalent in everyday history. 'Ordinary language' is an element of common sense, of 'what everybody knows', and that is not an innocent idea.

Common sense has one more implication for the paradigmatic changes discussed: many questions connected to the relationship between the historian and history-in-society did not come to view while analysis remained at the level of the profession as a whole. Like the divergent undisclosed elements of historical research, many of the individual historian's problems were, before the transformation at the end of the twentieth century, covered up by the traditional schism that divided the profession for almost two centuries. More generally, this disagreement blurred the issue of the historian's role in society.

Present-mindedness disciplined?

Overcoming the division between the 'objectivists' and the 'representatives of partisanships', as the German authority on historiography Reinhart Koselleck calls the two camps, was probably the greatest benefit of the paradigmatic change as regards historians' professional self-awareness.[26] This traditional schism had been created after historians gained freedom from producing examples and models from the past for political and rhetorical purposes, for instance, in the early nineteenth century. In reaction to the previously subordinate position of history-writing, they were united in the need to defend the autonomy of the new discipline, but disagreed about the degree of detachment from society.

The dominant 'objectivist' or 'orthodox' section demanded that no account should be taken of present conditions; it rejected the idea of studying the past in order to make sense of the present. The historians' agenda 'must be driven by the surviving sources of the past, not the intrusive questions of a present-minded enquirer'.[27] The 'representatives of partisanship' did not disagree with the demand of presenting the people studied 'on their own terms', but regarded the past as the key to understanding the present.

The weakness of the minority's position was the failure to distinguish between the two levels of a historian's relationship with society. One results from the function of the chosen topic in current debates, the other from the durable commitments every scholar has. The failure to make this distinction resulted in vulnerability to accusations that historical research had been turned into an instrument of political ideologies. This was, for example, the weak point of my 1972 book.

On the face of it, the paradigmatic change entailed the defeat of the 'objectivists'. Yet, far more important was the wiping out of the way in which 'historians' regarded their research as separate from the prevailing social and cultural conditions. There had been an unfortunate tendency to imagine that scholars were, a priori, intellectually in control of the circumstances in which they worked. In this inward-looking, narrow scholarly perspective historians' relation to their surrounding circumstances was reduced to personal choice: either they opted for 'objective' or for 'partisan'.

Yet, all the changes of the late twentieth century notwithstanding, traditional objectivity persists as a hindrance to adequate reflection on the context in which historians work. There are two influential guidelines, the first of which is encapsulated in the dictum 'extinguishing one's self', coined by the best-known of the discipline's German founding fathers, Leopold von Ranke.[28] This advice may seem, at first sight, innocent enough, but on closer examination it turns out to be insidious.

The significance of Ranke's advice lies in its invitation to historians to take their own concept of reality and their own discourse virtually for granted, that is, to consider them as objective and neutral. This stance, firstly, leads easily to the historian measuring the patterns of thought of the people studied against his or her own tenets and to concluding that they had primitive and undeveloped beliefs. Secondly, and far more importantly, there is the risk of importing the beliefs and notions of the historian's own culture to that under investigation; in other words, for instance, of inadvertently having eighteenth-century people adopt the logic of people in the era of the internet.

LIVERPOOL JOHN MOORES UNIVERSITY
LEARNING SERVICES

The demand that they give up these kinds of, mostly involuntary, anachronistic ways is where the significance of the linguistic turn lies for historians. Reconstructing the deeds of the people studied 'on their own terms', presenting a fair description of them (that is, the justification of the profession) is a far more demanding task than had hitherto been thought. The task is not only to set down the actions and thinking of those people under investigation: the historian must also outline his own discourse in setting the parameters of the study. Doing justice to the people studied is similarly hindered by the second fundamental dictum in traditional objectivity, 'deliberate abandonment of the present', as the Cambridge historian G. R. Elton puts it.

According to Elton, the historian is allowed to be concerned with later events 'only in so far as [they] throw light on the past studied'. To reverse this process, and to 'study the past for the light it throws on the present, is the cardinal error'.[29] As practical advice this, too, is counterproductive, since eradicating the influences present circumstances have on research is impossible, and leads easily to research governed by ulterior and hidden motives. Instead of trying to ignore the present circumstances, historians should attempt to avoid being unintentionally guided by them.

The principal argument of this book is that historians are so intimately involved in surrounding society that they must substitute managing their present-mindedness for objectivity. Disciplining one's thinking is absolutely vital since historical enquiry is in two ways inescapably conditioned by the social process of history-making: the questions specialists on the past seek to answer are embedded in society and their findings influence it. Managing this two-way connection entails developing *double detachment*, distancing oneself both from those interpretations criticized and the alternative one/s proposed. Unfortunately, as will be shown repeatedly in the following chapters, getting into grips with the social context of one's work has all too often been neglected, giving traditional objectivity as the excuse.[30]

It is not objectivity but the soundness of the knowledge produced that gives historians their intellectual authority. Nor does their stature depend on arguments based on their findings. The key element is, in the words of the Cambridge historian Stefan Collini, the trained scepticism that says 'it was not like that'.[31] This is the easy part of double detachment: the need to distance oneself from prevailing interpretations is also self-evident. How much effort this requires depends on the difficult part of double detachment, that is, the historian's own ideas: thinking over and taking a stand on the implications and consequences of the alternative interpretation proposed.

The means of disciplining one's present-mindedness is to start from uncovering *the initial idea* that gave birth to the project, and then elaborate it meticulously to formulate the *central idea* of the study. 'Exactly why do I want to argue for an alternative interpretation'? Answering this question, the historian sets in motion the process of finding out the significance of the deeds of the people to be studied. 'Why is it important to demonstrate where prevailing interpretations go astray? What makes the knowledge my study shall produce a well-supported novel contribution to history-in-society'? Whatever the historian's aim, the challenge that must be accepted is disciplining one's thoughts, and the key way to do this is to clarify continuously the point of the project.

While developing his or her alternative interpretation the historian must also avoid the all too common habit of scholars of reflecting on their starting points only in scholarly terms, a practice not only short-sighted but also dangerous. Neglecting the meanings transmitted by public and popular histories is equal to claiming that everyday history has not influenced one's thinking. Nor is it sensible to pretend that one does not have any intention of influencing those outside the scholarly world; and even in those rare cases where one does not have such intentions, it is worth remembering that the effects of historians' alternative interpretations are not limited to academia.

Double detachment emanates from practical need to manage the inevitable societal aspects of one's research and not from some 'theory', the kind of argument many historians have, partly with good reason, grown allergic to. On the other hand, when defining the parameters of their studies the same scholars act, most probably, in accordance with the role they have themselves determined of the historian's function in society. My point is that they only very seldom articulate that idea, and create by dint of this an unfortunate situation for future historians. Instead of being able to form their own concepts through assessing clearly defined divergent professional positions, they are forced to develop their own views of the historian's relation to society the hard way.

Another way of commenting on the historians' speechlessness, their reluctance to make their stances and methods transparent, is to say that they have not done justice to their own craft. This is the argument of the Australian historian Hugh Stretton: historians have failed to promote their professional skills generally, and have also kept hidden particular approaches which colleagues in other fields could take advantage of.[32] This lack of regard for the practices of their own craft seems to spring from the phobia about societal influences. Yet by not spelling out the foundations of their research and by inaccurately presenting how they see their role in relation to society, historians have misled not only their own students but also scholars in other fields.

As a result of their lack of candour, historians have conveyed, almost simultaneously, three different images of their work. There is little coherence, if any, between interpretations of historical enquiry based on historians' everyday discourse, their theoretical treatises and their practice. Neither *what historians say they are doing* nor *what they are supposed to do* according to the profession's articulated methodology matches *what they actually do in practice.*

Historians' relative indifference to the standing of historical research is a good example of their notorious aversion to secondary reflection on their research. It is with good reason that Thomas L. Haskell claims that historians, 'virtually alone among all the practitioners of the humanities and social sciences', are reluctant to acknowledge that 'their discipline has a non-empirical, "theoretical" dimension, [as] worthy of specialized attention as any other'. Like Haskell in the United States, I have had in Finland 'a long-standing quarrel with the mainstream of my profession, many of whose members pride themselves on a tough-minded, archive-based empiricism and openly disdain everything that smacks of "theory" or "abstraction" '.[33]

As Haskell states, when historians indulge their aversion to theory they have no choice but to fall back on common sense. Haskell's *Objectivity Is Not Neutrality: Explanatory Schemes in History* appeared in 1998, and starts from the observation that the profession's 'complacency about the theoretical dimension of historical practice' has become 'harder and harder to sustain over the past two decades'. Mary Fulbrook's *Historical Theory*, published in 2002, is another important sign of the changing times; she demonstrates 'the ways in which all historical writing is inevitably theoretical'. Haskell's very reasonable opinion, in turn, is that there is no need for a pretentious definition of 'theory'. The term could be understood to refer to 'a freewheeling recognition that events are interrelated in more ways than are immediately apparent or carry the sanction of common usage'.[34]

Having now introduced the secondary issue underlying this book, getting to grips with historians' unavoidable involvement in society it is now time to address its primary objective: to propose a pattern of thinking that combines the idea of history as a discipline with recognition of the purposes that bring about other types of histories? This aim is not new; it takes a step further the idea outlined by E. H. Carr in 1961.

'Before you study the history, study the historian. . . . [and] before you study the historian, study his historical and social environment'.[35] Carr's advice has directed my view on historical enquiry throughout the whole of my career, and dominates the present book too. The argument is that historians should shake off their professional blinkers, and clarify their relation to the ongoing social process of history-making. The logic to be followed is based on another piece of important advice from Carr, and was expounded in the previous pages: 'man's capacity to rise above his social and historical situation seems to be conditioned by the sensitivity with which he recognises the extent of his involvement in it'.

Historians as cultural critics?

Being an integral part of history-in-society is the lesson taught to the historical profession by the paradigmatic change in their discipline at the end of the twentieth century; historians were deceiving themselves in thinking that there was a vantage point outside the history they were studying. Acknowledging this means that, internally, in the world of research, historians must acquire double detachment, from both from the interpretations criticized and from those for the alternative interpretations for which they are arguing. Externally, in relation to those addressed, they must acknowledge the role of cultural critics, and delineate what this means in practical terms, that is, how they can accommodate this role alongside their disciplinary duties.

The rationale that animated the founding fathers of the discipline in the nineteenth century is still sustainable: experts on the past are there to produce sound knowledge, not to convey moral stories or political lessons, for instance. In the mainstream historian's view, this idea meant keeping public and popular histories at arm's length; judging non-academic histories was the most important part of their role with regard to the uses of the past outside academia. A positive interpretation of the founding fathers' rationale is to be preferred by considering the close link between historical research and surrounding society: historians are there to uphold history-making and to refine the ensuing accounts. Their job is, in banal terms, to demonstrate how to use and how not to use the past.

Regarding the historian's capacity as a cultural critic, Chapters 3 and 4 below discuss the various aspects of transforming the chosen topic into a subject. Here I deal with the historian's two-sided role on a general level. Being simultaneously a scholar and a cultural critic is, in my view, integral to his or her occupation: that is, the historian acts as the interpreter between two cultures, that of the people he or she is studying and that of the people he or she addresses. It is his or her job to demonstrate the relevance of the chosen fragments of the past in the present situation; to display the ways in which thoughts and actions yielded by different circumstances, together with their consequences, are connected to present and future conditions. The end result should be virtually a dialogue between the people studied and the audience.

The historian's contribution to the social process of history-making is twofold: to open new perspectives on the world of the people addressed, and to invite them to ponder their values. Utilizing the ability of historical enquiry to extend people's horizons, historians use their expertise analogously to the ways of actors or novelists who are experts in their particular genres. The difference is that historians are in the main, thanks to the multitude of public and popular histories, better aware of the thinking they seek to influence. In effect, their societal role means upholding non-academic accounting of the past as a basic social practice.

The task of supporting history-making outside the academic world is embedded in the rationale of historians' work in another way too. As specialists they are there (also) to provide critical analysis of the prevalent views of the past in everyday history; they act as referees, as will be displayed in Chapter 2. It is the historian's responsibility to highlight inaccuracies in existing knowledge as well as to draw attention to unreasonable or unfounded likes or dislikes of aspects of the past in public and popular histories. Thus the historian's work does not come to an end with the mere presentation of sustainable alternative interpretations: it is not enough just to reveal contemporary prejudices, for instance. Historians must also show which parts of the accounts criticized are inadequate, and why. In a way, the concept of the historian's work can be encapsulated as refining non-academic accounts of the past.

Still, the relationship between academic and non-academic research in the past is not one-sided. Findings produced by family history or highlighting the past of various localities, for instance, are sometimes, as the social science professor Ruth Finnegan at the British Open University stresses, 'as serious, original and carefully-tested as that of academics'. On the other hand, there are also people who stubbornly stick to their favourite interpretations, no matter the evidence and arguments which question their explanations. However, rather than dealing with the professionals' connection to laypeople comprehensively, in this book the focus will be on the issue of the upholding of history-making outside academia as a dimension of the historians' research practices.[36]

The crucial requirement for success in upholding history-making as a basic social practice is that the objectives of non-academic history-making are taken seriously, and this, in turn, raises a fundamental issue. Which kinds of ideas are best dealt with by specialists in the employment of the past for present purposes and which are not? This is an issue without an obvious answer, and one historians have not debated. It will be discussed from several angles in the present book. My own answer is to suggest a participatory historical culture, an idea originally put forward by David Thelen: cooperation between professional historians and their fellow citizens that builds on the shared histories which people have mutually created. This vision will be gradually developed in the following chapters and the potential embedded in it concludes the book.[37]

The thesis I seek to advocate is that upholding everyday history-making and refining the ensuing accounts presupposes taking seriously non-academic histories, but does not in any way endanger the epistemological foundation of the historian's craft. Like the American historian Bernard Bailyn I am convinced that 'history and memory ... may act usefully upon each other'. Making history should be, as another American colleague, Roy Rosenzweig, puts it, 'a more democratic activity that allows amateurs and professionals to learn from each other'.[38] Focusing on the relation between historical enquiry and history-in-society contributes, I hope, to debates on history as a discipline but it is not the basic rationale for this book. What is intended is not a new kind of comprehensive introduction to the study of history but an introduction to a discussion, from the vantage point of an individual study, about the heart of my profession. Ultimately, I am inviting everyone, and especially historians, as users of the past, to ponder 'why history?'. A useful starting point is discussion about the distinctiveness of historical research as a genre of history-making.

The structure of the book

Sound knowledge is what *distinguishes scholarly histories* from public and popular accounts of the past, but it is not meeting this standard that carries forward a research undertaking. Progress is made because the historian becomes gradually better aware of what he or she is pursuing, and realizes the point of the undertaking. When choosing a topic to be studied the historian often has only an inkling that the prospective results will be significant, but this dim vision is clarified as research progresses. Disciplining one's thoughts about the circumstances surrounding the research project leads at the same time to intellectual control of the context in which one is working and, in addition, to a better idea of the historian's role in society. Discussing all these aspects of the historian's rationale, in addition to the discipline's basic tenets, is the subject of Chapter 2, 'Historical Research'.

Different people appreciate different aspects of the past, and this means that selecting a topic also entails choosing one's audience. '*For whom are the research findings likely to be important?*' Having answered this question, the historian must acknowledge the presence of the target audience throughout the investigation. What is more, the people addressed are not just readers – if one recognizes that accounting for the past is a basic social practice. The audience consists of people who, in a way, are historians themselves – that is, they use the professionals' findings to create their own histories. These statements may seem, at first, odd but they will cease to cause surprise when one gives up the prevailing tendency to think about all history in disciplinary terms. The consequence of this is, in general, that one should take seriously the duty to uphold history-making in everyday life, and, in particular, that one needs to think meticulously about the audience for the specific research project. These are the themes of Chapter 3, 'The People Addressed'.

Analysing the research context that has prompted their study is how historians define their objectives. The aim is to specify the reasons for 'setting the record straight', that is, to think out the component that is always embedded in a historical study, to *demonstrate something contrary to what is claimed or believed to be the case*. The historian needs to establish his or her topic's position in the battlefield of rival interpretations, that is, in the politics of history which is the theme of Chapter 4. Historical advances result from meeting the demand of double detachment, from finding out why prevailing interpretations are insufficient and why a different kind of knowledge is needed to supplant them. It should also be noted that many crucial aspects of the investigation are likely to be marginalized or lost if in the critique of existing knowledge, the meanings on the subject conveyed by public and popular histories are neglected, as is the case with the work of many academics.

Deciding on the audience for one's study and developing the draft of one's alternative interpretation are the methods used to turn the chosen *topic* into the *subject* to be studied. Thinking about the people to be addressed and examining existing interpretations are the means used to work towards a critical awareness of the research one is actually intending to do, the rationale of one's study, and what its implications might be. The particular issue to be studied emerges gradually by setting out the boundaries of the subject to be tackled. This work is the substance of the planning stage of the project covered in Chapters 2, 3 and 4. The aim is for the historian to have gained intellectual control of the current situationof social history-making in the area of study before starting the second stage of the research process, that is, working on the primary sources. Most sensible historians will also take time to study all the available secondary sources too.

It is necessary to devote a relatively large amount of space to the planning stage also because that is when the crucial decisions are made. It is at this stage that the *initial idea*, the inkling that the chosen topic matters, is refined and developed into an outline of the *central idea* for the study ahead. Defining the study is complete when the historian is able to make convincing case both for the make-up of the audience and the alternative interpretation proposed. By then the historian has formulated the assumption he or she is striving to justify, has become aware of the substance of this pursuit and of the valuable qualities of the eventual findings. He or she has specified the potential significance of these findings, knows what kind of meanings he or she will be conveying. In a word, he or she has drafted the study's *message*. To reach this far does of course take time, since the work involved amounts to almost a mini research project in itself, but taking this detailed approach will save more time during the following two stages of the research project.

During the second phase the historian tests his or her assumptions, that is, assesses the strength of his or her message against the primary sources. This work will be finished when the historian has convinced him- or herself that the findings are sustainable. Having done this the historian moves on to convince his or her audience, that is, starts the third and final stage of the research project, producing the final account. In this book the second and third stages are covered by Chapter 5, but the essence of that chapter is denoted by its title, 'Cultural Critics'.

What is suggested here is that historians should give up the paradoxical view they hold of their profession: while historians continue to emphasize that people must be studied on their own terms, they abandon this principle when examining their own occupation, historical research. They have subordinated the study of history to general scholarly tenets. Approaching historical enquiry 'on its own terms' presupposes the opposite of the conventional approach: giving up what appears to be the near emulation of philosophers. The historian's practice should be the starting point of thinking about the discipline, not the variable factor. Historical research should be characterized by uncovering and analysing the key elements in what historians do, through unfolding the rationale of their work.

In contrast to what is commonly thought to be the case, the historian's pursuit is not, primarily, epistemological, to present the chosen fragments of the past as accurately as possible. The historian's work is prompted more by cultural objectives: it seeks to make sense of matters of the past and to demonstrate their relevance. This should be the starting point for the historian seeking to define the subject to be studied, while the role of disciplinary conventions is auxiliary: they lend support and bring regularity to the research practice. In practical terms, this implies that professional history-making should be thought of as a process, as a project that starts with an initial idea and ends in the final account that conveys the historian's message. Too many aspects of the historian's work, ways of explaining and the final account, for instance, have often been discussed separately from the project as a whole, and in this sense, in a distorted context.

Reconstructing the past on the basis of primary sources has been, for good reason, the stronghold of scholarly historians. Yet, working with primary sources is only the second of the three stages of the historian's work, and not the most important one. The effort of producing the final account has been underrated just as the planning stage has been. In an attempt to remedy this weakness, Chapter 5 ends with a discussion of this key problem.

The final account has two contradictory dimensions which cannot, when writing the text, be separated: these are, the tension between reasoning and rhetoric. This illuminates the historian's basic predicament, the temptation to compromise the demand of soundness in order to make the message more convincing; the dilemma is there from the very outset of the project. The way out is to approach, at the last stage of the research process, the final account in two phases. First, the presentation should be thought through in the perspective of mere reasoning, as a complex structure or of arguments and their grounds. Only after the historian has chosen the elements that can in no case be left out of the account is it reasonable to approach the presentation in the rhetorical perspective, as an instrument seeking to convince the audience of the sustainability of the message.

The final chapter of this book returns to the historical situation at the beginning of the twenty-first century that gradually, while working on my final account, turned out to be the most important starting point. The core of the discussion in Chapter 6 can be encapsulated in the twofold meaning of 'impact'. On the one hand, the term has, and with good reasons, awful connotations for an increasing number of academics. On the other hand, it is also possible to look upon the impact of historical research in a positive light, interpreting it as referring to the vision of a participatory historical culture.

2
Historical Research

It is the choices historians make that define the parameters of their studies and this gives them a great responsibility. They are, in relation to their own society, guardians of sound knowledge of the past, and in relation to past societies, instrumental in making sure that justice is done to the people they are studying. On both counts, their moral principles are constantly tested by the predicament embedded in the past-present relationship. The challenge is to respond to current concerns – but not at the cost of presenting a fair description of the people studied.

The candid historian admits that there is always a temptation to sacrifice the obligation to do justice to the people studied in order to buttress the message. To succumb is to knock the bottom out of learning something from the dissimilarity of the two cultures, since all historical research is based on a recognition of the gulf between the past and the present. Fairness is entailed by this divide, and rules out the use of present patterns of thought and ideas in describing those of the past.

Before the recent paradigmatic change scholars used to, as the Cambridge historian Peter Mandler puts it, keep public and popular histories at arm's length. Nowadays professional historians' work complements rather than overrides these accounts, and there is no need for this 'collaboration to blur [their different] roles'. Historians have 'gatekeeping and quality-control functions' in the information-rich society of the early twenty-first century. Their job is to oppose the tendency to project contemporary desires onto earlier times and to dispute the unwarranted use of bygone cultures. They are 'the past's advocates, constantly jabbing the modern observer in the side with the strangeness and difference of the past'.[1]

As a branch of knowledge, history has been allocated high value in everyday life, probably from time immemorial, and the historian's craft seems to have had an equally long lifespan. A milestone was reached in the early nineteenth century when historical enquiry emerged as an academic discipline with its own epistemological standards. Even so, specialists on the past did not lose their traditional role, although the significance of this was considerably reduced. The connection to earlier practices has been articulated by the Dutch historian Johan Huizinga, among others. History, he writes, differs from other disciplines in that its 'privilege and heavy responsibility is to remain comprehensible to all civilized people'. At the same time history is, as for example the Cambridge historian Richard J. Evans underlines, by its nature, 'a critical, skeptical discipline' with regard to existing histories.[2]

The distinctiveness created by the integral connection to prevailing societal knowledge has been a permanent element in historians' debates about their discipline, an issue for even the staunchest 'objectivists'. It is also hard to imagine a future when this distinguishing characteristic will not feature in historians' discussions – even after the traditional schism between the 'objectivists' and the 'representatives of partisanships' has lost its immediacy.

As indicated in the introduction, this book seeks to contribute to debate on the nature of history as a discipline by offering a new starting point with changed priorities: historians should reflect on their profession in the first place as a cultural institution, and only secondly as a scholarly discipline. This suggestion is, as will be demonstrated in the present chapter, in agreement with the rationale of the profession's founding fathers and does not entail essential changes in research practices. What follows from the suggested change is the need to recognize the roots of historical research as being in the culture where the research is undertaken; accepting that the fundamental rationale of historical enquiry is the inherent criticism of the present assumptions of the world. True, this requires theoretical consideration, but not the kind of analysis many historians have rejected as useless. Reflection on the scholarly practices of history must take place on *historians' terms*, and be directed and dominated by historians' rather than philosophers' issues. The obvious place to begin is the practical context of any historian's work: history-in-society.

Making histories

Events since the end of the 1980s testifies to the ubiquity of public and popular histories: it is easy to demonstrate that the past can provide many messages for those who turn to it for support. Ethnic groups in the former Yugoslavia provide a good example: all of them 'appealed to history to help boost their cause, justify the present, or reinforce the dream of an alternative future'. But the past can also provide an imaginative escape from the present, 'a kind of tourism of the mind' or a 'seductive home . . . for those in search of nostalgia'.[3]

History is not something 'official' nor is it limited to what are usually considered significant local, national or global events. In short, it is fairly obvious that life cannot be lived without a consciousness of the past. The American historian Roy Rosenzweig underlines that there is nothing 'abstract or antiquarian about popular history-making'. The dialogue between the past and the present is the context for dealing with 'pressing current-day questions about relationships, identity, immortality, and agency'.[4] The various ways in which people engage the past in their lives, actions and thinking have, especially during the last few decades, given birth to several extensive fields of research. On historical consciousness, for example, there are a great variety of studies on memory and narratology.[5]

The custom of calling attention to the past makes every person an active agent in creating histories. Looking into local history is a common way of getting to know the area where you live. Making histories is actually quite a simple practice: one person relates a past event or matter to another because they think it is, for one reason or another, relevant to that person. They produce their interpretation by selecting the items to be used in the description and showing how they are connected to each other. The depth of comment on the items ranges from passing references to a careful explanation, and that blurs the difference from trained historian's account. It is justified to conclude, as Rosenzweig does in the title of an article, 'Everyone a Historian'.[6]

The variety of purposes these everyday histories have is also great: there is no uniformity either in the substance or the angle of the accounts. The past is, as David Thelen puts it, a reservoir of alternatives to the present: by recovering things from the past or by looking at experience differently we can see how to think and act differently in the future.[7] No wonder people appreciate different aspects of the past: what is worth remembering for one may well be unimportant for another, and a matter one finds puzzling is crystal-clear for another. Logically, then, differences between the various perspectives can commonly produce discrepancies, rivalry and even contradictions in interpretation. History is a complex and contested field.

The incentives to create histories vary from fear of oblivion to curiosity about photographs or artefacts from the past. People may simply be fascinated by former lives; they may use the past in constructing themselves and their lives; they may be engaged in community, local and family history projects; they may trust in history while negotiating the present and navigating the future. People have, to use the American historian Warren Sussman's phrase, multitudes of 'usable pasts'. According to Roy Rosenzweig, 'the past is (for people) not only present – it is part of the present'.[8] It would not do any harm if professional historians followed David Carr's suggestion quoted in the Preface (see p. xii) and reflected on the connection they have to the historical past prior to adopting a particular research interest.

While in Germany in 1997 I stopped off at Weimar, for me the symbol of the birth of the German republic and the fall of the empire, to see the former concentration camp, Buchenwald. While there, I could not escape learning that for Germans Weimar was before all else the town of Goethe and Schiller. And instead of finding a memorial to the parliament that proclaimed the republic I was confronted with dozens of culturally significant remains of the past. The visit reminded me that what is worth remembering and seems historically significant varies from one country to another and that within any society diverse groups value different aspects of the past. Staying in Weimar also underlined that buildings themselves, for instance, are but mute remains and that their historical significance depends on what one is told about them.

My experiences from Weimar illustrate also the nature of shared histories, a concept introduced in Chapter 1 (see pp. 9 and 12–13). They are accounts of the past without a specific author which various communities (families, neighbourhoods, nations and so on) have mutually created to cope with the present. People's sense of history is also moulded by references to the past in the media and by the politicians, even if their influence is not as great as that of shared histories. Anyone following political debates, for instance, knows that the various stances taken are usually tied up with both general assumptions and specific claims about the past. It is easy to recount cases where past events have been seized upon to justify a particular course of action, albeit not always adequately. There is also good reason to observe in this context the importance of state action and direction, as for example the British historian Jeremy Black emphasizes.[9]

In addition to everyday popular and public uses of the past, our sense of history is also influenced by historical novels and films as well as by numerous institutions – not least among them schools and museums. Further, historical information is conveyed by sources that were not designed to convey information of the past. These include various artefacts, such as statues and buildings, built environments, everyday ephemera and so on. They signify several different pasts and contain many divergent stories depending on the person or group referring to them. The Ruskin historian Hilda Kean's *London Stories*, based on, for example, 'shards' of her ancestors' lives, the various stuff, bits and pieces they left behind, is a good example of the richness of such potential starting points for history-making.[10]

All in all, there are an infinite number of various kinds of histories, each with its own purpose. There are also many different kinds of historians, even if the term is reserved, as is reasonable, to cover only those with a continuous interest in presenting the past as distinct from casual history-makers. The different types of histories have emerged as responses to the many kinds of present-day concerns people have, and the huge amount of them testifies to the countless number of historians there are at any given moment. It goes without saying that the social making of histories is in constant process, rather than being static. And in the middle of these never-ending activities to account for the past are the specialists endeavouring to demonstrate 'that is not how it was'.

At the beginning of this book everyday history was divided, in order to make the historian's practical context simpler, into three categories: public, popular and scholarly. At this point I would justify an additional simplification. The variety of everyday history notwithstanding, this book focuses on one type of history-making: scholarly history and its numerous aspects. This limitation should, however, allow the opportunity to deal relatively comprehensively with the role of all history and all historians in society. For the idea is to suggest a viable standpoint for the scholarly historian's practice among the multitude of history-makers.

The pasts present

The social process of history-making is maintained by a myriad of interacting people among whom scholars amount to a clear minority. What then constitutes the trained historian's distinctiveness? The answer is the same as for the founding fathers of the discipline in the nineteenth century: experts in the past are there to produce sound knowledge. True, it is possible to evaluate many kinds of histories by epistemological criteria but the scholarly genre is the only one in which such an assessment is obligatory. The same aspiration of producing solidly researched historical accounts that led to the birth of the discipline has not lost its validity, even though historians have neither considered it in all its aspects nor updated it in every respect needed.

The need for the historian's expertise is created by the absence of the past. Certainly, the past is present as *remnants* which can be used as historical *sources*, and these remnants also establish history as an empirical genre of knowledge: they exist independently of any later thinking about them. But the remnants are mute or, to paraphrase Paul Ricoeur, they are *traces* that signify something without making it appear. Consequently, it is the ability to infer what the available remnants signify that is the logical goal of trained historians.[11] Nevertheless, practical research does not start from these inferences, the references of the available remnants as traces, but from the historian's questions or assumptions, as Figure 2 demonstrates.

It is the assumption that a remnant may yield fruitful information and can be used as *evidence* that instigates the historian's reasoning as regards this potential source. The next step is to make sure that this does not remain a mere supposition, that the remnant also qualifies as a *source*. One has to analyse the remnant as a *trace* in order to establish its purpose or function since without this it is not possible to decide whether the potential source can be used as evidence. The decision about the remnant's validity, whether it can be used as proof of the historian's assumption, is based on the influence of that purpose or function has had on the information conveyed by the remnant.

Since all remnants are mute, the crucial element in reading sources is inference of their purpose or function. The historian cannot take for

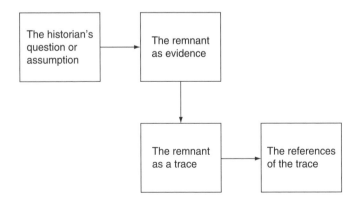

Figure 2 The emergence of the source

granted the nature of the remnant's relation to the circumstances as it appears to be; the *references* of the potential source are always results of reasoning. The historian has to evaluate every inference he or she has made in the light of all relevant previous findings. To establish the soundness of reasoning based on the available sources is essential because other people rely on the specialist's inferences and deductions, on his or her interpretations. It is this presumption that justifies the existence of the historical profession.

History is a genre of empirical knowledge that is based upon the remains of the past, and when devising the subject of study, the historian must always make sure that there is sufficient material accessible to work on and that the primary sources needed are available. The late twentieth-century disruption within the discipline widened the range of sources as the metaphor 'realms of memory' indicates. Archives are no longer thought of as the sole repository of potential evidence. It is the socially cherished tangible and abstract tokens of the past that the metaphor, coined by the French historian Pierre Nora, refers to. It depends on the historian's choice of subject whether statues, vehicles, ephemera, civic rituals, holidays, folklore or hit music, for instance, are deemed fruitful sources.[12]

Yet 'realms of memory' is symbolic of a long-incubating change. The grounds for rethinking what materials could be considered valid historical sources were well in hand before the end of the twentieth century: any historian who had bothered to stop and think about it would have realized that the profession had artificially limited both the concept of history and the range of sources. Still, the supremacy of written texts was broken only when the 'new histories' were granted access to the mainstream. The training of historians then had to be reformed: the analytical skills for using archival documents alone were no longer sufficient and, in addition, there emerged the need to weigh carefully the methodologies of close disciplines. The result was a trend towards a rejuvenation of historical enquiry, maintained by the expanding range of sources and by the blurring of traditional disciplinary boundaries.

The widened range of sources and taking seriously the innumerable genres of everyday history stimulated important new ways of looking at the past. The important point to remember here is that in the singular the notion of 'the past' is valid only in theoretical discussion. With concrete, empirical studies, there are always *many pasts*. Use of the plural may be surprising, but it is only to be expected when one remembers that every person has his or her unique past.

Oral histories illustrate another theme of the rethinking prompted by taking everyday history seriously.[13] True, personal reminiscences are sources for the past, even though use of them for this purpose is not straightforward. The fruitfulness of these sources, however, lies in their nature as accounts: they are not actually remnants of the past. Oral histories are, as the British historian Eric Hobsbawm has it, 'about the retrospect to (the past) of some subsequent present'.[14] Oral histories are first-hand sources of the moment and place where they have been mentioned or written down. They tell us what in the informant's view was significant in the past, how he or she arranges connections between the various elements, what is in his or her view the adequate way of presenting distinct matters, and so on. In other words, oral histories allow the historian to draw a host of conclusions – *about history-making*. This is further discussed in Chapter 3.

Current attitudes towards oral history also introduce the present mainstream way of looking at source material: the *fruitfulness* of information takes priority over truthfulness. People's recollections are no longer discarded as a priori unreliable evidence: instead of starting from the notion that people simply will remember wrong most historians today realize that it pays to analyse *the significance of remembering in a certain way*. This change in reading sources is quite recent. Back in the 1950s and 1960s, many historians (among them myself and my future, also foreign, colleagues) were trained to think that memories are the least reliable source and to give priority to sources with fewer 'subjective' elements, such as official documents, in order to find out 'what really took place'.

The hegemony of 'reliable sources' had its origins in the aspiration of the founding fathers to produce histories free of bias and hearsay, and the methodological term for this was *source criticism*. However, well before the disruption of the late twentieth century, historians had begun to realize that following the original logic of source criticism led to virtual dumping of potentially fruitful information. One was discouraged from pursuing what the sources sometimes invited one to do, that is, one was told to discard the clues revealed by the 'subjective' elements of the source. Reading sources (of whatever kind) would, in fact, quite a long time ago, have been a more accurate term than source criticism.

Today, the mainstream way of using sources is radically different from the ideas propounded by the discipline's founders. This is the situation in spite of the historians' failure to update their thinking: the implications of toppling the primacy of reliability have not been paid the attention they deserve, nor have historians altered their professional

ways of speaking accordingly. The usefulness of a source is not determined by its reliability in a general sense, but by its validity for *answering
the scholar's question*. When it comes to drawing inferences, it is crucial
to distinguish between first-hand and x-hand sources and not confuse
these with primary and secondary sources. The dividing line in the latter
case refers to differences in the historian's source material: scholarly histories, for instance, are quite often secondary sources but primary ones
in studies of history-writing.

That the fruitfulness of the sources has taken priority over truthfulness reflects a latent change in historians' self-awareness, a shift in
priorities. Historians seek to make sense of some past matters, and to
demonstrate their relevance; presenting the pieces of the past studied as
accurately as possible is the result of this effort, not its guiding idea. The
change has, in other words by no means led to sacrificing accuracy: correctness has merely lost its previous status as an independent criterion.
First, the degree of exactness needed depends on the historian's question. Secondly, factuality, as discussed later in this chapter (section *'The
enigmatic truth'*), must be thought of in terms of the cultural dimension
of truth.

The crucial change that characterizes the present mainstream thinking is giving up the original division into reliable and unreliable sources.
A new point of departure has been adopted: all sources are tendentious
and it is the historian's job to reveal these characteristics. The objective
is not, however, as with the original source criticism, to discriminate
between the source's various elements in order to discard some of them.
The new idea is to provide the historian with the possibility of answering the crucial question: does the information in the source warrant my
hypothesis, force me to modify it, or compel me to work towards an
alternative one?

The all-important point is that any source is, in principle, usable
as evidence. This means that the validity of a source is not an absolute but a relative characteristic, and it calls for specification – which
research question can it be used to answer? Once it is accepted that a
source is valid for answering one question but not another, the scholar
becomes a crucible of history-writing. The historian's subject takes pride
of place: questions precede sources and not vice versa. Sources really do
not – even though many historians still maintain they do – 'speak for
themselves'; they speak what the historian has made them speak.

Notwithstanding the many changes in historians' relation to their
sources, the original rationale of the discipline, to produce sound knowledge, is still valid. It is still sensible to argue that there are patterns of

thought that must be criticized by historians and that there are debates in which they are under an obligation to intervene as experts. True, they have to see the context of their work in a different light than the historian did in the nineteenth century, but this change has not undermined their role as a kind of referee in everyday history. The notion of sound history continues to be valid in spite of the necessity to acknowledge the plurality of pasts, to accept that different people have different pasts.

Still, there remain open questions about the historian's role in society, which the following chapters seek to answer. Deciding the historian's responsibilities is one of them. That there is no consensus on this reflects the current situation and demonstrates that the profession has not adequately discussed its connections to society. A good example of this failure is the issue about the boundaries of the historian's role as a referee.

The expert as a referee

The problems created by everyday history as the practical context of the historian's research work have been illuminated by, among others, the Cornell historian Barry Strauss. His claim is that historians do not have the option of remaining aloof from the 'burning of Troy'. History is no one's private property but owned by us all, and in these circumstances specialists on the past are expected to serve as referees. That unavoidable task is, however, far from a straightforward one.[15]

One side of the problem refers to reconstruction, is about the soundness of the historian's description. Troy is an extreme case since the scarcity of sources has led to professional disagreement over whether the Trojan War really took place about 3,000 years ago or not. What some scholars might call 'the likeliest interpretation of imperfect evidence' becomes, to others, 'unproven'. As regards, however, the other side of the problem Troy is not an exceptional case. It is the significance of the past event or matter that shows the huge toll of acting as a referee. Not even Troy is not the preserve of the specialists.

Once hailed as a sign of Europe's triumph over Asia, Troy has now been put into service as a bridge between East and West: the Anatolian character of the city has been called in as support for Turkey's quest for admission to the European Union. In the United States in recent years, 'both prosecution and defence have called Homer as a witness in debates on the nation's wars' in Vietnam and Iraq. So, it is apparent, if professional historians disregard the public uses of Troy and 'shy from interpreting imperfect evidence, amateurs will surely rush in'.[16]

It is, as Strauss puts it, the scholarly historian's job to 'create and debate plausible scenarios that connect the dots represented by the few facts that happen to survive from ancient times'. Dealing with recent history, at the other extreme, is actually quite similar. No one is able to manage all the available sources when trying to discover, for example, what took place in 1968 in virtually every western society. Still, the difficulties notwithstanding, it is producing sound knowledge that distinguishes professionals from the other history-makers. To historians to act as referees of everyday history accords also with the rationale of the founding fathers: there is a social demand for criticism of unreliable histories.

'Excluding supernatural interventions and legendary and mythical elements' from accounts of the past was a conspicuous aspect of historical research in the early days of the discipline. Another demand called for by the requirement for sound knowledge of the past was rigorous examination of the 'veracity of the sources on which (historical) accounts rested'.[17] The view that emerged within the profession on its work has been aptly crystallized by Paul Ricoeur: 'through documents and their critical examination of documents, historians are subject to what once was.' The task is, as historians themselves put it, to present the object studied in its own terms. Ricoeur is also right when he characterizes the profession's aspiration as far as representing the past is concerned: 'if history is a construction, historians, by instinct would like this construction to be a reconstruction'. A necessary part of the balance sheet of good historians is this 'plan to reconstruct something in constructing it'.[18]

The magnitude of the historian's task is revealed by the linguistic turn of the late twentieth century, a transformation common to all disciplines studying society and culture. The core of the nowadays conventional way of thinking is that language is not a neutral mode of conveying information. The content of knowledge is not independent of the form in which it is presented, nor is it possible for the scholar to master all aspects of a text. To what extent scholars are at the mercy of a discourse, however, is an issue that has given rise to heated controversy. In any case, once one accepts that the comprehension of reality is conditioned by the language used to express one's beliefs it is hard to regard scholarly attempts to reach an 'objective reality' as viable.

There is no acceptable excuse, at any stage of the research process, for not asking 'whose reality?' and 'whose discourse?', to paraphrase the Dutch philosopher of history Frank Ankersmit. It is this that is, with respect to history-making, the message of the linguistic turn.[19] The most profound change in relation to the way of thinking prevailing before the paradigmatic change of the late twentieth century is the requirement to regard the scholar's basic tenets as an integral part of the research done. If historians forget that their discourse is not neutral, and consequently that their concept of reality is not objective, they are unable to describe the people studied in their own terms. In addition to the historian's comprehension of reality and his or her way of expressing it, readers' beliefs must also be incorporated – if historians aim to contribute to their understanding of their own world.

The argument of this book, all the consequences of the linguistic turn notwithstanding, is that there is no reason to give up the objective of reconstruction. True, it is an epistemological impossibility to make transparent something that is inherently opaque. This is the argument that supports the postmodernist demand that *construction* is substituted for *reconstruction*. However, the impossibility of mastering another person's thinking does not prevent the historian from attempting to reach out to that other person's concept of reality and discourse. Still less does it hinder the scholar from reconstructing the circumstances in which that person lived. On the contrary, if research is carried out properly, the resulting account is a fair description. Performing these methodological operations is what the rationale of historical research demands.

In Paul Ricoeur's view, the requirement of presenting a fair description of the people studied reflects the 'robust conviction animating (all) historians', that they are 'moved by the desire to do justice to the past'.[20] The point Ricoeur makes, from the perspective of the present book, becomes clear when one thinks about what happens when this is not the case. Being unfair to the people studied results in at least one, but in many cases two, scenarios. One possibility is the spreading of propaganda, where those studied have become the historian's pawns, their views and actions misrepresented to serve the historian's message. The other is where historians have deceived not only themselves but also their audience by strengthening prevailing prejudices. Failure to produce a fair description is really to lose the very point of historical research.

As regards the audience, it is useful to refer to what I presented in Chapter 1 (see pp. 18–19) as the ultimate end of historical enquiry. The virtual dialogue between the people studied and the people addressed is possible only if the historian displays to the latter party the way the former party understood its reality and expressed its beliefs. What this means in practical terms is no novelty for an experienced historian: he or she has made it clear to him- or herself where one can use one's own words. What is suggested here is just taking a step further: to convey to the people addressed the need to exercise the same care in history-making. This means also showing to one's audience the self-defeating nature of traditional objectivity.

Fairness, presenting a fair description of the people studied and their culture is the *sine qua non* of historical research: without explaining reasonably the situation of the people studied and their intentions, there is neither sense in the historian's profession nor any justification for it. On the other hand, 'the cobbler must stick to one's last'. The professional historian's training gives him or her a mandate to judge whether everyday accounts of the past are fair or not, whether past people's actions have been presented on their own terms or whether an event has been situated in a justifiable past context, for instance. This mandate does not, however, include judging the significance of past phenomena in the present: the historian does not have any privileged position in determining their meaning and importance. When assessing the relevance of past matters for the present, the specialist must adjust to a situation where his or her arguments are on a par with the arguments of other history-makers.

To sum up, in scholarly vocabulary: the historian has the right to act as referee only as far as the epistemological *soundness* of knowledge is concerned. One's duty is to attempt to ensure that the people studied and their culture have been described appropriately and given a fair hearing. As regards the *meaning*, of the past matters, the historian does not have a privileged position. The significance he or she attaches to what has taken place in the past is only his or her reasoned opinion, and equally, it is not his or her job to state which fragments of the past are noteworthy and which are not. The implications of this distinction between soundness and meaningfulness are discussed in many contexts further below. Here is the place to discuss the historian's way of managing the meaningfulness that carries his or her work forward.

The specialist's personal contribution

Opposition to the idea that history is a reservoir of examples to be used for rhetorical purposes was the rationale for Ranke's famous dictum, *'wie es eigentlich gewesen'*, be content with explaining 'only what actually happened'. The historian's job, as this founding father put it 1824, is not to 'instruct the present for the benefit of the ages to come'. He reacted against the way of thinking about the past that had dominated history-writing up to the nineteenth century and was symbolized by a phrase coined by Cicero, Historia magistra vitae, history as life's teacher.[21] Ranke's justified pronouncement did not, however, mean that nothing was left in historical research of the original instructive role. On the contrary, even if many historians have kept their silence on the subject, the incentive for choosing one research topic over another is the historian's feeling that his or her prospective findings will make a difference. The idea of all the subsequent research is to test, refine and expand this notion.

The historian's message, the meanings he or she conveys in his or her work, sets forth the significance of the subject studied for the present situation. The idea, however, is not that the findings would be relevant only in the current circumstances; on the contrary, they should also serve in the future as 'a resource with an open-ended application'. The guidance and perspective embedded in the message are not intended as firm predictions and unequivocal generalisations; their role is to offer 'a surer sense of possibilities latent in our present condition', as John Tosh puts it. This is the way 'every manifestation of the human spirit in the past' evokes the claim on our attention.[22]

Specialists on the past act as intermediaries between two cultures, interpreting the thoughts and actions of those living in very different circumstances to people living in a later time so that they can make use of that knowledge. Today, such strong emphasis on this aspect of the specialist's role may sound odd but that emphasis was certainly not self-evident in the early 1960s when I was learning my craft. My generation was told that truth-seeking was, in Thomas L. Haskell's words, 'a matter of emptying oneself of passion and preconception, so as to become a perfectly passive and receptive mirror of external reality' – erasing one's self, according to Ranke's dictum.[23]

Worth noticing is that the scholar's message need not have an immediate bearing on the current situation or on a broader audience. Here an example is provided by the Canadian historian Jeffrey R. Collins's recent work on Thomas Hobbes, which was rated highly by one of its reviewers in 2006. In fact, 'not for nearly half a century... has there been so challenging an interpretation of the relationship between the political thought and the revolutionary events of seventeenth-century England'. This judgement was based on the scholar's message, which 'invites fresh approaches not only to Hobbes but also to the movements of ideas to which Collins relates him, and in which he repeatedly identifies patterns and correspondences that cut across expectation'.[24]

In contrast to Jeffrey R. Collins, the Finnish historian Juhani Suomi had to work with a quite different kind of audience in mind when preparing his multi-volume biography of the late Finnish President Urho Kekkonen. The reception of his works was dominated, as was to be expected, by politically interested lay readers. This comparison between the two historians serves as an introduction to Chapter 3, 'The People Addressed': not only is there is no such thing as a universal audience but the composition of the prospective readership makes a great difference from the scholar's point of view.

The works of Collins and Suomi illustrate a key aspect of this book's central idea. Culturally, the historical profession has two functions: to contribute to people's sense of the past and to advance the discipline. On the one hand, scholars evaluate public and popular accounts by relying on epistemological norms and, on the other, improve disciplinary methods and enhance knowledge, aims which are only indirectly connected to public and popular histories. Neither of these functions is more valuable than the other; in contrast, an ideal study makes a notable contribution to both.

A perspective on the historian's intentions is shown by a recent discussion I had with the New York scholar Ronald J. Grele, an internationally leading figure in the field of oral history. In interviewing Cambodians about their experiences during the time of the Khmer Rouge, he had met several local people who had been politically active in those days and their views had given him cause to think about the concepts of justice and vengeance. This made me respond: 'you arrived at precisely the point at which it is the historian's job to lead his or her readers. Instead of taking your own values for granted, you began to reflect on them.'

In his paper at the conference during which we had our discussion Grele referred to the studies of two American anthropologists, Susan Harding's (Santa Cruz) of an evangelical Christian community and Dennis Tedlock's (Buffalo) of Maya. For Harding the attempt to bridge the gap between herself and her interviewees 'led her to seriously question her own religious traditions'. Tedlock, in turn, has argued that 'there is no way of understanding Maya unless one accepts the validity and truth of magic'. For Grele these are works in which the scholar takes 'at face value' the world view of the people studied instead of 're-colonizing them' with anthropological or historiographical methods.[25] My formulation of the same approach is that fairness demands that the historian expounds the views of the people studied before proceeding to argue for the current significance of their ideas.

As regards the historian's personal contribution, as indicated in the Preface, making comments on specific contemporary developments is my personal preference. My position does not, however, imply that this is a book which argues for speaking to current issues through scholarship as the historian's obligation. Writing about the past with no explicit intent to affect the present is quite legitimate; concerning such studies the argument of the present book makes just three points.

First, it is worth the historian's while right at the outset of the research project to think about his or her actual reasons for doing it. Secondly, even an historian working without the specific aim of influencing current debates is inescapably involved in society, and they should give serious consideration to what this entails. And, third, one's contribution will have consequences irrespective of one's intentions.

History as 'an argument without end'

Historians may serve, as Mary Fulbrook puts it, a wide variety of purposes, 'from entertainment to argument, from information and understanding to empathy and emotive arousal'. They may aim for example 'to argue a particular case in a wider context of controversy, to solve a puzzle within an existing framework of knowledge, to present a particular interpretation against other views, to reconstruct the 'unknown', to evoke a certain atmosphere or arouse a set of sympathies'.[26]

Fullbrook reminds us that the never-ending social process of history-making provides the historian with a multitude of incentives to research; the historian works surrounded by innumerable everyday activities to account for the past. There is also a wide variety of purposes to choose between. The end-result, too, may be of many kinds since there are several options to choose between when composing the final account that conveys the one's findings. The bottom line is that there is not only one way of conducting a historical enquiry; it is of great import to emphasize that the kind of research a historian performs is the result of his or her choices.

Selecting a topic to be studied, of course, is a practical necessity, but it is also the point when the sensible historian starts to think about his or her responsibilities. Why this particular research? The common tendency to keep silent about one's intentions is self-defeating since the choice of focus is no coincidence, and once you have got a hunch that the topic turns out to be fruitful, why not build on it? It is in the historian's own interest to uncover as early as possible the actual reasons for selecting a particular topic. The task of the following chapters is to assist in this effort by way of discussing the various connections the historian's objectives have and by elaborating their implications.

'Self-overcoming' is Thomas L. Haskell's term for the attitude that is required. The scholar needs a capacity to achieve distance from his or her own preferences 'to ensure collision with rival perspectives'.[27] The question is of disciplining one's thinking by means of dissecting and organizing those preferences. Such 'self-overcoming' refers, in the vocabulary of this hook, to the hard side of double detachment discussed in the Introduction (see pp. 15–16). Doing research in history is to straddle the uneasy juxtaposition of arguing for an interpretation that conveys one's message and detaching oneself from the positions embedded in that message.

The practical way of performing 'self-overcoming' is meeting the conventional part of double detachment, critique of prevailing knowledge. Why is there need to demonstrate that the past matters were contrary to what they are claimed or believed to have been? Analysing the interpretations targeted has to sides. The (relatively) easy one is about soundness, to highlight their weaknesses as explanations while the hard one refers to their meanings. The real challenge lies in exposing the uses to which these interpretations have been put, especially since it is not always easy to discern the contexts where they have been exploited. These are issues to be discussed more thoroughly below in Chapter 4, *Politics of history*.

In the present chapter the focus is on historical enquiry in the perspective of theory of knowledge, and this theme is introduced by two general remarks on the epistemological status of the historians' alternatives. The first thought-provoking perspective on historical research is opened by the sensible contention of the Swedish historian Rolf Torstendahl. According to him all answers to the issue 'what is history?' actually come down to the question 'what is historically significant' – which means that there are many different concepts of history among historians.[28]

Today's situation takes Torstendahl's point to the extreme. The diversity of scholarly orientations with regard to 'historically significant' has hardly ever been as great as it is in the beginning of the twenty-first century – and new perspectival paradigms continually emerge in the wake of the one-time 'new histories'.[29] In addition, none of these orientations even tries to claim similar hegemonic position as the nineteenth century variant of political history, with its focus on high politics and great men, had for such long a time.[30]

The second general remark on the results of historical enquiry is the perspective opened by the rationale of criticizing prevailing knowledge.

The idea of alternative interpretations lies in offering new historical knowledge in the sense of producing more compelling explanations than the previous ones. The argument is that, irrespective of whether the aim is to upgrade or criticize existing interpretations or to present an entirely new one, the historians' 'truths' are by their nature qualified, since they are always provisional. The findings are not absolute but conclusions open to modification.

It is actually only since the 1960s, thanks to E. H. Carr's *What Is History?*, that it has become a mainstream notion that 'the priorities and findings of historical enquiry inevitably change over time'. Carr thought of history as an unending dialogue between past and present: 'to learn about the present in the light of the past means also learning about the past in the light of the present'. In his view the most significant 'pointer to the character of a society' is 'the kind of history it writes or fails to write'. As an example, Carr referred to the work of the Dutch historian Pieter Geyl on the judgements of nineteenth-century French historians for and against Napoleon, which reflected the patterns of political life and thought in their country.[31] Geyl himself presented history in an albeit worn out but very apt formulation, as 'an argument without end' and it is from this perspective that one has to consider the nature of commenting on existing interpretations.[32]

According to Geyl and Carr, histories emerge from a continuing dialogue between present and past: changes in the historical situation are reflected in the demand for knowledge. As a result, any interpretation, no matter how well supported, is liable to be amended. The comprehension of the episode in the past which is studied changes when attention is focused on untried aspects of it, popular and public interests get a new direction, there is a shift in scholarly perspectives, new source material becomes available, and so on.

On the other hand, one must not forget that producing alternative interpretations entails accountability: historians must justify their choices and decisions in a way that is open to evaluation. Those who will come to evaluate the work must be provided with the reasons for the questions asked as well as the approach chosen. They must also be able to assess whether, within the conceptual framework selected, the reasoning is impeccable and whether the people studied have been dealt with fairly. A new interpretation can only be more compelling than previous ones if it passes epistemological scrutiny. In other words, the provisional nature of the explanations arrived at does not give licence for theoretical ambiguity.

Still, it is not only with time that interpretations of the past change. The provisional nature of the historian's truths must also be considered from the perspective of there being many pasts, as discussed several times above. Accepting that different people have different pasts means recognizing that there are always different points of view from which the past can be analysed. The ensuing multitude of histories does not warrant the claim of a limitless relativism in the sense of 'anything goes'. Rather, the sensible conclusion is that history is a social form of knowledge, as Raphael Samuel has argued.[33] In Chapter 3 it will be demonstrated that there exist in any society several divergent *shared histories*, meaning that there are, simultaneously, many different perspectives on the past. The significance of this is that those who research human history cannot think in terms of a single truth.

The enigmatic truth

Their qualified 'truths' has led many historians to despair over the knowable past. The American historian Arthur Schlesinger Jnr., for instance, expresses this when he speaks of what 'all historians know in their souls': the past is 'a chaos of events and personalities into which we cannot penetrate. It is beyond retrieval and it is beyond reconstruction.'[34] This is why it is unreasonable to maintain, as many historians still did at the end of the twentieth century, a belief in the 'untiring and unending accumulation of hard facts as the foundation of history, the belief that facts speak for themselves'.[35]

Towards the end of the twentieth century such unreasonable claims by historians incurred a backlash. Some postmodernists even went so far as to suggest that scholarly works on history constitute a distinctive genre of fiction. It was often asserted that like reality, history is a chimera. To historians these allegations were unfair: to discredit myths, correct distortions and authenticate events beyond reasonable doubt, for instance, is not useless. The past is not just a plaything of the present as postmodernists seem to think.

'Hybrids' characterizes the position of Raphael Samuel in the late twentieth century on the nature of historical knowledge. What historians produce is for him the opposite of 'immaculate knowledge'. They always syncretize 'past and present, memory and myth, the written record and the spoken word'.[36] In my opinion, this stance of Samuel's is reasonable, since it is impossible to adequately compare the findings of historical research against the kind of knowledge produced by the natural sciences. Nor is it sensible for historians to confuse their own issues with those of philosophers, as they did from the 1950s until the 1970s by, for example, importing the Covering Law Model to historical enquiry.[37]

Instead of disregarding the difference between their field and that of philosophy, historians should remember that the context of their work is history-in-society. They should, for example, avoid imprudent use of the term 'truth' in defending the profession against claims that overstate the relativity of all historical knowledge, and keep in mind that there are many different types of knowledge. The 'truth' of the date of an event, for instance, is of a different order to the 'truth' of the description of that event. Truth, in other words, should always be ascertained in terms of the question asked. In addition, one should also remember that there are many terms (accuracy, correctness, veracity, reality, certainty, and so on) to describe the different tenors of 'truth'.

In similar vein, historians should remember that people attach different meanings to truth. There are, for example, those who think about responsibility or guilt, and those for whom 'truth' refers to what is essential in the course of history. In other words, historians should avoid simplifying 'truth' by treating it as a one-dimensional notion. The issue studied is often clarified when the scholar treats the various dimensions of truth – ethical, epistemological, methodological, cultural, pragmatic and political – as different, separate aspects of a single entity.[38]

As regards the truth of historical interpretations, the point is that the issues dealt with are indistinct when compared with those of philosophy. It is seldom, if ever, that a question is as clear-cut as the requirement for agreement between a statement and 'the way things are', for instance. The challenge the historian is confronted with is a very different. What is possible to achieve can only be characterized in terms of a 'never-ending argument'. The historian aspires to deliver an interpretation of the past that makes better sense of it than previous ones, and that not only holds good now but also in the future.

When evaluating interpretations, it is sensible to give up the notion of truth, and to think instead in terms of the distinction introduced above: there is on the one hand the *soundness* of the knowledge produced and on the other the *meaningfulness* of the findings. This distinction is based on the arguments used by historians when evaluating the studies of their colleagues. The British philosopher Stephen Toulmin refers to the same dividing line when he speaks of the *criteria* and the *force* of arguments.[39] Historians rely on three criteria in assessing each of the two dimensions of interpretation:

```
┌─────────────────────────────────────────┐
│ Soundness of knowledge                   │
│                                          │
│ 1. Impeccability of reasoning            │
│ 2. Cogency of interpretation             │
│ 3. Plausibility of description           │
│                                          │
│ Meaningfulness of the findings           │
│                                          │
│ 4. Truthfulness                          │
│ 5. Fruitfulness                          │
│ 6. Lesson, or moral of the study         │
└─────────────────────────────────────────┘
```

Figure 3   The criteria used by historians in evaluation

Impeccability of reasoning is a criterion underrated by historians and hardly understood at all by scholars in other fields. Its rationale derives from the nature of the historian's final account, which has not been paid the attention it deserves. The exposition is, with regard to its reasoning, structurally complex, consisting of several intersecting trains of argument, often with common elements. Making sure it is coherent, avoiding internal contradictions and unnecessary repetitions is far from an undemanding task. The difficulty of the exercise is increased by an 'absence', the undisclosed elements of reasoning. All historians have to assume, for example, so as not to underestimate readers, that certain parts of the argument are familiar to them.[40]

The second criterion of soundness is *cogency of interpretation*, and this is evaluated by reference to previous findings, the prevailing knowledge. Is the new explanation more convincing than those to date, does it make better sense of the particular aspect of the past than did its predecessors? The third criterion is the *plausibility of description*, which refers to the culture of the people studied. Here, it is evaluated whether adequate consideration has been given to the available, relevant knowledge on the particular culture. However, tapping all the sources and examining previous findings is not the only requirement; the description must also be fair, as has been emphasized above.

It is this ethical dimension of plausibility that continues to subvert the very idea of historical research: the temptation to compromise fairness to past people has often proved irresistible to both professional and lay historians. Since it is easy to mistake politics for ethics, some of the most heated debates among historians have been about the plausibility of an interpretation. Avoiding unjustified use of power assumes an honesty among specialists in the sense that they do not bring their reconstruction of the past to an end before they are sure they have grasped thoroughly beliefs of the people studied and the ways they were thinking.

Knowledge that is sound but not *meaningful* does not make sense. While soundness is a necessary component of the historian's findings, it is not sufficient on its own. The way historians evaluate each other's works demonstrates that it is the *fruitfulness* of the knowledge produced and the *lesson* or *moral* embedded in the study that decide whether an enquiry is considered worthy of merit. The findings are fruitful when they upgrade or invalidate existing interpretations and/or present a new one. The results are also fruitful if they have been achieved by employing new methods or approaches, opened up new perspectives for research or posed new questions.

Fruitfulness is, by its nature, always particular, in the sense that it is connected to a certain subject and its context, whereas the same lesson may be produced or the same moral conveyed by several different studies. Yale authority on slavery David Brion Davis gives a good example of history being instructive, in his review of the Pittsburgh historian Seymour Drescher's *A History of Slavery and Anti-Slavery*, a work he praises for showing that slavery has 'an amazing capacity to endure or suddenly become resurrected'. According to Davis, 'if Drescher's profound history of human nature gives some cause for hope with regard to moral progress, it should also end complacency and put us on continual alert'.[41]

Truthfulness, the third criterion of meaningfulness, is, like impeccability of reasoning, something that has not been paid the attention its exacting nature deserves. The results of historical research must, first, be presented in a discourse that matches the audience's understanding of reality and their way of speaking about it. Since plausibility of description also means being true to the same traits of the people studied, it is reasonable to speak of a *requirement of double truthfulness*.

To sum up: evaluating new interpretations of history is anything but straightforward.[42] First, the truthfulness (don't forget its double form!) of a work is only one aspect of the historian's interpretation, and history is more accurately regarded in terms of 'an argument of end'. Thus, the historian's job is not to disseminate absolute and unconditional versions of the past but, rather, to furnish materials for serious debate. Secondly, it is not simply whether a new explanation makes better sense of sources on the past than previous ones that gives it validity, but whether the research findings are fruitful and provide lessons for the future as part of an ongoing struggle for the relevance of the past. The following section in this chapter (*'The historian's basic predicament'*), explores these criteria further and demonstrates the central role played by the historian's point of view on the topic at hand.

The six criteria needed to assess the soundness and meaningfulness of the historian's findings demonstrate that the profession needs, to use Stephen Toulmin's term, a field-dependent approach of its own for evaluation.[43] This contention is supported by the fact that epistemological soundness is connected to both what sources are available and the nature of debate within the discipline. Every historian knows that new, more cogent and more plausible interpretations emerge with the discovery of new sources. Yet, this does not mean that the study of history is simply to fill the gaps in the existing body of knowledge.

Nor is it viable to claim, even though many scholars still do, that once a gap has been filled there is no need for further discussion. This is equal to thinking that history is 'an argument *with an end*', to discuss interpretations in terms of a single 'truth'. The professional historian's duty is the opposite: to make it clear that there are no absolute and authoritative views on the past. Rather, it can be approached from many points of view, with the chosen perspective always supported by convincing argument. This is how historians can counteract the tendency, especially in the media, to oversimplify complicated historical issues and to play down the complex nature of history in general.

The historian's job is to argue, when appropriate, that common interpretations are insufficient; or even, where necessary, to demonstrate that received scholarly opinion is inaccurate. It is reasoning, not beliefs, that occupies pride of place in history-writing, while there is also a wide space for epistemologically grounded argument about the past. The scope of supranationally shared professional criteria is broad enough to make it possible to distinguish well-supported historical contributions.

It is thus reasonable to conclude that lay expectations of specialists in the past are not unrealistic – provided experts work systematically towards an awareness of exactly what they are doing. Those addressed must be sure that the accounts offered are not merely accurate but also carefully weighed. Historians, in turn, must make it clear that the past is a terrain which does not allow for debates in terms of 'truths':[44] what is within the bounds of possibility are findings that are both sound and significant, *knowledge* that is *sustainable*.

The historian's basic predicament

The persistent ideological conflict between 'the objectivists' and the 'representatives of partisanships' has diverted attention from the historian's basic predicament. The rival camps created a situation where two sides of the same coin were separated from each other, and de facto thought of as unconnected issues. One faction laid emphasis on treating the people studied on their own terms and the other on producing meaningful new knowledge for the researcher's contemporaries. What was lost was the historian's predicament: to reconcile the conflicting demands entailed by these different objectives. The challenge to be met is to respond to current concerns – by way of presenting a fair description of the people whom one is studying.

The relevance of the topic the historian chooses is not predetermined, but depends on the circumstances. Recently, quite a few fresh works on the abolition of slavery were published; the apparent reason for bringing them out was the bicentennial of the Abolition of the Slave Trade Act, passed by the British parliament in 1807. It is quite possible that these books were initiated by the publishers, but that does not exclude historians also having their own reasons for opting for this particular theme. The point is that there were several alternative approaches to the *topic*, all highlighting different aspects of abolitionism.

Among these recent works, the American author Adam Hochchild's looks upon British abolitionism from the point of view of its leaders, while the British historian Simon Schama's 'heroes...are black loyalists (in America) and a handful of white British abolitionists'. Their reviewer, the Washington (D.C.) historian Eric Arnesen in turn, would have preferred to 'look for insights into the emergence and spread of antislavery thought or the reforming impulses of evangelical Christianity'.[45] The relevance of the study depends, in other words, on the way the scholar specifies the topic and turns it into a *subject*.

Creating the *subject* takes place when the historian selects one of the several possible contexts for discussion of the topic, in this case, abolitionism. Hochchild, Schama and Arnesen made different choices. The heart of a research project is thus not provided by the topic or given in some other way, but created through the historian's thinking. It is selecting the *point of view,* choosing the explanatory context that defines the focus of the enquiry. The questions the historian sets out to answer do not originate either in the topic or in the context alone but in the connection between them. This combination of topic and point of view is the most important decision made at the planning stage since the whole research process revolves around it.

Another example illustrates the pivotal role of the historian's decisions. In the case of seventeenth-century Swedish witch hunts, it is possible to discuss them in the context of, for example, contemporary religious groups, or popular beliefs in magic, or prevailing gender relations and so on. In other words, historians have several points of view at their disposal but opt for only one of them. True, it is also possible to deploy simultaneously several points of view in approaching one's topic, but never all the conceivable ones. In any case, it is the topic and the explanatory context, both denoting the past, that constitute one's subject, but what must not be forgotten is that their combination is created in the present by the historian.

The origins of my own doctoral thesis illustrate the incentive to a create a subject. In the mid-1960s I wanted to criticize the tendency to ignore the prevailing circumstances of any given time in debates on the then Finnish forign policy options. The topic I chose was Finnish cooperation with other Scandinavian countries, and the objective was to show that not even this orientation was self-evident but depended on the historical situation. My way of corroborating this was to analyse relations between Finland and Sweden in the 1920s. I compared systematically the foreign policies of the two countries and demonstrated that the contemporary international situation had made these neighbours choose, as I expected, profoundly 'different roads' (the title of the book).[46]

What I managed to show was that those responsible for Finnish and Swedish foreign policy had profoundly different views on the Soviet Union, the status quo in the Baltic region, and the international situation. Given these differences, there simply was hardly any room for cooperation in terms of security. Viewed in this light, prevailing explanations for the lack of diplomatic and military collaboration between the World Wars were clearly deficient. It was not plausible to ignore the completely different assessments of the foreign context the two countries shared, and to account for their different policies with reference to political attitudes. Bitterness caused by the dispute over the sovereignty of the Aland Islands and the ethnic conflict in Finland, the struggle for entitlements between Finnish-speaking and Swedish-speaking Finns, were clearly secondary.

The point to be made in this section is that the issue the historian chooses to study emerges with a view on swaying the people to be addressed. The focus of the investigation, the particular combination of topic and explanatory context, results from *the aim of calling the audience's attention to it.* The idea is to demonstrate that the subject thus created is connected with matters relevant to those thought to be interested in it, and to argue that it is worth thinking about. In the vocabulary of this book, it is this connection, the relationship between the subject created and what matters to the audience that constitutes the historian's *message.*

True, it is often only gradually that historians become aware of the issue they are actually pursuing: identifying one's intentions is not always easy, let alone explaining them to others. And the draft of the message will also normally change many times while the project is being planned. Yet the time consumed on defining the audience, subject and message at the outset of the research project does not, contrary to what many colleagues argue, testify to unnecessary haste in defining one's subject. The rationale of the study is not to be found in the primary sources, it is created in the historian's thinking. The point I am making – which this whole book seeks to substantiate – is that sensible historians keep on elaborating their message until the research project ends. Still, the crucial phase is creating the subject during the planning stage.

The main objective of *Making History* is to draw attention to the implications of the scholar's attempt to draw the audience's interest to the selected subject and to persuade them of its relevance. Irrespective of the make-up of the audience, the predicament every historian will have faced is the temptation to compromise fairness to the people studied in order to convince the audience of the cogency of his or her 'message.' It is the making of one's point that, quite reasonably, directs one's work.

3
The People Addressed

The rationale of historical research is, from the historian's perspective, to call the audience's attention to one's selection and arrangement of particular past matters in order to demonstrate their present relevance. From the vantage point of history-in-society the same rationale can be given another formulation: historians meet the demand for knowledge concerning the past. This perspective has, however, been underrated by the profession.

'Whose history has been written and whose has not?' This question illustrates the position from which I criticized the profession's establishment in the 1970s. The response was that such an approach is not justified since the historian must be neutral in relation to the different groups in society: rather than showing preferences, one has to abstain from taking a stand. More pertinent to the present chapter was that the premise of my approach was regarded as inappropriate too. Historical enquiry should not be thought of in terms of its 'relevance'; its starting point was not in the present but in the past.

This was the dominant pattern of thought, but it did not mean that all historians took literally the logic of 'history for its own sake'. Many admitted the importance of looking after 'the nation's memory', for instance, and some were even of the opinion that professionals are there to dispose of myths, to correct misinformed interpretations and to meet the demand for knowledge.[1] These kinds of tasks were from my point of view halfway measures: the rationale for historical enquiry was thought of in terms of the profession as a whole, hardly ever in terms of the individual historian's work.

My dissatisfaction remains the same forty years on: prospective historians are left to their own devices as regards their relation to society. Choice of the audience, for instance, cannot be avoided, but to discuss the ensuing issues has been taboo. The purpose of the present chapter is to demonstrate the various ways in which approaching the audience poses questions which have hitherto not been discussed. The most crucial failure from the individual historian's angle is that the role of the audience in the research process has hardly been tackled at all. Yet, the rationale for the historian's work is centred upon those interested in his or her subject.

As emphasized in Chapter 2, different people have different pasts in any society, which means that when historians choose a topic to be studied they also select their audience. In other words, the relevance of the knowledge produced does not depend only on the matters dealt with but also on the people addressed. Or: the message that the historian's study will eventually convey is not important for everyone. Furthermore, advances during the research process are also connected to the audience, since it is the historian's increasing comprehension of why the eventual findings will be significant to those addressed that carries the research work forward – even if historians do not articulate the logic of their work in these terms. Besides, the audience is continuously present in the investigation.

Initially, it is the people to be addressed that the historian has in mind when thinking about the significance of the research – albeit not the audience, as such, but indirectly, by way of evaluating the meanings conveyed by the planned study. Similarly, it is the audience that historians think about when considering which particular aspects of the past should constitute the subject to be studied, and which point of view is best adapted to highlight the relevance of the matters embedded in the topic to be explored. Historians start their work by trying to decide what in particular they want to study and finish the planning stage of the project when they know which matters should be investigated and why these particular matters are significant. By then they will have made up their mind as to what is the study's the central idea and what they want to say by means of their research – that is, to whom it is addressed.[2] This virtual dialogue with the chosen audience continues in the two following phases of the research process.

While the people studied are historians' main 'companions' during consultation of the primary sources – their main task is now to ensure that these people will be given a fair hearing – the people addressed are present at the second stage too. At the same time that historians test their central idea, they collect information with the help of which they can make sense of the beliefs, motives and actions of the people studied in their final account – an essential aspect of making sure their account is fair. This also introduces the third stage that is dominated by those addressed: it is with reference to the audience that historians select the material to be included in the final account and decide how it should be presented. The text must fulfil two tasks: convince the audience that the findings have a sound basis and be readily understood. The idea of this stage is encapsulated, as the American historian J.H. Hexter puts it, on how much knowledge the people addressed already possess and their patterns of thinking.[3]

Thus, the historian's virtual dialogue with the audience lasts from the beginning of the research process to its end. At the same time, the people studied are also present in the investigation, but the dialogue with them (virtual, too, of course) is of a different kind and the stakes are higher. The issue one is now negotiating is about are the deeds of the other party, performed in the past culture, and it is necessary to reach an agreement (in the sense of a fair description) to get the permit for conveying one's message. Mary Fulbrook has aptly characterized *the simultaneity of the two dialogues*. 'The historian is the creative intermediary between selected elements of the past and selected audiences in the present; and we would hardly be likely to have any interest in history if this were not so.'[4] The historian's message is based on a particular point of view but he or she must (virtually) make sure that the people studied do not veto it.

That the historian selects his or her audience has been tragically covered up: it is an issue disregarded by the profession even though every historian is confronted with it. True, there has been discussion of the distinction between professional and lay audiences, but that has been conducted in terms of the historian's style (to be discussed at the end of the Chapter 5), not as a dimension of defining the subject. As regards the research questions asked, a universal single audience remains an undisclosed premise. This is to deceive oneself, and the more frank historian will admit that his or her readers constitute often only a particular group. The varying consequences that selection of the audience has for elaborating the subject to be researched is discussed in Chapter 4. In this chapter I deal with the general implications of choosing the people to be addressed.

Selecting the people to be addressed from the large number of conceivable audiences should actually be thought of as a task on a par with two other exercises performed during the planning stage: defining the subject and delineating the message. And, as with the other two, specifying the audience is not self-evident: all three elements depend on and influence each other. Thinking about the ways in which they interrelate is the substance of the series of steps that eventually leads to formulating the central idea of the research project.

It is the narrow understanding of the professional's rationale that explains the logic leading to the premise of a single universal audience. Regarding the accurate description of the past as the dominating idea of scholarly history is, as such, a task that has no necessary connection to any specific audience other than fellow scholars in the same field. Making sense of the past is very different since it calls for analysing the need of and responding to the demand for historical knowledge. The crucial issue is then about whose view it is that is in need of correction. However, this question has been surpassed by epistemological soundness; accurate description has been thought of as the guiding idea of research instead of being treated as the result of historical enquiry. The same limited ('ivory tower') rationale is evident also in the critique of the prevailing interpretations: it is their status epistemologically that matters, not the stances and policies they sustain.

The conventional inward-looking pattern of thinking also explains why choice of the audience has been covered up; it reveals the blind spot in the rationale of scholarly history. The present relevance of past matters to those potentially interested in them has not been part of mainstream thinking whereas attaining a clear view on why the study is needed is what the professional historian gains from focusing on the people addressed. The following pages seek to demonstrate that, hitherto, in specialist eyes, the audience has actually had no role in the making of history. Instead of thinking about the people addressed as creators of their own histories, professionals have simply regarded them as consumers of academic studies.

Developing a viable concept of the historian in society has been, in retrospective analysis, a task with which I have been preoccupied since 1979, when I was appointed historian of Paperiliitto, the wealthy trade union of the paper and pulp industry. The commission was no coincidence since I had pointed out in my works the virtual total neglect of labour history, a special characteristic of Finland at that time. The key experience of the seven years as an official in Paperiliitto, as far as this book is concerned, was to grasp the built-in elitism of my profession: we considered all other genres of history-making as subordinate to that of our own discipline. It was not the only lesson that I learnt, the hard way, about the scholar's premises during the 1980s (they are explored in the following chapters).

It was with the questions raised by our professional arrogance as the vantage point that I reflected during the 1980s and 1990s on the vortex humanities were drawn into. Without actually knowing it at the time, I was an active agent of the paradigmatic change in the discipline of history. The way I designed my commission in Paperiliitto made me one of the proponents of the 'new histories' in Scandinavia, as will be evident from the next pages. Experiences from working in the trade union movement also determined my response to the linguistic turn as its consequences began to unfold. Rather than being upset by postmodernist positions I discussed our basic tenets in the light of the unfolding disruption within the discipline in dozens of publications.[5]

The risk of patronage

I started my work as the historian of Paperiliitto in 1979 by declaring in the union's newspaper that it was neither scholarly questions nor those of the union leadership that should be answered: a professional historian had been employed to investigate what was significant for the members. It is to the great credit of the governing body of the union that this prerequisite to approach history 'from below' was unanimously accepted. The method to be employed was the study circle, the traditional form of self-education for the Scandinavian working-class movement. The new element was that the groups did not study ready-made materials but produced the substance of the work themselves by creating their own histories. Like their Swedish counterparts, these peer groups came to be called research circles.[6]

The idea of research circles worked in practice: at the end of 1986 there were forty groups at thirty-three of the union's sixty-two local branches: over 200 workers engaged actively with history in different parts of the country. The plan was, in other words, a success and it inspired similar initiatives in other unions. My final study, published by Paperiliitto in 1986, was based on the experiences of the workers involved and conveyed my interpretation of the current challenges facing trade unions. It is a treatise that describes the transformation of Finnish society since the 1960s – from the local perspective. However, what is important as far as the present book is concerned is that these results were achieved quite differently from how I had initially envisioned it.

Instead of submitting their queries to me, as I had originally suggested, so that I would approach them as a professional historian approaches his own questions, local activists were encouraged to initiate research themselves. Swedish colleagues in workers' adult education had convinced me that the necessary motivation could only be secured by giving the peer groups full freedom to choose their own subjects. As a result, rather than their becoming de facto research assistants of mine, the research circles conducted their work independently. What they created were histories in their own right. The Swedish advice caused me to develop a novel concept of history that I managed to persuade the workers to accept.[7]

It took roughly one year's campaigning at the various branches all around Finland to prove to the workers that history did not mean narratives of past ruling groups, and that they too had a role in history-writing. Local activists had to be convinced that the substance of 'history' was not predetermined and that what had taken place in their factory and their neighbourhood was history too. Once they had accepted the idea that they had the same right to define the substance of history as a professional historian, the circles proliferated. This agitation was the hard way in which I discovered that the traditional academic concept of history that I had taken for granted was, by its nature, patronizing. What the workers had been taught at school, in turn, made me reflect on my own lecturing at the university and led to awareness of another problematic nineteenth-century legacy. Given the multitude of pasts, there are also many histories, and one must therefore reserve 'history' in the singular for theoretical and philosophical contexts.

A further lesson about how history is conceived was taught by what aspects of the past turned out to be important for the workers in the paper and pulp industry. Half of the more than 200 people engaged in the project, both social democrats and communists, were primarily interested, to my great surprise, in the transformation of their locality. Most of these towns or villages had originally emerged around a small factory on a stretch of rapids. For one-third of the circles the important theme was changes in their work: this was the time when production was being computerized. The really unexpected matter was that only one-fifth wanted to study the history of the union or labour movement policies – despite the fact that practically all those involved were activists, in addition to being a member of the branch of their union, in at least one of the other local working-class organizations.[8]

The way Paperiliitto activists defined 'their own history' bears in two ways on history-writing, and the first of these is connected to the role of history in the traditional working-class movement. My surprise at their choices revealed that I had in fact shared the socialist version of 'history from above' or 'the history of great men'. In the 1986 book published by the union I coined the term 'the imperialism of the enlightened worker', to indicate a tendency common to all heirs of the Second International from the late nineteenth and early twentieth centuries. It was not only communists who regarded themselves as the vanguard of the workers' movement but social democrats too – albeit expressing their views in a different way. This is a theme to which I will return (see pp. 63–5) in connection with public histories.

The other perspective on history-writing opened by the Paperiliitto activists can be summarized as a piece of advice: beware of patronage. It was apparent that it was the workers' own situation that might engage them with the past, not the history of their union or of some other formal institution. That the risk of patronage is a permanent one has also been demonstrated by, for example, Roy Rosenzweig and David Thelen in their project on the popular uses of history in American life in the 1990s. When people had the opportunity to approach the past on their own terms, that is, 'not as a classroom progress from election to election', they 'grounded historical inquiry in the present circumstances, perceptions, and needs'.[9]

The fundamental message was that the substance of 'history' must not be taken for granted. Scholarly historians should really explore how, and why, the past becomes history. In a more practical perspective, I learned that the professionals must always beware imposing his or her views upon the readership. To make this warning explicitly is called for by the often unintentional nature of patronizing attitudes. The paradoxical difficulty is familiar to any non-authoritarian teacher: to strengthen the student's own motivation while conveying the skills you master.

That the work of the research circles was separate from mine did not, however, preclude cooperation – rather the reverse. Taking the members' ideas seriously led in the long run (it took three years of full-time work!) to a situation where I could communicate with them freely and without misunderstandings (that they were people of roughly my own age and spoke Finnish as their native language was no distinct advantage). At the same time the trust put in me made it increasingly difficult to distance myself from their views. The dilemma has aptly been characterized by Roy Rosenzweig: it really is not easy to be simultaneously 'a trusted insider and a dispassionate outside expert'.[10]

My role in the Paperiliitto history project was that of a supervisor. In addition to taking part in the circles' discussions about their projects, I set up a system of three-day or four-day intensive courses for the circle leaders. Actually, I worked much in the same way that I had done at the university – but free from academic formalities. What ensued in practice, besides guiding the research, was that I had countless diverse conversations in a variety of contexts from the angle of my own research work – the key means by which I acquired the information needed for it.[11] I also took on a new way of thinking about the role of professional historians in society. Rather than just transmitting knowledge, our main contribution is to encourage and support non-professional people engaged with history – and to be available when needed.

Supervised research done by people without academic training proved to be possible but, on the other hand, also raised several issues and problems calling for novel thinking – resulting eventually in the present book. The fundamental lesson was that sensible historians do not think about their audience as mere consumers of 'specialists' findings, but as people who create their own histories – most often, without our participation. What I learned is a good example of the usefulness of reflecting on aspects of the historian's work that conventionally are taken for granted, not to speak of problematizing them in the training of historians.

Not just readers

Whose sense of the past do I intend to influence and why? Along which lines should I proceed? These questions dominate the sensible historian's work when planning a research undertaking. He or she recognizes that history is a mode of making more sense of the world and one's place within it. The grounds for this being a premise for my profession were strengthened while working for Paperiliitto. The new element that entered my thinking during those seven years was a keen awareness of the authoritarian tendency embedded in our work: the risk of slipping into patronizing attitudes is far greater than historians believe.

Avoiding arrogance and condescension calls for taking seriously the views of the people addressed, but this is something historians have to learn the hard way. They are not trained to tackle either the make-up of the audience, or the significance of the topic at hand for the people they are addressing. Hardly any attention has been paid to the particular way the audience, chosen by the historian, approaches prevailing knowledge. Historians are trained to think about the historical interpretations they intend to criticize in scholarly terms, and only imprecisely, if at all, in relation to those outside the academic world.

There was an element of 'from below' in my initial idea of writing the history of Paperiliitto, but it was only gradually that I learned to take into consideration the audience's particular way of thinking. Insight into the role engagement with history plays in people's lives was not only provoked by my experiences at Paperiliitto, however; the key factor was learning a new aspect of the social process of history-making. Today I am able to define this clearly: the everyday casual habit of calling attention to the past was transformed into the purposeful creation of histories. In the early 1980s I learned that there were, in practically all developed industrial countries, a large number of projects where 'ordinary people' were producing various kinds of histories. Professionals were involved in some initiatives, like the best-known one, the British History Workshop movement, but by no means in all of them.[12]

When it gradually became apparent that the kind of historical practice I was initiating in Finland was actually part of an international phenomenon I considered the deliberate non-academic history-making on a par with the 'new histories'. Their historical significance lay, it seemed, in their function as indicators, and as essential parts, of a wider change in western culture. The world that had been created and was still thought about in terms of the great nineteenth-century ideologies – liberalism, conservatism and socialism – was breaking up: the 'modern' social orders were crumbling. It was actually only later, in the latter half of the 1980s, that I began to think systematically about the new history-connected activities as a challenge to scholarly history. Still later, only through Raphael Samuel's *Theatres of Memory* (published in 1994), did I realize that this was the resurgence of an old phenomenon: the novelty was in its proportions.

Thanks to the intensive Scandinavian cooperation, it was easy to get acquainted with the Swedish counterparts to the Paperiliitto history project. Here, the patrons of the activities were the powerful national organizations for workers' adult education and for the preservation of local arts and crafts. Many initiatives were inspired by the writer Sven Lindqvist's internationally acclaimed book *Gräv där du star* ('Dig Where You Stand') the point of which was that, in any job, the specialist was the person who actually did the work. For me, a more inspiring writer, in fact, was the architect Gunnar Sillén, whose ideas were intriguing from the professional historian's angle (and to which I will return, see pp. 72–3).[13]

The starting point for the purposeful non-academic history-making was, according to Sillén, that many aspects of industrialization and the past conditions of workers were unknown. Or, as Raphael Samuel put it: in industrial archaeology and the retrieval of oral memory one could see that it was a sense of cultural loss that animated the growth of popular enthusiasm for study of the past. The spur for research was not, as many academics think, the ethos of continuity and unity of national culture but rather its unexplored diversity.[14]

It is worth emphasizing once again that creating histories is a multi-faceted practice and that scholarly enquiry is only one genre of making history. As to research done by those without university training, it is reasonable to highlight two matters. On the one hand, the basic demands on any historian are not alien to present-day common sense: what is required is taking seriously the thinking of past people and being fair to them, as well as learning to construct an account based on sound reasoning. On the other hand, acquiring the necessary skills takes time without a trainer. This line of thinking actually leads to the vision of history-making discussed at the end of the book (see pp. 159–64). The idea is that of a participatory historical culture: one of collaborative practices where specialists ensure the soundness of the knowledge produced, and where diverse genres of histories are encouraged to flourish.

The expansion of purposeful non-academic history-making at the end of the twentieth century is a laborious subject to be researched because the nature of these activities makes acquiring the information needed difficult. The basic rationale of most projects is intimately connected to their regional, local or familial context and there is seldom any ambition to reach beyond these confines. Connected to this feature is apparently some distinct sense of belonging, an interesting but poorly researched phenomenon. Today, at the beginning of the twenty-first century, these kinds of initiatives seem to be so common that they do not attract special attention. Those who participate come from all walks of life; they are no longer only workers or previously marginalized groups. Scholars from many different fields are also involved.[15]

Even if deliberate extra-mural history-making remains a poorly investigated theme, there has emerged academic interest in popular concepts of history all over the world during the 1990s and 2000s. A pioneering status is enjoyed by the project directed by Roy Rosenzweig and David Thelen on the popular uses of history in American life. Further studies, at least in Australia, Canada and Finland, followed.[16] One of the interesting findings in the American project was the ubiquitous nature of active history-making. Out of 1,453 Americans interviewed about their relationship to the past, 'more than one third had investigated the history of their family in the previous year; two fifths had worked on a hobby or collection related to the past'.[17]

An important finding by Rosenzweig and Thelen is that people are keen to insist that others have no right to foist on them alien opinions of what is important in the past.[18] The issue at hand is, of course, that patronage that does not observe national borders. In Britain, Samuel criticized leftist writers for confusing the commodification of heritage with genuine popular interest in the past. As regards academic historians, there is a strong tendency to dismiss occupations like family history and the collecting of old photographs. These kinds of activities, as John Tosh puts it, are 'largely independent of the cultural *dirigisme* of the major heritage institutions'.[19]

Changes in history-in-society at the turn of the twenty-first century have shed new light on the traditional issue of what should be considered the principal aspects of history, something on which there seems never to have been agreement among historians. The political nature of this question was revealed, and emphasized, by the disruption within the discipline at the end of the twentieth century: the profession could no longer turn a blind eye to societal distinctions and the relative positions of different types of historical research. And, as this book argues, upholding history-making should be accepted as the historians' duty. The audience addressed, however, are not just readers of academic studies, but creators of their own histories, too.

The present pasts of the audience

Giving some thought to the history taught in schools is a rewarding exercise for anyone interested in the uses of the past: one learns that it is a far from straightforward task to decide which topics are important enough to be given attention. That there are alternatives to the history taught in school was something that encouraged quite a few Paperiliitto activists to join the research circles; the curriculum of their (or my) grandchildren today is also of a very different kind to what we were taught all those years ago. This reference to changes in educational policies acts by way of an introduction to the questions confronting historians about to select their audience.

Lists of bestselling books provide another kind of clue to what aspects of history people are interested in, but the sales also provoke reflection (this is covered in the next section). Yale historian Jay Winter, for instance, dealing with studies on the First World War, found that the books that are read most widely are not the ones that took years of research effort, but rather those that allowed families to see the way in which the war affected every British and French household, leaving traces and wounds palpable to this day.[20] The point here is that the historians' findings cannot be separated from other influences, that the reception of historians' works is also determined by readers' previous knowledge.

The example above prompts comment, too, on the mode of presenting the past. It is probably in the overlap between the information that historians present and what is contained in family narratives that the widely disseminated stories of the First World War have their origins. There are certainly other kinds of process too that affect the reception of the historian's work, even if our knowledge of them is limited. What seems certain is that it is not only the way the findings are presented that counts, readers also interpret what they are told in their own way.

The way the historian's results are received is also influenced by the audience's sense of the past. There are many different concepts of history even among professionals, not to speak of the lay readers. However, the variety of ways in which history is understood and the past is used are too great to be summarized in this book.[21] What seems certain is that there are a host of factors that impact upon a work's reception, making it unpredictable, but this does not preclude trying to anticipate the nature of the response. It is, thus, the meaningfulness of the historian's interpretation that is now key: the more intriguing the connection of the subject to the interests of the intended audience, the more eagerly the work will be received. As to how the research project is taken forward, this is the same for both professional and lay audiences.

Ideally, historians start creating the parameters of the subject to be studied knowing what in the past is significant for the people they intend to address, and why. Even if their knowledge of the audience's sense of history is only partial, sensible historians seek to develop the subject starting from the meanings attached by those addressed to the historical interpretations being criticized. Later on, the work is directed by the historian's increasing comprehension of the significance of the research findings for the audience. Normally, the role of the people addressed in this dialogue is passive, but there is nothing really to prevent organizing an actual exchange of views.

As to the historian's role in the dialogue with the prospective audience, the key thing to remember is that 'history is an argument without end'. It is also crucial to bear in mind that there are no 'proper' points of view: in Paperiliitto, for instance, I kept learning of new approaches to the changes that had taken place in the local communities. The point is that history works as 'the citizen's resource', as John Tosh puts it, when historians remember that their job is not to convey absolute statements but well-founded and carefully weighed conclusions liable to be modified.[22] The idea is to open new perspectives on the world of those one is addressing and to invite them to consider whether their existing concepts and values continue to hold true.

The historian looking for an attentive and thoughtful audience to be addressed has been provided with a practical guide on the subject by Roy Rosenzweig and David Thelen in their book *The Presence of the Past*. This summarizes their findings from a large project on the popular uses of the past in American life, and demonstrates their complexity. With an eye to providing some pointers to historians pondering their own relation to the people addressed, the American history professors stress that readers are more attentive when the historian has ensured that those addressed feel they are being invited to approach the past *on their own terms*. In other words, for historians to beware imposing their opinions on readers is not enough; they must also take the audience's concerns seriously.

The historian must also avoid being misled by scholarly hegemony and remain open to the unexpected. The dichotomy between 'personal' and 'national' is an example of the kind of carefulness needed when treating with consideration the thoughts of the people studied. Separation of the public past from the private does not always make sense; public events are often remembered and perceived as personal ones. A grandmother's story of an event and a meticulous academic study of the same event are very different kinds of histories, and yet, for an individual user of history, they may have the same function.[23]

While developing the subject of the study, the sensible historian also pays attention to the nature of everyday histories as sources for *history-making*, something mentioned above in the context of oral histories (see p. 31). A person's reminiscences do not only tell us which fragments of the past he or she considers relevant in the present, but also reveals the processes by which they are turned into history. The wealth of possible references becomes apparent when one realizes that every historian is surrounded by an infinite number of histories, each with its own purpose. It is worth the historian giving these serious consideration when elaborating their chosen topic.

When historians reflect on the deliberate production of histories by non-professionals, something now quite common in western countries, they would be wise to take on board Raphael Samuel's point: 'The past that inspires genealogists, local historians and collectors is not random' but connected to what for them is important. For many of the local trade union activists whom I trained, the engagement with history resulted from their political views. They were worried about the future of the working-class movement and wanted to restore its traditions. The means to that end was to explore their personal life experiences and to establish connections between these and those of the earlier generations.

It is also good to keep in mind that the sense of the significance of the past and the relevance of history varies depending on the people addressed and the subject studied, a point illustrated by Hilda Kean's description of British 'researchers of family, locality and place'.[24] Some engaged with history are looking 'in a vague way for a wider family', others for an 'educational hobby' and some 'for filling in gaps in family stories'. But there are also those who seek 'the fantasy of connection with someone in the past'. When developing the chosen topic into a subject it is worth the historian's while to reflect on this variety of concerns among the potential audience. As crucial as acknowledging the multitude of different interests is looking at their present impact; it is current concerns, the relevance of the past in the present that is the starting point of all history-making.

People and their Pasts, a collection of essays edited by Paul Ashton and Hilda Kean makes two important points, the first of which is encapsulated in the plurality of pasts in its title. The second significant aspect of the book is to introduce an issue that hardly appears at all when research conducted is based on conventional premises: how does the past become history, by which processes are histories created?[25] The conclusion of Ashton and Kean, the crucial role of defining history, is illuminated by my change in strategy when engaging the members of Paperiliitto with the writing of their union's history. They had to have the right to study *what in their view* was *their own history*, rather than take for granted a ready-made concept of it.

History provides people not only with a way of learning about 'the external world they inhabit' but is simultaneously for them, as Raphael Samuel emphasizes, a mode of shaping an 'understanding of themselves'. For him, what becomes the content of history is 'directly related to who researched and wrote history'. If history 'is an arena for the projection of ideal selves, it can also be a means of undoing and questioning them, offering more disturbing accounts of who we are and where we come from than simple identification would suggest'.[26] The rationale of engagement with history in case of the local trade union activists whom I trained to be their own historians was similar to that of Raphael Samuel – with the difference that they were not, and had no ambition of becoming, professional historians.

Public histories

'The problem of the working class movement here and now', as I formulated it in the union's newspaper on 14 November 1979, was the starting point for my work at Paperiliitto. Which elements in societal development had made it 'increasingly difficult for the movement to adhere to its original nature as the working people's collective instrument' for improving the conditions in which they lived and worked? Why had the movement failed to help the workers in 'getting a grip on the society and their place in it'? The 'imperialism of the enlightened worker' encapsulated, seven years on, my answer to this (see pp. 55–6). Both social-democrats and communists patronized their supporters by way of sticking to standards of the early socialist movement instead of having the prevailing social conditions as the foundation of their policies.

During my seven years with the union I came to the conclusion that one of the many functions of history is as an instrument of power. 'History is on our side' was the conviction and emblem of the traditional working-class movement. This belief entailed, for both social democrats and communists, the duty to root out social evils; although to be sure, they interpreted the real interests of the working people in their different ways. The method, however, was the same: the parties were there to turn into policies the grievances and demands their members had articulated – since the parties understood the connection between the workers' conditions and the course of history. This was the core of the 'imperialism of the enlightened worker'.

The first step towards recognizing the propensity of the workers' parties to order about their members was to realize the patronizing nature of the traditional historical enquiry that I had come to accept without question. As the work of the research circles and my discussions with those active in them progressed, my perspective widened to cover the 'modern' social orders. 'We have the knowledge' as the prevailing idea among decision-makers and 'from above' as the dominating characteristic of western politics in general gained strength over time. At the twenty-fifth History Workshop in Oxford in 1991, I personally laid the hitherto labour movement to rest in a paper titled 'History-writing, power and the end of the traditional left'. In 2009 my study titled 'Denial of politics as government policy', that highlighted the currently increasing meaninglessness of the idea of responsible use of power was published in the English volume of the *Parliament of Finland Centennial* series of studies.[27]

Opposition to social, cultural and political predestination was from my perspective, as a contemporary, the crucial dimension in the disruption within the historical discipline at the end of the twentieth century. I came to share the view, common to 'new histories', that history should be thought of as a resource with open-ended applications instead of serving as a course indicator. In his *Identity and Violence* (2006), the Nobel laureate in economics, Amartya Sen argues along the same lines regarding moral philosophy. He highlights the current contradiction in which, on the one hand, 'we are becoming increasingly divided along lines of religion and culture', whereas, on the other, the many other ways 'people see themselves, from class and profession to morals and politics' are ignored.[28]

Sen's point denotes the ontological insecurity characteristic of western societies at the turn of the twenty-first century. People are groping around uncertainly in the circumstances in which they find themselves today: what entities actually exist and what is my relation to them? They have created this dilemma themselves in the sense that people now insist on making their own choices. The type of society in which life was culturally predestined has lost its justification; the idea that one's social position dictated one's way of life and thinking has been refuted. True, the possible choices are limited and the liberty experienced is all too often just the creation of skilful marketeers. Still, people refuse to give up their hard-won rights; they want to retain control over their lives.[29]

With the benefit of hindsight, one can argue that it was the ontological insecurity described above that the research circles and myself were confronted with in Paperiliitto during the early 1980s. In the beginning, the project was instigated by the received idea that it is the function of history to tell 'who we are' and 'how we came to be what we are'. Gradually, we had to accept that being able to complete such a task was illusory and that identity poses a real challenge to anyone who is sensitive to the circumstances in which he or she lives. This has been aptly described by Peter Mandler: the collective identities that people once inherited and had to live with, whether they liked it or not, have broken down: 'community', religion, social hierarchy and class, ideology, 'nation.'[30]

Paul Gilroy's recent work on the aftermath of the British Empire is also a good example of the problems an historian has to deal with today. It is, in his opinion, not only the racial hierarchy that must be rejected but also 'the very idea of dividing humankind into homogenous and easily distinguishable biological and cultural groups'. In a similar way 'a healthy distance, even estrangement' is needed from the 'politically over-integrated nation-state'. This is where the sensible historian keeps in mind Stuart Hall's remark, that far from being 'eternally fixed in some essentialised past' identities result from the interaction of history, culture and power.[31] Raphael Samuel referred to the same point in different terms (see p. 63): history is an arena where identities can be both constructed and deconstructed.

The sensible historian also takes note of the most powerful characteristic of public histories – their ubiquitous nature. One meets references to the past anywhere and anytime. In Finland, for instance, scholars have produced excellent studies of descriptions conveying interpretations of history: images of an ancient Golden Age (Derek Fewster), paintings (Tuula Karjalainen) or photographs (Maunu Häyrynen).[32] These are just some examples where interpreting the past has been intentional, but the same effect is also imparted by artefacts which were not designed as contemporary representations of past phenomena. It is also worth remembering that politicians are not always consciously interpreting the past when they refer to it as a reason for a particular decision.

The challenge posed by identity to historians is to bear in mind that it is extremely difficult to separate giving people knowledge that enables them to construct an identity and suggesting one. Defining one's distinctive identity is today an individual affair, in the sense that people are 'freer to tailor it after their own fashion' than before. This is why it is so important, for example, to think carefully about the context in which one uses concepts like middle class, working class and so on. And all the time one must also keep in mind that it is not the historian's responsibility but that of the people addressed to clarify in their own mind who they are and what they want to become.[33]

In historical circles, debates around public histories have been of a different kind. One, actually a continuous debate, is about the competition, if not rivalry, between academic and popular historians. The popularizers aim, in academic eyes, 'at producing compelling and dramatic narratives that will hold the interest of non-professional readers'.[34] Their narratives, according to another common argument, serve 'no higher intellectual purpose' than 'to describe and entertain'. In the opinion, for example, of Exeter historian Richard Overy, it is popular history, not academic history, that is 'really disengaged from the real world'.[35]

The target of Overy's criticism is the mode in which many of the bestselling works have been written, and one of the academic's arguments is that the popularizer's accomplishments come easily, but at a cost. What is lost is 'an analysis of cultural, religious, or economic developments'. The opposing side, in turn, complains that too many academics 'do not wish to make the effort to relate their little picture to the context provided by the ever-present big picture'.[36] The perspective in this discussion is that of the professional producers of historical knowledge, and, as a result, its field is rather narrow. A wider perspective, that of popular understanding of the past is embedded in another academic debate.

Criticism of people's ignorance of and indifference to history became common in western countries towards the end of the twentieth century. In rebuttal, it was claimed that the problem was in the substance of historical studies, which was rejected as dull and irrelevant.[37] This debate about the historical awareness of 'ordinary people' has also taken place among professional historians; the views of the people addressed are anybody's guess. Absent is an analysis of the particular patterns of thought among the people addressed and the reasons for them. Why do people, for example, make connections between the various aspects of the past in the way they do?

Why the media and politicians make political use of the past is relatively obvious and will be discussed in Chapters 5 and 6. What is not so obvious is why popular histories flourish. Why do so many people regard professional histories as insufficient? Why do people find it necessary to create their own history themselves? It is to these questions that I next turn.

Popular histories

Thinking about ways in which the people addressed deal with one's topic calls for an analysis of everyday history, the multitude of diverse histories prevalent in any society. The practically useful concept here is the social process of history-making, since it both visualizes the context of the historian's work and points to the interplay between public, popular and scholarly histories, their rivalry in 'the terrain of truth'[38] and their competing influences on people's sense of the past. It is positioning one's topic among these different kinds of histories from which sensible historians take their cue for developing the subject of their research. True, public and popular histories are only analytical categories, each of which includes widely divergent types of histories, but they are, at the same time, useful precisely because they encapsulate such varying accounts of the past.

Introductory textbooks on historiography do not devote many pages to everyday history, nor to the various uses accounts of the past are put.[39] Nor do they discuss the problems confronting the historian as a referee in this field – in fact, the traditionally dominant pattern of thinking discourages assuming such a role. 'The task of history is to understand the past, and if the past is to be understood it must be given full respect in its own right...[which] involves, above all, deliberate abandonment of the present.'[40] A great many historians (the majority?) have disobeyed this tenet, however, as has been demonstrated in the section dealing with the specialist's personal contribution, but this has not resulted in a systematic discussion of the professional's role in everyday history.

Thanks to the conspicuous presence of public histories, historians are well aware of these accounts of the past even if they normally disregard them in their writing. The decision to overlook them arises, to some degree, from the undisguised partisanship peculiar to many of these interpretations, but there is also a strong tendency to regard them as unworthy of consideration. In contrast to public histories, historians pay far less attention to accounts that fall into the second analytical category, that of popular histories.[41] These presentations of the past encompass many genres, too. They include, for example, reminiscences of their youth by the elderly or tales and stories of past events learned in the neighbourhood or at one's place of work. They are histories one gets stuck into.[42]

My own sense of the past provides an unmistakable example of the way popular histories are passed on. In the early 1980s I was already an established historian, and it was only to be expected that my aunt should rely upon me as a specialist to assess the manuscript of the biography she had written of her father, a notable Finnish politician in the 1920s and 1930s. To my great surprise, I was confronted with a reconstruction of my own views on Finnish politics during the interwar period twenty years earlier, when I was a young student. As a schoolboy I had not been particularly interested either in politics or history, and my own recollection was that I had tried to avoid listening to my father and his sister talking about my grandfather – yet clearly I had been influenced by their discussions.

It is important to note that popular histories are by and large not meant to be presentations of history, as such; probably much less so than public histories. Notwithstanding this, the interpretations embedded in these accounts influence people's conception of history at least as effectively as those of public histories. A good example in this respect is provided by Jonathan Steele's article in the *Guardian* of 15 April 2005 with the intriguing subtitle 'It was Mikhail Gorbachev, and not Pope John Paul II, who brought down communism.'

The *Guardian*'s correspondent was irritated by the image of the late Pope's dealings with communism conveyed in the obituaries of him. According to Steele, 'the notion that anti-communism was always a consistent part of his motivation is off the mark'. What was ignored in the obituaries was that 'the way Poles saw Communism in the 1970s is not the way they see it now. The Polish Catholic Church was in regular dialogue with the communist authorities, and both worked subtly together at times to resist Soviet influence.' The accounts Steele discusses are public histories dealing with the late Pope; but his article demonstrates that these accounts share an important feature with popular histories. They too are normative by nature, and as a consequence easily become stereotyped. Still, popular histories are probably more effective in conveying customs and traditions, patterns of social behaviour. As Anthony Smith has remarked, 'it is to their ethnic symbols, values, myths and memories so many populations turn for inspiration and guidance.'[43]

As historical sources, both public and popular histories are problematic if our criterion is one of sound knowledge. Their significance for the historian lies in the meanings they attach to the past. They portray social agreements as to what features of the past are considered, by the people who share these accounts, to be indispensable in the present. These aspects of the past support a normative order, common to the people in question, in accordance with which the individual is expected to think and act in the present. But the same norms also govern the perspective on the past. They tell us what to remember and how, as well as what to forget, exclude, render unthinkable or regard as insignificant. In this sense, public and popular histories are political by their very nature.

The meanings attached to the past by public and popular histories are valuable for the historian from two angles. First, in attempting to avoid being unintentionally directed by current circumstances, an understanding of prevalent ideas on the 'right' or 'proper' way of thinking about the past is crucial. Secondly, when one is trying to uncover the functions performed by the interpretations to be re-evaluated, nonscholarly accounts of the past serve as important cues. They help in understanding the meanings currently attached to the topic chosen to be studied.

Attention has been paid to the cultural significance of public and popular histories, but not adequately. There are a host of treatises on the [public] uses of history[44] and on popular accounts of the past,[45] but not on the most significant characteristic of these presentations: the way in which they constantly modify each other while shaping people's sense of the past. This neglect of the interaction between public and popular histories is actually surprising, since it was one of the main points taken up by the well-known Popular Memory Group, active at the turn of the

1980s at the Centre for Contemporary Cultural Studies at the University of Birmingham (UK).[46] Yet, it is the very interaction of public, popular and scholarly histories that defines the position of the historian's topic in the social process of history-making.

There are today, as will soon become evident, an almost innumerable amount of studies on memory (by scholars other than historians) but, comparatively few dealing with popular conceptions of history. The small number of such works actually points to the continuing presence in professional thinking of the idea of 'real' history as an academic preserve.[47] The low academic opinion of everyday history is also demonstrated by ignorance of the variety of lay views on the nature of history; the same controversies that have divided professional historians abound outside academia but in different guise, for instance.

Scholarly histories

Analysing the particular aspects of the past that the intended audience feels are relevant to their current concerns is one of the professional historian's tasks when planning his or her research project. However, a paramount aspect of upholding history-making as a basic social practice must be borne in mind: starting from the histories those addressed have created or cherish does not mean taking them at face value. On the contrary, is it not an essential part of the trained historian's job to try to prevent people from using prejudiced, simplistic or outdated interpretations of the past? Is it not their role to demonstrate and correct weaknesses in prevalent histories? And to provide the people addressed with the knowledge and new interpretations they need?

Discovering that is possible to produce one's own history often creates an enthusiasm that can be self-defeating: the resulting work can strengthen one's prejudices instead of improving the ability to make informed assessments of interpretations dealing with what one is interested in. This was something I had to emphasize repeatedly in the early 1980s to those involved in the various initiatives. While encouraging efforts to create new, sound interpretations that replace one-sided or otherwise questionable ones, I had to underline that the first step is to put aside one's own prejudices. Taking up a marginalized or forgotten theme was just the starting point and finding new as well as previously undervalued sources only one of the means to the goal. Sound reasoning was the thread running through the intensive courses the research circles of Paperiliitto were given.[48]

The often justified professional concern about the pitfalls in producing popular accounts of the past must not prevent us from acknowledging their potential usefulness. I share Ruth Finnegan's doubt as to 'whether there really is some marked divide between the processes of knowledge creation outside as against inside the universities'.[49] Only arrogance and privilege denies those who do not have academic training the status of 'real' historians: it is argument not authority that counts. This is a theme to which I will return. Here I discuss other aspects that have arisen on the relationship between professionals and lay historians.

One issue is about the historian's relationship to the people he or she is addressing in an age when the internet is on its way to becoming (or has already become?) the key media. How should one go 'about imagining your audience if it is worldwide and online and probably searching for something you wouldn't expect'? It is perfectly reasonable that this issue should be explored thoroughly, but it is, however, beyond the competence of someone who was already about to retire when the internet became an everyday medium. The same is true of the other considerable effects of electronic communication on historical research.[50]

In any case, it seems probable that the printed word has already been replaced by radio and television as the most influential channel for communicating history. On the other hand, historians such as Simon Schama and David Starkey are still today only a tiny minority; the overwhelming majority of us have to confine ourselves to the world of print. This was the situation to an even greater degree thirty years ago and that is why the research circles in Paperiliitto greatly surprised their academic supervisor.

By far the most popular way for the circles to convey their findings was to put on an exhibition of commented old photographs, which was then visited by hundreds (in some cases even thousands) of people, even in relatively small locations. This medium turned out to be so effective that a special course on displays in general had to be organized for the groups with a specialist from Swedish Travelling Exhibitions. The circles also conveyed their research results in plays, processions, video and music programmes, recitations, as well as one long-playing record. True, there also emerged several books and dozens of articles, but an academic used to thinking in terms of written texts was confronted with unexpected questions about ways of disseminating an historian's findings.

Communication skills have, however, acquired a new kind of status in the university training of historians since the 1990s, especially in the United States. The curriculum gives emphasis to the use of non-traditional evidence and formats in the recreation and presentation of history. Conventional methods have been expanded by using not only photographs, oral histories and museum exhibitions, but also television documentaries, multimedia, websites and by reworking traditional historical knowledge into modern, computer-based formats. In this sense, public history (in the singular; see the section '*The profiles of cultural critics*' in Chapter 5) refers to a distinctive way of acquiring and disseminating historical knowledge.[51]

In addition to the exhibitions and other forms of presentation used by the circles, an incentive to rethink the professional historian's relationship with his or her audience also emerged in the 1980s from a public debate I had with Gunnar Sillén, one of the authorities for the Swedish research circles. Criticism of professional historians was an integral part of his credo: 'don't regard history as a problem, make it alive instead!' My defence of the specialist referred, in addition to the need to overcome common prejudices, to the role of historical enquiry as critic of a distinct type of using power: there was an obvious need for knowledge about social entities as opposed to dividing society or any other social whole into ever narrower sectors.

In another perspective, the debate with Sillén acted as a stimulus to consider, once again, the relation of historical research to various artistic forms, an issue to which I return in Chapter 5.[52] As regards the present chapter, Sillén prepared the ground for assuming the message of the linguistic turn. In his words the historian should present his or her findings 'as situations one could re-experience', that is, in ways which made it possible to understand and share the feelings of the people studied. Maybe this was the secret of the remarkable popularity of the circles' exhibitions.

Thinking about the historian's connection with the people addressed also caused me to ponder the question 'what is history for?' from a novel angle. After the historian has, in R. G. Collingwood's words, 're-enacted' a piece of past thinking he or she should present it to the readers in a way that makes, in Sillén's terms, 're-experiencing' possible. This suggestion accords with Markku Hyrkkänen's understanding of 'reflecting' in the Collingwoodian sense: history can give a human being the incentive to 'start thinking about one's own thinking'. What comes out of this is close to Raphael Samuel's view of the relationship between history and historian quoted above (see p. 63).[53] In any case, every historian has reason not only to define their view on the responsibilities of the historian's role as a cultural critic but also to elaborate their personal relation to history.

An additional useful idea, stimulated by Sillén, is connected to the difference between empathy and sympathy. The former means, according to the *Concise Oxford English Dictionary*, 'the ability to understand and share the feelings of another', while sympathy means 'feelings of pity and sorrow for someone else's misfortune'. It is empathy that describes the historian's relation to the people studied, while sympathy, or rather concern and even solidarity, refers to one's relation to the people addressed.[54] This distinction serves as an introduction to Ranke's early nineteenth century maxim *wie es eigentlich gewesen*.

Later generations have failed to notice that there are two elements contained in Ranke's maxim. The one that has attracted historians' attention the most refers to empathy as the required attitude, and has been expressed in our days by, for example, the American historian Gertrude Himmelfarb. Instead of providing lessons the idea of the historian's work is to make 'a strenuous effort to enter into the minds and experiences of people in the past, to try to understand them as they understood themselves, to rely upon contemporary evidence as much as possible, to intrude his own views and assumptions as little as possible'.[55] This refers to empathy, or fairness, as the historian's fundamental duty that was discussed in Chapter 2. The element that has been largely ignored is the logical premise of Ranke's maxim.

Ranke's 'eigentlich' ('actually') should really be understood as 'contrary to what is claimed or believed', and is the necessary, albeit unexplicit aspect of Ranke's maxim. This refers to the historian's task of producing alternatives to existing interpretations, whether the aim is to improve upon or critique existing histories or to present completely new ones. The historian may have many motives for presenting an alternative interpretation. To condemn these kinds of motives, as the 'objectivists' used to do, is arbitrary. Chapter 4 is devoted to the many aspects of the historian's objectives, and the issue will be further elaborated in Chapters 5 and 6.

The two aspect's of Ranke's maxim refer to the historian's basic predicament, often expressed in the previous pages: responding to contemporary concerns without compromising fairness towards the people one is writing about. Peter Mandler provides an example of resolving the dilemma in reviewing the 1859 bestseller of the Scottish author and reformer Samuel Smiles, *Self-Help*. According to him, the book provides one with many relevant ideas about developing 'the self – its powers, range, creativity and diversity' for the present day. However, up to its reissue in 2002 the book's title had been enough to label its author a 'Thatcherist of the crudest ... sort', and since no one has come up with 'anything coherent to say about the positive inspiration provided by *Self-Help* the Thatcherite mud still sticks'.[56]

Demonstrating that something is contrary to what is claimed or believed to have been true means that the idea of persuading the audience is always embedded in the historian's work. 'The chief product (the historian) has to sell', as Stefan Collini puts it, 'is the trained skepticism that says "it wasn't like that"'. Pauli Kettunen, in his turn, underlines that the works historians publish 'open or close, broaden or restrict the perspectives of human agency'.[57] The crucial point here, albeit referring to a neighbouring field, has been aptly made by Ricca Edmondson (teaching at the University of Galway) in her *The Rhetoric of Sociology*:[58]

> ... in place of objectivity sociologists in fact proceed as follows: they try to tell the truth in a manner which complements and is complemented by, the knowledge and dispositions which their (selected) audience already has. Consciously or otherwise, writers try to gauge the personal and political commitments of the audience they wish to address, or are forced to address, and they adapt the personal and political tenor of their own communication so as to complete or correct their readers' views. Strictly speaking, truthfulness is a product of the joint communicative efforts of both.

As a genre, scholarly histories are on a par with public and popular histories when looking at the different sources of influence on people's views and knowledge about the past. The three categories (all are plural terms) simply represent an analytical division to help historians assess the practical context of their work, everyday history. *Shared histories*, however, open up a different perspective on the social process of history-making.

Shared histories are not analytical tools like public, popular and scholarly histories; they are not coarse categories the historian needs for managing the prevailing knowledge, when organizing the context where his or her study will be conducted. Rather, shared histories are on a par with individual scholarly studies in the sense that they convey substantial interpretations to be evaluated – with the crucial difference that there is no specific author. They are jointly produced collective views of the past, conglomerates of various public, popular and scholarly histories.[59] Analysing the nature of shared histories in the next two sections means studying the elements and mechanisms involved when the people addressed develop their own views on history. The results of this history-making, the various interpretations shall be discussed in Chapter 4.

Shared histories

During recent decades there has been marked progress in the historical profession if the criterion is the upholding of history-making as a basic social practice. This is not only due to transformation in historical research, and primarily the emergence of new themes and actors, but also to changed views on gathering knowledge of the past. There seems to be a greater awareness that history is not only taught in a classroom, but learned in a multitude of places, and in a variety of ways.

An increasing number of academics have begun to wonder whether history is something to be approached along the lines suggested by Raphael Samuel. For him history is 'a social form of knowledge', the work, in any given instance, of a 'thousand different hands'. If this is true, he claims, professional studies in history should be discussed in a context created by 'the ensemble of activities and practices in which ideas of history are embedded or a dialectic of past-present relations is rehearsed'.[60] In this book I refer to this 'ensemble' as the social process of history-making.

Nevertheless, shared histories have attracted only a small amount of research. True, a great number of scholars have been interested in the ways in which social groups create their images of the world, but the studies produced concentrate on the various aspects of the agreed upon versions of the past. The shared histories themselves have escaped analysis. As a result, the following discussion of the elements and mechanisms involved when the users of the past create their collective histories are based on studies dealing only with the various aspects of the ensuing whole. This notwithstanding, many scholars have suggested that some shared history is probably a necessity for any community. Michael Howard, for example, writes that 'all societies have *some* view of the past; one that shapes and is shaped by their collective consciousness, that both reflects and reinforces the value-systems which guide their actions and judgements'.[61]

Shared histories then, are the means through which the various groups and communities get to grips with the present and the groundwork for them is done outside university rooms and libraries. It is from the diverse public, scholarly, and especially popular histories and their interaction that these collective forms of knowledge about the past emerge. Often the key role is played by various stories and other forms of folklore, usually passed on by word of mouth. Characteristic of these histories is that they tend to be stereotypical in nature; through constant repetition they become fixed and widely held. Being composite in form, shared histories describe the particular identity of, and often constitute, a community, be it a family, neighbourhood, workplace, institution or nation. They are mutually constructed accounts of the past and, as such, akin to Benedict Anderson's famous imagined communities.[62]

As noted, scholarly accounts of the past contribute to shared histories too. Still, it is important to remember that only a tiny fraction of existing interpretations of the past can be traced back to the work of professional historians. Thus, shared histories remind us that, contrary to many academics' understanding, scholarly works are not the ultimate source on which people's conceptions of the past are based. Professional contributions are not even necessary for shared histories, as the researcher of folkloristics Anne Heimo has demonstrated in her study of a southern Finland municipality.[63] One must not confuse history with the results of historical research.

It is reasonable to depict shared histories as constructions on three levels. First, there is individual remembrance, secondly, public memories and thirdly, frameworks for organizing the ensuing accounts as wholes. During the last three decades a vast number of studies examining these elements has appeared, but hardly anything on the interaction between all three. This disconnection reflects perhaps the most unfortunate effect of the present division of current research on culture and society. There are an almost infinite number of academic 'disciplines', 'traditions', 'orientations' and so on, in addition to the many formal organizations such as 'departments', 'schools' and 'institutes', each guarding jealously its own territory or preserve.

For shared histories as composites, oral history is the most fruitful scholarly orientation even if its emphasis is on the level of individual remembrance. The narratives studied are autobiographical, often organized by the individual lifespan, and these memories reveal, as was indicated above (see p. 31), ways in which individuals reconstruct their past, create histories. A similar perspective on the methods of history-making is opened by works like Thelen and Rosenzweig's *The Presence of the Past* with its focus on the divergent popular uses of history.[64] What all this points to is that providing a *site for personal recollections* is the first necessary prerequisite for shared histories. It is the possibility of making sense of one's own experiences with the help of these collective accounts on the past that makes them shared ones.

The idea of reminiscences or life stories is to make sense of one's past, or rather, as American historian Michael Frisch underlines, to attach personal experiences to their social context. His Italian colleague

Alessandro Portelli, in turn, has demonstrated, from the historian's angle, that the significance of the 'errors, inventions, and myths' which characterize these accounts is that they 'lead us through and beyond facts to their meanings'. On the other hand, it is important to keep in mind what specialists in oral history Paula Hamilton and Linda Shopes point out: neither scholars nor people remembering necessarily reflect on 'the process by which the articulation of memories takes place or how they become public'.[65] In highlighting the process through which remembrance is expressed, Hamilton and Shopes prepare the ground for my next point: *unrestricted availability* is the second precondition of shared histories.

The emphasis on the unrestricted availability of shared histories reminds us that remembrance does not take place in a vacuum. On the contrary, individual reminiscences are sustained by *public memories*, for example various memorials, monuments, places and rituals or, in other words, by heritage. This support to individual remembrance (actually history-making) by public memories is the function of *the second level* of shared histories. The question is now of collective remembrance that is the focus of a distinct field of research, often called memory studies that has boomed since the 1990s.[66] This 'memory scholarship' has a very different historiographic trajectory from oral history, and removing the disconnection between the two is what is suggested by the collection edited by Hamilton and Shopes, *Oral History and Public Memories*.[67]

The third level of shared histories, frameworks which organize these accounts as composites, is the least discussed aspect of the topic. True, there are plenty of studies dealing with the different concepts of history, but their function in arranging individual remembrance and public memories has not been systematically analysed. In shared histories the role of these frames is, first of all, to give an impression of the *underlying continuities in history*. An interesting approach in this respect is suggested by Joseph Mali in his *Mythistory*. Another fruitful starting point is provided by the 'schematic narrative templates' (for example, the mode in which the official Soviet narrative of the Molotov-Ribbentrop Pact was presented) suggested by James V. Wertsch.[68]

The most frequently used framework for shared histories is provided by the idea of nation. Not only is the nation frequently taken for granted by historians, it is also often presented as a predetermined condition of anything else in history. The tendency is so strong that historians studying popular views of history (for example, Rosenzweig and Thelen as well as Ashton and Kean) have called into question 'the concept of a common story and national character'.[69] These criticisms of unreflect-ingness lead to two remarks and with them to the current significance of shared histories.

The liquid social fabric

My first comment on the misuse of the concept of 'the nation' is similar to the point made by Amartya Sen in his *Identity and Violence* (see pp. 64–5). The historian's challenge is the strong tendency, even in this globalized world of ours, to divide people along national lines, and to ignore the ways in which people see themselves. What this means is that historians face the task of demonstrating that nations, communities and ethnic groups change over time and, therefore, should not be taken for granted. Historians must not forget that part of their job is to scrutinize the historical perspective, for example, of political visions and statements and, where necessary, to show that they are anachronistic.[70]

My second comment on the misuse of the nation refers to situations in which the different shared histories are subordinated to a single national narrative – for example, by discussing 'the English' or 'the Finns'. Together, my two comments introduce the key challenge of twenty-first-century politics: customary concepts describing people's associations with each other cannot any more be taken for granted. Not only have nineteenth-century notions of social/class structure become obsolete, but much more recent concepts may also have lost their validity. Culturally different parts of the social fabric, highlighted by the 'new histories' at the end of the twentieth century, can hardly any longer be regarded as fixed.

Shared histories help us in characterizing this dilemma. It is reasonable to assume that those living in circumstances similar enough to want to use the past as a means of coming to terms with the present feel affinity with each other. On the other hand, it is equally obvious that people belong to, and are active in, at one and the same time, several overlapping communities. From the political (or the historian's) angle, these alliances are intriguing not only because the multitude of them exist simultaneously but also because they are characterized by the concurrence of polyphony and unity.

As composites, shared histories allow people to exert control over their present circumstances, but in a counter-intuitive way, similar to that argued by the German sociologist Norbert Elias: individuals are larger than groups because individuals contain within themselves so many different identities. David Thelen agrees and continues:

An individual could be a woman, lawyer, Republican, Chicagoan, lesbian, Irish-American. Each piece of her identity carries with it materials and traditions that the individual, alone or with others, could turn into a collective past with constantly evolving individual variations. And yet to describe any one of these groups is also to fall far short of describing any individual who contains so many potential identities and locations between identities with which to describe where he or she has been.[71]

The point, from the perspective of politics and history, seems be that no shared history is a uniform, consistent interpretation of the past, but rather an amalgam of different and often contradictory views. Even so, it is good to remember Elias's point above. Examining shared histories in their capacity as challenging and special forms of knowledge is the scholar's headache: the people studied (and scholars in their private life) do not have any trouble in coping with them in their everyday life.

It seems, to paraphrase the Palestinian-American literary theorist Edward Said, obvious that shared histories are 'as protean, unstable and undifferentiated as anything in the actual world'. Nevertheless, past experiences are arranged with their help, and shared histories also assist in negotiating the present and navigating the future. The problem seems to be our tendency as historians to think almost only in terms of stable identities; to understand 'individuality as a process of becoming and therefore fluid' is unfamiliar to us.[72] With regard to the multitude of oral history and memory studies, however, I would like to take the risk of suggesting that it is the 'fluidity of the self' as their context which gives shared histories the guiding role they have. From this perspective it is unfortunate that scholars have pulled apart the mutually constructed composites of views on the past rather than analysed the ways in which the connections between the different levels within them have been arranged. Nor, because of the lack of studies that focus on shared histories themselves, have the contradictions been examined that result from the heterogenuity of the communities which have produced them.

The trouble with shared histories is simply the lack of research on them. My own work in Paperiliitto opens one perspective. Having directed the union activists while they were doing research in what in their view was their own past, I could have presented their various shared histories – had I known of the concept. Yet, during the first half of the 1980s, 'world view', for instance, was still regarded as a sufficient concept. Shared histories only seem to have attained the key position they hold today with the changes in the structure of western societies during the last two or three decades. I will return to the implications of this situation at the book.

I now turn to negotiation as a mode of reaching an interpretation of the past since this method highlights the nature of historical knowledge. The meanings the historian discovers in shared histories emerge through an interactive process, as the researcher of folkloristics Elina Makkonen has demonstrated in her study of popular and oral history projects in three eastern Finland locations. She shows, first, that parties arguing over, for example, a past event or deciding on its meaning move in a hermeneutical spiral, with the result that the explanation arrived at is not reducible to any of the original viewpoints. Her second point is that the resulting interpretation is not a final one, but the starting point for new discussions and interpretations.[73] In other words, Pieter Gevl's 'an argument without end' (see p. 41) seems to characterize shared histories, too.

As regards the historian's own work, shared histories remind the him or her, firstly, of the necessity of critical detachment from their own position in the social process of history-making. Historians must not forget that they too have been brought up with several shared histories. In other words, David Carr's point highlighted in the Preface (see p. xii), that a human being has 'a connection to the historical past, as an ordinary person, prior and independently of adopting the historical cognitive-interest' has to be taken seriously. Secondly, historians must remember that an awareness of this is crucial so as to keep one's own views separate from those of the people studied – thus, analysing one's own thoughts is necessary in order that one produces sustainable knowledge. Such scrutiny is *sine qua non* for carrying out the historian's fundamental duty, doing justice to the people studied.

A further prerequisite for producing sustainable knowledge is that the historian keeps in mind that the audience is always present when he or she conducts the (virtual) dialogue with the people studied and negotiates with them over the meaning of their thinking and actions. Even if the people addressed are, as often is the case, close to his or her own position in terms of locality, ethnicity, political allegiance and so on, their views must not be excluded from critical evaluation. On the contrary, the specialist's obligation is to subject all meanings attached to the past to analysis, and this applies especially to those histories upheld, often even cherished, by people near him or her.

Shared histories emerge from the various comments on and interpretations of the past instigated by the current concerns of those under consideration.[74] The prime function of these mutually constructed accounts is to contribute to the people's daily activities and thinking, not to knowledge in general, and it is from this everyday function that they acquire their significance. Still less are shared histories there to enhance the discipline of history – even if studying them might lead to this. Professional historians have to be content with their duty to replace prejudices and strive to contribute to the sustainability of new interpretations and knowledge.

From the perspective of upholding history-making as a basic social practice, shared histories are useful in the sense that they serve as bridges between the historical understanding of trained historians and the laity. As to supporting the efforts of non-professionals in creating histories, I share the conclusion drawn by Rosenzweig and Thelen. For them, 'the most significant news' of their project was that 'we have interested, active, and thoughtful audiences for what we want to talk about. The deeper challenge is finding out how we can talk to – and especially with – those audiences.'[75] Such an intercourse, involving shared histories as objects of mutual study, entails reassessing the profession's conventions and commencing research work from the perspective of the anticipated significance of the research findings. The problems connected to this approach will be discussed in Chapter 4.

Creating such a participatory culture (see Chapter 6, pp. 159–64, for further exploration of this) would help to put an end to the scholar's monopoly on history-writing, and to release the study of the past from the one-sided grip of the professionals. At the same time, the move would entail an epistemological issue that has been taken up by Michael Frisch, albeit in connection with oral history, in his 1990 book, *A Shared Authority*. The implications of the close link between authorship and interpretative authority are a thread running through the following chapters. Here, Frisch's questions serve as a useful introduction to the Chapter 4, which deals with the politics of history, the historian's relation to the struggle between various interpretations of the past.

> Who, really, is the author of an oral history, whether this be a single interview or an edited book-length narrative? Is it the historian posing questions and editing the results, or the 'subject', whose words are the heart of the consequent texts? –What is the relation between interviewer and subject in the generating of such histories – who is responsible for them and where is interpretive authority located?[76]

4
The Politics of History

'Setting the record straight' is for quite a few historians the rationale for their work. Others speak of demonstrating 'that's not how it was'. Whatever the expression, criticism of prevailing knowledge is the absolutely essential element of a historian's work. If the findings do not demonstrate that something is *contrary to what was claimed or was believed to have been the case* the research project does not make sense.

When setting out their alternative interpretation historians need to keep in mind that it has two aspects, as shown in Chapter 2: one, the soundness, and the other the meaning of the knowledge at hand. 'Setting the record straight' refers only to the first of these, the description of the past matters studied with the historian acting as a referee on that particular area of history. This task is straightforward when compared with tackling the meanings of those past matters, since here the specialist has to adjust to a situation where his or her arguments are on par with those of other history-makers.

As regards the significance of the chosen topic, the historian's first task is to analyse this. The topic must be positioned with regard to rival interpretations, that is, the historian must establish where his work fits into the current politics of history. The next, and crucial, step in planning the study ahead, outlining the questions to be asked, is to uncover 'exactly why do I want to argue for an alternative interpretation?' The inadequacy of the prevailing explanations must be expounded and the implications of the alternative/s offered must be examined systematically, that is, the historian must meet the requirement of double detachment. What follows in practice is for the historian to begin his or her analysis of the functions performed by the interpretations criticized, a quest for both the obvious and the imperceptible stances they sustain.

In 2006 Cambridge historian Paul Cartledge published *Thermopylae: the Battle That Changed the World*. This book presented, in the view of his Oxford colleague Jasper Griffin, the first stage in what would be, and would long remain, 'an archetypal showdown' between East and West. The events at Thermopylae 'still cast a long shadow in the present', they were the 'first round' in a long series of 'return matches' in which East and West have 'in turn invaded and conquered each other'. Opposing the West were the 'Eastern hordes, subjects of a despotic ruler, driven on into battle by men with whips, and the forces, much smaller but resolute, of free men, fighting freely in defence of their freedom.'[1]

This pattern of thought was taught to me, a schoolboy in the 1950s, as one of the cornerstones of western civilization. Half a century on, I tend to side with those researchers who are critical of the interpretation that was once taken for granted. The British author Tom Holland in his *Persian Fire*, for instance, urges us to steer clear of the notion that the impact of the ancient opposition between Persia and Greece is 'confined within rigid notions of East and West'. After all, he argues, monotheism and the notion of a universal state, democracy and totalitarianism can all trace their origins back to both warring sides of the Persian Wars. Holland's American reviewer, the historian Victor Davis Hanson, reminds us of the impact 9/11 has had on world affairs. With 'Americans in the Hindu Kush and on the Euphrates, and Europeans attempting to dissuade an ascendant oil-rich Iran from obtaining nuclear weapons', historians had better remember that talking of free Greeks fending off enslaved Persians means 'treading over a mine-laced ground'.[2]

Interpretations of the Persian Wars demonstrate clearly that, for the historian, it is not only the descriptions of past events that count; what matters too are the functions that they serve. In fact, it is often the claims made and the stances taken by the various interpretations that are important. This example also shows that the historian's work can easily take on meanings that are unintentional, and this underlines the necessity of carefully defining one's central idea. Becoming aware of and specifying one's objectives is evidently closely connected to the basic rationale for doing the study. The historian's wish to awaken the audience's interest in the selected topic must, even if not the main objective, be developed into a reasoned exposition of the inadequacy of existing interpretations.

When the historian analyses current knowledge, it is useful to differentiate between the two levels on which interpretations may clash. One is illustrated by the examples of the Persian and Trojan Wars (see Chapter 2, pp. 33–4), and comprises perpetual debate about diverse issues. To elaborate these is not necessary for the purposes of the present book. What suffices here is to contrast the persistent nature of some arguments with those related to the particular circumstances in which the historian creates his or her subject. It is the latter level of meanings in the never-ending social process of history-making to which the concept the politics of history relates. It denotes the clash between rival interpretations of the past in a particular situation where the 'right' or 'proper' way of thinking about that area is at stake.

The emergence of the subject to be studied from analysing the position of the chosen topic in the politics of history is the theme of this chapter. Discussion focuses on the historian's attempts to specify the reasons for proposing an alternative interpretation to prevailing ones.

Concerning the meanings attached to the past, it is reasonable to start with the historian's feeling that the knowledge he or she aims to produce makes a difference. This is his or her initial idea that will be discussed from various angles in this chapter; the idea is to tip in establishing the central idea of the study. What this entails is a research-like process during which the accumulating knowledge provides grounds for expanding some aspects of the original topic, and for contracting others. Creating the subject in this way involves selecting between the many aspects of the chosen topic, as well as clarifying the particular aspect of the past to focus on: period, people, and area. In other words, defining the 'what' of the study takes place simultaneously with answering 'why'.

The criteria and grounds for the choices that turn the initial idea into the central idea are provided by a critical analysis of the prevailing interpretations. The other side of the same exercise is to define the room for one's alternative exposition, to designate the objectives of the study. Thus, the historian carries out two tasks simultaneously: distances oneself from the functions sustained by the explanations criticised, and anticipates the implications of one's alternative interpretation. Meeting the demand of double detachment in this way helps the historian in attaining the capacity needed to conduct the study: getting intellectual control over the circumstances where the research has to be done.

The most dynamic element of creating the central idea is honing the significance of what will be studied, that is, elaborating the meanings embedded in in one's message. At the same time, the historian turns the chosen topic into a clear-cut subject, and selects the people to be addressed. These three operations, delineating the message, defining the subject and selecting the people addressed, produce a multitude of arguments for the selections made. It is the expanding of these grounds that leads to the assumptions which will be tested against primary sources at the second stage of the research process.

Assessing histories

Constructing and developing 'a good question', as some historians aptly put it, is what unites the different parts of this chapter, which suggests different ways of disciplining one's thoughts when elaborating the chosen topic and thinking about one's central idea. This emphasis on keeping one's work in check is justified by the driving force of the research process: the historian seeks to make his or her point.

Here we meet a good example of the self-defeating nature of the profession's traditional self-awareness: motivation is one's main asset and yet, ways of availing oneself of it have not been discussed. The reasons for this were discussed in the introductory chapter: the historians' missing candidness about their work caused by the phobia about societal influences (see pp. 16–17). There is an obvious contradiction between historians' eagerness to comment on public debates and the counsel about keeping away from current debates.

Cambridge historian Christopher Clark's *Iron Kingdom*, dealing with the history of Prussia, shows one way of tackling the typical starting point of the historian. There are two traditional perspectives in German history-making common to public, popular and scholarly histories. One is laudatory, celebrating the 'heroic destiny' embedded in the past; the other is critical and 'decries the villainous destiny'. The historian, however, is not obligated to choose either of these two traditions, but can opt for the route taken by Clark. He has consciously avoided hindsight and 'sought to restore to Prussian history an openness, a sense of possibility and ambiguity, of unintended consequences and unused opportunities'. Instead of burying his head in the sand, as the conventional counsel actually suggests, Clark has done what the sensible historian cannot avoid doing, and what he or she should do: rather than keeping away from the current politics of history he has commented in his own particular way on the two traditions.[3]

That the number of works on the history of Islam has rocketed since 9/11 shows that historians seek to meet the demand for knowledge of the past – in addition to trying to increase the sales of their books. That there are trends not only in fashion but also in historical research is displayed by the growing number of books on the environment and gender relations, prior to the boom created by the Islamists. On the other hand, one must keep in mind that the very idea of history is linked to reflection on ordinary everyday concerns and to the need to acquire a sense of proportion on current events.

It is also part of the historian's job to provide the context for current events. A good example is James Reston Jnr's recent study of Columbus, the Inquisition, the downfall of the Moorish caliphate – and the year 1492. In his prologue, the author points out that the bombers who killed 191 Spanish commuters on 11 March 2004 justified their actions by invoking the defeat of the Moors in 1492. According to one reviewer, the events in this book 'may have taken place more than 500 years ago, but there are times when they seem chillingly familiar'.[4]

The first step in research is to take advantage of all the existing knowledge – especially, but not solely, the works history specialists have produced. Previous studies are sources of useful information on issues since they result from making sense of one's area of research. In addition to increasing the historian's knowledge, these histories contain information on areas the historian's own research project need not cover. In other words, the historian must distinguish between existing knowledge that is sustainable (until there is reason to question it) and that which is not, but needs to be criticized. Keeping in mind the fundamental distinction between the soundness and meaningfulness of knowledge is helpful here.

A common, but oversimplified understanding of that distinction is the opinion that historians often agree about 'the facts' but give them different meanings. What makes the situation much more complicated is that the 'what' and 'why' components of a study are not independent of each other. A meaning that diverges from the established one normally also presupposes changes in the subject matter, period, people or area dealt with; in addition, explanations that contradict existing ones often share a great deal of supporting sound knowledge. This is why historians must be extremely careful every time they meet references to the 'same' in the material they are using.

The case of Finland during the 1970s provides an example of two conflicting interpretations, in the post-Cold War world, of the 'same' period. According to the 'Finlandization narrative' the main characteristic of that time was national humiliation and political corruption connected to the country's foreign policy, while in a rival exposition it was during the 1970s that the Scandinavian model of a welfare state was completed in the country. The difference lies, in this case, in the selection of supporting references.[5] A more complicated example of the problematic nature of 'the same' is provided by western orientalists.

The British historian Robert Irwin's *For Lust of Knowing: The Orientalists and Their Enemies* illuminates the connections between academia and the 'outside' world in a useful way. The book was published in 2006 and criticizes heavily Edward Said's interpretation of western research on the Middle East. Irwin, on one level, presents and analyses orientalist studies from medieval times to the present and, on another, defends these scholars against the way Said characterizes them in his famous *Orientalism,* a work that Irwin found 'richly imagined, but essentially fictional'. In reviews, Irwin's book was regarded as 'indisputably erudite' and a 'generally convincing riposte' to Said's work.[6]

'The main flaw in an otherwise meticulous and impressive book', according to Middle East specialist Christopher de Bellaigue, is that its author does not confront Said on his central idea, 'that orientalist scholarship helped define the character of the European empires of the nineteenth and twentieth century, and that it was itself influenced by Imperialism.' To anticipate and defend in advance against this kind of critique would by no means have been an insurmountable task. Irwin's omission is, according to de Bellaigue, all the more odd since he gives evidence of 'strong and complex ties between Orientalism and Imperialism'. In Harvard historian Maya Jasanoff's view, Irwin's approach s explained by his faith in the detachment of pure scholarship from real world problems.

Jasanoff's main argument is that Irwin has missed Said's most enduring legacy: present-day western scholars are aware 'that their work has political substance and ramifications, whether or not it might appear to be political a priori.' This comment by Jasanoff and that of de Bellaigue bring to the fore a key aspect of the paradigmatic change in the discipline at the end of the twentieth century. Scholars nowadays are expected to satisfy two requirements: they have to pay systematic attention to both where their points of view emanate from and the probable consequences of their findings. As has been underlined above, awareness of these two aspects of the historian's work, double detachment, is a necessary prerequisite for gaining intellectual control over the context of one's work.

A further comment on assessing previous histories is that the historian must not confuse the lines dividing the various genres of history with the distinction between soundness and meaningfulness. The scholarly interpretations evaluated are hardly ever independent of public and popular histories; often their involvement in the non-academic battleground of rivalling interpretations is very close indeed. In spite of this, however, many historians assessing previous interpretations still think about them in terms of an isolated academic domain, separate from public concerns. This is tantamount to giving non-academic interpretations almost unrestricted, but unnoticed influence on the scholar's research.

The problem with public and popular histories is that they are often resistant to updating in the light of new empirical evidence and inter-subjective debate, whereas the fundamental criterion of scholarly history is that the work is open to argument, revision and advancement.[7] Nevertheless, it is not only professionals who satisfy this basic requirement of soundness.

A useful reminder of this is the above-mentioned article by Jonathan Steele in the *Guardian* of 15 April 2005, dealing with Mikhail Gorbachev, Pope John Paul II and the collapse of Communism (see pp. 68–9). One of Steele's many perceptive observations pertinent to discussion of the historian's relation to society concerns the nature of obituaries. 'The deaths of the powerful elicit extravagant claims, and many of the tributes to the man buried in Rome last weekend [John Paul II] have been little short of grotesque. In their eagerness to define a clear legacy, obituary writers often produce simplifications that take no account of change.' It is useful to bear in mind that this tendency is not only seen in obituaries, but also marks many stories of the past told in one's own neighbourhood, for instance. Comparisons between different situations in the past are often oversimplifications because they disregard the passage of time. Still, Steele's article shows that not even presenting plausible descriptions is the professional's preserve.

Previous histories are always involved when the topic to be researched is chosen, and they often help in deciding which of the available alternatives should be given priority. This kind of selecting between many possibilities dominates also the later work during the planning stage. When the historian develops his or her initial idea it always turns out that the planned project has more of relevant connections than was obvious at the first sight. Creating the study's central idea means opting for some of these overlapping and often contradictory potential lines of enquiry, that is, at the heart of this exercise is selecting the point of view for the discussion of the topic. The historian has found the crucial combination of past matters (see pp. 47–9) when he or she has worked out which period, people and area he or she has to concentrate on, and when he or she has decided who should be people to be addressed. The central idea has been clarified when the historian has managed to formulate the draft of the study's message.

LIVERPOOL JOHN MOORES UNIVERSITY
LEARNING SERVICES

Elaborating the topic

The rationale of historical research has been aptly crystallized by Mary Fulbrook: 'historical debates are about issues which matter; and therefore the nature of historical understanding matters.' The subjects professional historians deal with are not just academic puzzles; they are also politically and morally informed.[8] This means that historians need to anticipate the implications of the alternative interpretation they are suggesting. The context in which the research is undertaken will have many aspects, as Amit Chaudhuri, a specialist on contemporary literature at the University of East Anglia, has demonstrated.

When reviewing Indian historian Ramachandra Guha's *India After Gandhi: The History of the World's Largest Democracy*, Chaudhuri comments on the tendency of a nation or a community to 'rehearse its history, the very reasons and outcomes of its existence, to itself'. The subject matter of these histories is 'endlessly familiar', and yet they have a strong appeal. The pleasure conferred by interpretative freshness and the surprise of archival research is one explanation, but another is the chance to speculate. It is 'precisely the possibility of what might have happened that gives an immediate but inexhaustible magic to some...historical narratives'.[9]

'Virtual history' is another name for the speculation about which Chaudhuri writes. In the post-communist part of Europe such conjectures have taken on an aggravated political character, but the reimagining of twentieth-century politics has also dominated many public debates about history in countries west of the former Iron Curtain. From the historians' angle, this tendency for counterfactual theorizing, discussions in terms of 'what if', is useful since it reveals currently topical issues.

These debates are well illustrated by the recent argument between Harvard historian Niall Ferguson and Sheffied historian Ian Kershaw over the latter's *Fateful Choices: Ten Decisions that Changed the World 1940–1941*.[10] 'Who knows how it might have turned out (had Stalin sided with the Western Powers in 1939)? The guessing game is pointless.' This argument by Kershaw against the popular 'what if' history is sound, but it is no licence to neglect the reality Niall Ferguson underlines. The course eventually taken was only 'one of the...number of histories that did not happen but which were, if only briefly, plausible futures for contemporaries.'

The specialist's role in this kind of debate is, first, to make explicitly clear the area for which there are no sources and to refute unwarranted speculation. It is on this count that Kershaw is right. Ferguson, in turn, refers to the second task of the historian: the specialist has also to demonstrate that there were alternatives, and that the defeated ones were, up until the point at which the battle was over, no less likely to win than the actual victors. In other words, 'the losers' history' is not situated in the domain of 'what if' at all.

At the same time, Ferguson's stance also raises a fundamental question. Is it possible to demonstrate, beyond reasonable doubt, that his interpretation of Britain's entry into the war is more sound than Kershaw's? The 'reason Britain fought was not because Churchill decided to [claims Ferguson]. It was because he was articulating a collective popular aversion to the alternative of French-style subjugation to the Third Reich.' Or does this question belong, as Mary Fulbrook puts the issue, to those 'areas of debate which will never be resolved', that is, does the choice between Kershaw's and Ferguson's explanations remain 'ultimately a matter of faith'?[11]

From the historian's angle 'what if' histories' are an incentive to examine what it actually is that bothers people: are they really interested in 'what might have happened if', or do they pay attention to matters of history because they have a bearing on the current situation? These are just two examples of questions which assist in demarcating the area where one should act as referee, in fixing the boundary between soundness and meaningfulness. Same questions also help the historian to specify his or her reasons for calling people's attention to particular past matters. Why exactly is there need to 'set the record straight'? What precisely are the claims or beliefs that do not present the past 'how it was'?

When analysing what is not adequate in prevailing knowledge the historian has many potential foci. One example is people's knowledge of the topic he or she has chosen, another the interpretations that dominate public histories. A meticulous search pays off since what one finally discovers is the audience for one's work. This is a crucial point: the researcher knows now how to evaluate the prevailing knowledge – not in general, but from the particular perspective of the people addressed. The historian has now also grounds for assessing the choice he or she has arrived at. Does my point of view possibly entail participation in debates or taking positions I would rather avoid? What are the ensuing implications in general? What kind of commitments do I make? In practical terms, defining one's point of view is a way of avoiding time-wasting; historians too often think that there is no alternative to a process of trial and error.

Yet there is no standard procedure to be followed in specifying one's research, and historians have like other people their particular manners. Notwithstanding this, there is a common logic that can be illustrated by asking two questions. The answer to 'what' will elicit the study's subject matter, period, people and area to be investigated, while 'why' leads one to the grounds for pursuing research. Thinking about these two components, 'what' is normally considered to be rather unproblematic, in the sense that the very idea of a historian's work is to produce new knowledge. In contrast, the meanings embedded in the component 'why' have not been paid the attention they deserve since the profession has refused to take the historians' involvement in the politics of history seriously enough. The rationale informing their projects is that the interpretation/s criticized lead people astray.

The connection between the 'what' and 'why' aspects may be ambiguous at the outset of the project and one's initial idea, the impetus for the enquiry, may be related to either. The historian may simply be interested in an aspect of the past, or dissatisfied with prevalent explanations for it, and develop ideas about the actual relevance of the study only later on. Or the relationship between the two aspects may be the other way round, although it is not so often that the historian starts from the relevance of the intended study or a demand for the knowledge sought. In any case, these two aspects of the study are connected to each other, and the sooner one is able to define the link between them the faster the process of elaborating the chosen topic proceeds. By the time the historian is able to formulate his or her assumption of the significance of the the planned study, the 'what' and 'why' aspects have become inseparable.

It was the 'what' question that initiated my interest in the links between the state and the economy, an issue that has dominated my empirical studies since 1971. I was asked by colleagues at Stockholm University to instigate research into the political consequences of the Depression of the 1930s in my country. In Sweden, Norway and Denmark those years marked the beginning of the welfare state, with Social Democrats as the driving force. Nothing of the sort took place in Finland and it was on the reasons for the difference that the research project concentrated. What ensued was a host of questions specifying the 'why' aspect both of the original undertaking and several later ones. What turned out to be especially significant were the implications of questions about Finnish history which had not previously been asked by historians.

The narrowness of Finnish historical research on this period was revealed by its focus on the extreme right-wing Lapua movement while hardly any research had been done on the Depression, not to speak of the relationship between the two. The Lapua movement turned out to be principally a reaction to the restoration of democracy (established in 1906) after the 1918 Civil War, forced upon Finland by the Entente powers as the condition for recognition of independence. The rationale of right-wing radicalism was not connected to the Depression and instead of being a useful tool the movement soon turned out to be an embarrassment to the export-oriented big business. As to the Social Democrats, their economic policies were quite similar to those of the British Labour Party at that time.

It also became apparent that historical knowledge of the state-economy relationship in the decades before the Civil War was insufficient. In particular, the contrast with nineteenth-century western European developments, the accent on 'from above' rather than 'from below', was a great personal surprise. There was, for example, nothing comparable to the political revolutions, and the Russian emperor's decrees were crucially instrumental in the coming of the industrial revolution to Finland. A common theme in my own recent empirical writings is that by the end of the twentieth century my country had reached, in relation to the rest of Europe, the other extreme when compared with the situation in 1800s – a theme to which I will return in the final chapter of this book.

Actually, what followed from the 1971 Swedish initiative shows the 'multipler effect' of a well-founded unconventional question. In this case the incentive for research came from the academic battleground of clashing interpretations, whereas in the case of my doctoral thesis the impetus had been provided by politics (as explained in Chapter 2, see p. 48). At that time, in the mid-1960s, my starting point lay in the 'why' component, while the 'what' component, the lack of coopeation in terms of security between Finland and Sweden in the 1920s, had secondary status.

In addition to an analysis of the current politics of history (that serves mainly the attempt to attain intellectual control over the social conditions of the project), scholarly discussions and traditions provide a useful perspective for defining the central idea of one's study. This is illustrated by the way I argued for the findings in my doctoral thesis. Inspired by American studies on foreign policy analysis, I constructed a conceptual frame of reference for comparing the foreign policies of the two countries. That this method proved useful testifies to the fruitfulness of the theoretical self-awareness for which Mary Fulbrook argues in her *Historical Theory*. Unfortunately, far too many historians have only a slight, and many of them hardly any, interest in the various theoretical instruments relevant to their research. Colleagues with this inclination should think about the repercussions of Fulbrook's convincingly substantiated conclusion: 'processes of historical investigation and representation are inevitably, intrinsically theoretical enterprises'.[12]

A more recent personal experience demonstrates the usefulness of the kind of reflection that Fulbrook suggests for defining one's central idea. In February 2010 I watched an interview with the South African artist Candice Breitz (who specializes in video works and installations) on Finnish television and realized that there was an interesting similarity between us.[13] She focuses on the 'emergence of Madonna' while I am interested in the 'emergence of history'. What we share is dialogue as the arena in which our foci emerge: for Breitz between the artist and the fans, for me between the historian and his or her audience. It was the difference between us that was important with an eye to the present book, since it reminded me of the confines of my project by pointing to its heart. Breitz concentrates on the end result of the dialogue whereas the rationale of my effort is about the historian's position in the dialogue and the ways his or her choices affect it.

The main argument for the suggested approach to elaborating the chosen topic is the same as that that motivated the previous section: the necessity of bringing the context of one's research under intellectual control. Justification of this aim is simple: the historian must avoid a situation where he or she is unintentionally governed by the surrounding circumstances. The method employed is to answer two crucial questions. The first relates to the existing knowledge: 'what makes the planned project worth undertaking, where lies its relevance?' Discussing the various connections of this issue started at the beginning of Chapter 3 and was completed with this section. The second question will be explored in the following sections and is about the consequences of one's alternative interpretation: 'what are the implications of the way in which the historian specifies the chosen topic?'

Histories offered

'For all its antiquarianism, al Qaeda is as much a creation of modernity as globalization and the World Wide Web.' This is Oxford historian Christopher Tyerman's sharp comment on current debates where recent political conflicts in the Near East have been said to derive from the crusades. In his view such interpretations are valid only in the sense that the protagonists believe them to be true.[14] According to another historian, Jonathan Phillips from the University of London, George W. Bush presented, by referring to the crusades in the aftermath of 9/11, a 'propaganda gift to Osama bin Laden, who for years had been talking about Jewish-Crusader attacks on Islam'. A third British medievalist, Thomas Asbridge, makes the same point and emphasizes that this use of the crusades is an alarming and dangerous example of the potential for history to be misappropriated, misrepresented and manipulated for political ends. Both Phillips and Asbridge refer to the language of the crusaders' Muslim contemporaries: 'the wars of the Franks'.[15]

Using historical analogies, and metaphors as a special case of comparisons is probably the most widespread form of historical thinking – and the most prone to distortion. The example above demonstrates that similarities quite often turn out to be unfounded when the past subject matter is put into its historical context. On the other hand, the making of historical analogies is not necessarily futile, provided we do not look for a perfect fit between past and present. Respecting the otherness of the past, it is possible, in the words of John Tosh, to 'enlarge our sense of possibilities by reclaiming some of the richness of the past experience'.[16]

The fruitfulness of 'leap-frogging', as Tosh puts it, in search of a parallel is displayed by Anu Suoranta, who juxtaposed labour relations between the two world wars with those of the twenty-first century. Focusing on female employment in the Finnish textile industry in the 1920s and 1930s, she demonstrated that systematically irregular labour conditions create economic and social insecurity. Hiring a workforce solely with the company's interest in mind is no novelty in the globalized world of today, nor are the consequences of this kind of employment unprecedented. Giving emphasis to the differences between the two periods, the analogous argument of Suoranta's bestselling book transformed the debate on the conditions of employment between the trade unions, the media and scholars in present-day Finland.[17]

When developing one's subject, it is worth paying special attention to interpretations of history which have been deliberately subordinated to political or other specific purposes. Such accounts are plentiful in any society, and are used by governments, politicians and various social groups, for instance. These histories illuminate a category which is called in German *Geschichtspolitik*, a term that could be translated as *the expedient use of history*. There are a host of works dealing with this type of account of the past, among which M. I. Finley's *The Use and Abuse of History* is a kind of classic.[18]

The expedient use of history is a concept with far narrower scope than the politics of history, and emphasizing the difference between the two concepts is important because professional historians have a strong tendency to cover up their unavoidable political involvement.[19] Since the influence of current circumstances and the various consequences of research findings are always present in their work, every historian participates in the politics of history, irrespective of his or her intentions. This inevitable involvement of the historian in society has been hidden, and unnecessary confusion created, by drawing a sharp, unfounded distinction between the (virtually by definition) 'uncontaminated' scholarly historiography and the various (virtually a priori) 'impure' expedient (that is, political) uses of history. The historian's objectives, or 'partisanship' as it used to be called, are a separate issue, discussed in Chapters 5 and 6 of this book.

Carefulness is also required in respect of 'official history', an ambiguous concept that has at least three senses. One refers to the commissioned history of the past of an institution or organization, which should not to be confused with an unauthorized account. Another kind of 'official history' refers to mainstream historical research and is a term frequently used by those in other scholarly fields studying society and culture. The point is that this usage, which usually simply reflects intellectual laziness, should not be taken for granted. The third sense of 'official history' refers to the hegemonic position of some interpretation and should actually be approached as a special case of expedient use of the past. A good example of this usage is provided by Finnish history.

For a half-century after the1918 Civil War both 'White' and 'Red' interpretations, or 'truths' and 'lies' as the two traditions called them, had a vigorous life, but in very different ways. The 'White' version was the 'official' one up to the 1960s, and its dominance was so overwhelming that there was hardly any room in the public sphere for 'Red' accounts. It was only in the 1970s that the interpretation of the Civil War as a 'national tragedy' reached the status of an 'official' representation of the war of 1918 – even if it has never acquired as strong a position as the 'White' one occupied during the preceding decades. These versions of 'official history' clearly refer to power over history, the dominant position of an interpretation.

A cautious approach is also urged by silences on the past in general and in particular by the common confusion of traumas and taboos. Historical traumas are overwhelming and catastrophic or extremely painful past experiences (for example the Holocaust), whereas taboos stem from present-day considerations. Taboos are silences on the past regarding occurrences, people or situations that must not be mentioned. The difference between past and present origins of silence is easily disregarded, with the result that people frequently talk about historical traumas when they in fact mean taboos. This confusion has been exploited by some historians, who in fact invent 'traumas' in order to offer 'treatment' for them, and thereby increase demand for their works.[20]

The historian's relation to the public domain is by no means limited to interpretations sustaining obvious policies nor to bigoted explanations. Another kind of challenge is connected to received ideas, which often convey imperceptible stances. This is demonstrated for example by the Atlanta historian Ruby Lal's recent *Domesticity and Power in the Early Mughal World*. She describes a female world quite at odds with the usual image of harem life and of harsh and exploitative confinement of women. Mughal women were better educated and had a far more central part in court and diplomatic life than has previously been recognized. Calling into question many stereotypes, Lal's work is likely, in the opinion of her reviewer William Dalrymple, the New Delhi historian, to 'rewrite completely the social history of the period'.[21] She has, as the historian should do according to the British historian Ian Mortimer, made it possible for people 'to understand the human past differently, and what mankind has done differently, and thereby achieve a new vision of what mankind is'.[22]

A different example of interrogating current wisdom has been provided by the London historian Pat Thane with her studies of old age in English history. Hers is a convincing attack on the stereotyping of elderly persons 'as burdensome and dependent, requiring much but contributing little'. In fact, they have rarely been simply 'passive victims awaiting their fate at the mercy of others'; old people have 'consistently sought to take control of their own lives and find their own solutions to the difficulties caused by ageing'.[23]

Presenting unexpected connections between past phenomena is also a way in which the historian can give nourishment for fresh thinking. In his *Consumable Metaphors* the Birmingham historian Ceri Crossley demonstrates that in nineteenth-century France 'the meat-versus-vegetarianism debate reflected the same tension as those that existed between progress and conservatism, male and female, cynicism and belief, war and peace'. As a result of the vegetarian lobby's activities there emerged a situation where 'the tensions between Church and State, between conservatism and republicanism, were not so much effects of history, class and greed but a function of diet'.[24]

Attempting to position one's chosen topic in the politics of history is a logical starting point for the sensible historian when creating the subject, and a useful assumption to begin with is that the previous interpretations being evaluated are not there at random but have their own history. Finding out the reasons for their publication and continued availability is one way of developing awareness of what an alternative interpretation might signify. What are the probable implications of looking upon the particular matters from a different the point of view? Drafting a convincing explanation necessitates knowing this. What is involved in the effort to ensure that falsely interpreted, one-sided or otherwise unsound histories are not uncritically accepted, for instance? Are there some aspirations to authority, leadership and standards, or other hopes and objectives, that my planned study may criticize? Taking seriously these kinds of questions is also needed from the historian who writes about the past with no specific intention of influencing the present.

Looking for the uses to which histories connected to the chosen topic have been put points one towards the possible meanings that may be attributed to one's findings, but it is also, as the examples above show, a means of identifying factors likely to influence one's own reasoning. Here, it is good to remember two things. The first is that there are different kinds of discourses in which the past has been used. At one end of the continuum are debates about, to all intents and purposes, the substance of history and, at the other, controversies in which history is used only as one of many arguments supporting some position or action.

The second point is that the many diverse interpretations serve a multitude of functions and these purposes are by no means always obvious and unmistakable. Their often hard-to-make-out nature notwithstanding, it is important not to forget to look for them. Many historians have been rightly criticized for producing interpretations which have, for example, covered up inequality of the treatment of gender. Uncovering the meanings attached to the chosen topic thus entails doing research, even though the main questions of research are still only at the planning stage.

Treacherous time

Time is the inseparable companion to history, but also a precarious associate. It is an indispensable medium through which to make connections between various phenomena, but like a ruler it does not cause anything in itself. Criticizing unfounded views resulting from the passage of time is as important as attacking the common idea of there being a 'natural', that is, timeless state of affairs. Demonstrating that dealing with time is anything but straightforward is the first function of this section, while the second is to present the various risks and pitfalls associated with time.[25]

Defining time using similes, comparing it for example with a river in flow that carries events, entices people, even historians, to make artificial connections between events at different times in the past. The archetypical explanation of time in relation to history is that of 'historical continuity', a concept based on the logic that any past matter is explicable in terms of its origins and is recognizable through its consequences. The underlying assumption of this historicist meta-explanation, as I call it, is the idea that, in the end, everything in the field of history is bound together by the passing of time. In other words, confusion has arisen from muddling the continuities embedded in any phenomenon or state of affairs with the assumption of an overarching, a priori continuity.[26]

The historian's job is to demonstrate that the common tendency to take the nature of time as self-evident can be treacherous. A superficial understanding can easily lead, for example, to confusing the passage of time with causal connections, and to forgetting that these are two very different things. A preceding event may have given rise to the succeeding one – but it may just as well have not. A similar risk to watch out for is reducing history to processes leading up to a certain point. Such a trajectory is one possible historical explanation of the connections between various matters, but not a necessary element of a historical explanation. It is equally justifiable to approach one's subject in terms of a situation.

Worth keeping in mind is the historian's job as regards time: to uncover ways which people have understood and thought about time, contrasting present and past concepts of time, for instance. The task is not to discuss ideas of the actual nature of time even if its intricacies have enticed many historians. On the other hand, analysing the role time has played in the interpretations under criticism often provides the historian with a fruitful starting point for elaborating the chosen topic. Are there, for example, weaknesses resulting from not giving adequate attention to the various aspects of time or from not avoiding the always present pitfalls? It is also good to remember that every conclusion concerning interdependence mediated by time must be explicitly defended and that locating the matter studied in its adequate historical context is an indispensable element of the historian's final account.

'It is the winners who write history.' Demonstrating that this widespread way of thinking is not justified is what unites historians;

they strive to show that the lot of the losers is as important as giving an account of the winners' success. Nevertheless, there is a real tendency towards the 'history of winners' even in the works of professionals – especially when a process is examined with the eventual outcome as the starting point. This propensity is demonstrated by many works on various international phenomena after the Second World War, for instance. The term 'the prehistory of the Cold War' illustrates my point.

The same tendency often characterizes the writing of 'national' histories too. English historian Noel Malcolm has made this point in reviewing a recent work on Montenegro that covered the early twentieth-century fate of the non-Orthodox minorities there, for example. Their history became, in the book examined, part of Montenegrin history only after they were 'caught in the headlight of the oncoming expansionary state'. According to Malcolm 'old-fashioned histories of Britain' used to be like this. They 'would start with Anglo-Saxon and Norman England, and would treat the Welsh and the Scots only as 'noises off' until the English conquered them or united with them'.[27]

The historian always knows things that the people studied had no chance of being aware of and this makes hindsight a real pitfall. When looking at the past and producing one's account, there is sometimes a strong inclination to give the phenomena studied a more coherent shape than was actually the case, to rationalize events and to show causal links that are often unfair to the people studied.[28] This danger is multiplied by the term itself: the very idea of hindsight exposes one to the temptation to regard succeeding steps in the matter under scrutiny as inevitable. Such logic can easily lead one virtually to conclude that contemporaries knew what was going to happen.

Built-in determinism unites the history of winners and the notion of hindsight but the latter carries an additional questionable characteristic, the idea of teleology. The name of this term comes from the Greek word *telos*, an end, and with teleology the outcome is seen as implanted in the passage of time. A Finnish example is the tendency in twentieth-century history-writing to look upon various political activities preceding the declaration of independence from 'the peephole of 6 December [1917]', to see the aim of self-rule, even sovereignty embedded in these deeds. What was happening at that time has, in other words, been explained by the purpose those events were postulated to serve rather than by contemporary circumstances.

The 'Whig interpretation of history' is perhaps the best known example of teleological reasoning. Victorian historians of the English constitution regarded Parliament 'as the benign fulfilment of a centuries-long process of development' and misunderstood for example the structure of medieval English government because of their obsessive interest in the origins for their object of research. It is the inclination to 'project modern ways of thought backwards in time and to discount those aspects of past experience which are alien to modern ideas' that creates these kind of interpretations.[29] Peter Mandler uses the term 'historical bias' in this connection and refers to the likelihood that elements of continuity overweigh the explanations of historians. Scholars of the eighteenth century, for instance, tend to depict 'modernity' as if it was born in the period. This kind of process 'nearly always does violence not only to the present, but also to all intervening periods'.[30]

What unites the 'history of winners', hindsight and teleological reasoning is the tendency to see the sequence of events or matters analysed as inevitable; that is, they share a deterministic understanding of the passage of time. Connected to this is the risk of underestimating the differences between consecutive presents, or various different periods, and of forgetting that the study of intended actions is always about 'futures past', as the title of Reinhart Koselleck's famous treatise emphasizes.[31] Historians must always think very carefully about the implications of past actors not knowing what would take place in the future.

It is also important to remember that the future in the singular is a theoretical concept in the same way as the past in the singular; in empirical analysis there are many particular futures which must always be specified. The futures a historian presents must be plausible in the sense that they were unknown times ahead for the people studied. The Swedish historian Göran B. Nilsson has aptly summarized in general terms the historian's duty in the context of time: history must be written forwards, not backwards.[32] Written forwards, the years immediately following the Second World War appear as a period when aspirations for a peaceful, rational world were frustrated, whereas written backwards, it appears inevitable that the confrontation of the Great Powers would in due course be realized.

In the majority of everyday history, storytelling is the manner in which the past is related, and this mode is also partly to blame for specialists' tendency to present history as a smooth, linear development towards the present. Yet, as far as professional historians are concerned, to think of their work in terms of producing a narrative is questionable. The grounds for this statement are elaborated below in the section '*Composing the final account*', in Chapter 5. With a view to upholding history-making as a basic social practice, the main stress here is not on how the argument is presented, but on understanding the ways in which time is used to make sense of the past, to discover connections between different matters. This perspective is also useful for historians in delineating their subject.

The problems connected with periodization have been highlighted by the Oxford historian Clifford S. L. Davies with reference to Henry VIII. According to him the term 'Tudor' is an anachronism, 'a barrier to our understanding of contemporary thought'. The monarchs from Henry VII to Elizabeth I did not think of themselves as a 'Tudor dynasty'. Nor did their subjects, Davies argues, think of themselves as 'Tudor people' living in 'Tudor England'. 'Tudor' is a delusion, 'we must learn to do without the Tudors'.[33] Davies's point introduces an important issue: with what kinds of reservations is it justified, as many people outside the academic world do, to use terms like 'Tudor' and 'Victorian' as shorthand references for an historical period?

As expressions, 'Tudor' and 'Victorian' characterize the inescapable nature of historical knowledge: vast amounts of information have to be condensed into relatively brief phrases denoting, for example, a period or a pattern of thinking. There are 'the fifteenth century' and 'the sixties' as well as 'Newtonian' and 'Freudian', for instance. At the same time, one must never forget the status of these terms as later constructions, and the historian has to make sure that the audience becomes aware of this. No one at the time knew that they were living in the 'ancient' world, for instance.

'The Middle Ages never happened, they were just imagined later.' This statement by the British historian Alex Burghart reminds us that criticism of periodizations is a fruitful way to develop one's subject. He reviewed an inspiring book written by British medievalist Veronica Ortenberg with the European imagination as its focus, a work in which the Middle Ages blurs into the surrounding centuries and ceases to be a useful unit of time.[34] Christopher Tyerman, in turn, criticizes periodization from another angle when he claims that 'the medieval world, so often represented as crude, backward, superstitious, violent, was neither so inferior to our own nor so utterly different from it that understanding is unattainable.'[35]

The French historian Fernand Braudel's idea of the plurality of social time, his famous three timescales, or registers, is another instrument for specifying time in history. There is, first, the long term, *'la longue durée'*, an almost motionless framework of environmental constraints or of slow-moving cultural forms. The second tier is the history of conjunctures, movements in economics or demography over a cycle of ten to fifty years for instance; and the third, the history of events. Braudel's concept includes, among other things, the idea of the simultaneity of multiple times, metaphorically compared with music and the playing of an orchestra with its many different lengths of score and different rhythms.[36]

An unexplored approach to time in history, in addition to thinking of it in terms of music, is provided by shared histories. Historians like to refer to the twists and turns of fate when they criticize deterministic tendencies and they also point to contingency as an element characterizing history. Without questioning these, as such, it seems plausible to reduce the contingent nature of time in relation to history with the help of shared histories. Different communities or collectives in a society probably have different timescales too.

Historians should also ponder whether the Cardiff sociologist Barbara Adam's depiction of the contradictory relationship of social scientists to time characterizes the historians too. In their everyday lives social scientists are much like other people. They take time largely for granted in spite of needing to daily accommodate a host of different types of time and they also deal with this multitude 'as an interconnected whole'. And this mastery is not impeded by the actuality that some of these aspects 'have to do with synchronisation, ordering, sequencing or timing, others with control or measurement, and still others with the time aspects of machines and artefacts'. Yet, these everyday capabilities are not reflected in the scholarly works of social scientists. 'Not only does time seem to be a non-reflected aspect of social theory, it also lacks the multifacetedness displayed in thought, language, and the concomitant everyday life.' As scholars, social scientists reduce social time to clock-time.[37]

The historian, in addition to keeping in mind the many different types of time, should also be aware of the tendency to think, unintentionally, that time actually causes something to happen. It is also good to remember that past, present and future are just aspects of the experience of time passing and that it is not possible to define any of them without reference to the others. Time in history is neither linear, irreversible nor teleological, time is equal to the meanings people give to it.

Expectations of the specialist

Whose expectations am I going to meet? Whose understanding of history should be corrected? Has the debate on my chosen topic been one-sided or do I want to stimulate thinking about an historical issue by looking upon it from an unusual point of view? Considering these kinds of questions is helpful when historians create their subjects since specifying the expectations of specialists and relating them to one's own views puts the topic chosen into perspective. The result is a vantage point from which to assess scholarly and other interpretations as well as the differences between them. It is also necessary to take on board current historical debates, if one takes participation in these seriously and is not satisfied merely with catering to the fleeting demands of the market. Arriving at a deliberate stance on the history expert's public role also helps in the often troublesome relation with the media.

Pointing out deficiencies in lay histories is what probably still dominates scholarly attitudes towards everyday history. This view is also in line with the expert's role as a referee (discussed in Chapter 2), since part of the professional historian's function is to tackle and correct weaknesses in prevalent interpretations of history. Lay curiosity in the past is also acknowledged by professional historians. 'Was it really Gorbachev's reforms, perestroika and glasnost that brought down communism?' 'What actually was the role of the Polish-born Pope in the downfall of communist rule in Poland?' Being confronted with questions like these is part of my everyday experience as a specialist in recent history. The demand for knowledge is more modest in the case of antiquity, for instance, but it is there and my colleagues in this field also respond to lay questions.

One of the functions the specialist has is to arbitrate between conflicting interpretations; another is providing an historical context for an event. There are also expectations connected to historical traumas and taboos. Another fruitful theme for developing one's subject has been suggested by the Columbia University historian Susan Pedersen, who invites historians to analyse and ponder what readers expect from biographies. 'Impartiality is all very well, but we read (and write) biography not in order to judge people – or at least not only to judge people – but to understand them. ... to try to walk around in the person's shoes.' A slightly different formulation of the same aim has been provided by Gordon S. Wood, according to whom George Washington 'has finally become comprehensible' in two recent (2010) biographies.[38]

Historians are professionals who have to abide by scholarly norms but, on the other hand, they are also specialists who are consulted when knowledge of the past is needed. One can even argue that some patterns of thought must be criticized by historians and that there are debates in which they have an obligation to intervene. The problem lies in identifying such cases and in defining the boundaries beyond which the historian must not trespass. The position informing the present book in this neglected issue is that selecting the topic to be studied is not the professional's prerogative: embedded in the notion of history-making as a basic social practice is the argument that historians do not have the privilege to decide what historical issues are significant. They should, rather, accept that themes important to 'ordinary people' may be as worthy of research as those discussed within the profession and, as a result, that members of the public should have a say in deciding what is to be researched. Logically, this leads to the notion of a participatory historical culture, an issue discussed in detail in the last section of this book.

The historian's contribution to current politics of history must remain within the limits of his or her expertise, a requirement that is not always self-evident. The challenge here is illustrated by the tendency of those in the media and many others to approach the past in terms of praise and blame, of innocence and guilt. Facing the emotional and ethical dimensions of the public discourse shows the point of clarifying in one's mind what the historian can and cannot do. Making a sound contribution to current debates presupposes that specialists on the past have thought through, on a general level, the relation between the study of history and passing assessments on public issues as well as making moral judgements.

It is perhaps questionable to call history a judge even if history is akin to posterity. What is certain is that it is not viable to think about the role of the historian in this way. The logic dominating research is different from the way of thinking prevailing in the courtroom. Historians' assessments are based only on interpretations, not laws. The function of their evidence and arguments is to explain and not to arrive at a resolution. The idea of the historian's work is to use the available sources to create a sensible argument that enhances understanding, while for the judge establishing the facts is paramount.[39] Empathy towards those studied is necessary for the historian, and this applies to all sides when examining a conflict: the historian is simultaneously prosecutor and defence counsel.

Nor is it the historian's task to moralize, that is, to impose one's own standards when assessing the past people studied. The scholar's first task is to make sense of their thinking and actions in terms of their own norms. The second task is to place these values alongside with one's own moral standards, with the idea of encouraging readers to reflect on their own. The method is, in other words, to defamiliarize the past and thus to stimulate the audience to reflect on and evaluate its own values. In order to be successful in doing this, the historian must have clarified his or her own ideas of right and wrong, as well as good and bad.

The potential of history lies in making sense of the deeds and thoughts of people who have lived under very different conditions. The object is to give the people addressed new insights into their own culture by way of comparing it with one in the past, awakening their interest to the differences and similarities. To what extent are the alien characteristics connected to the different social conditions or strange beliefs, for instance? To implement this concept of historical research is more difficult the closer the culture studied is to that of today; a problem illuminated by the common tendency to assess policies during the Cold War era in terms of conditions after the beginning of the 1990s. Historical research is justified only when the people studied are given a fair hearing, and blurring the distinction between the past and the present jeopardizes this fundamental obligation. The historian's job is to make sense of the past, not to act as judge or jury, nor to provide society with a moral compass.

Unfortunately, passing judgements and making moral assessments has often been reduced to a simplistic banality in historical circles with reference to Hitler or Stalin. Of course, the historian is fully justified in disapproving their deeds even in his or her role as a specialist on the past – provided he or she has explained and presented to the audience the circumstances and ideas which led to their actions. However, these are relatively straightforward cases compared with the intricate situations with which the historian is normally confronted – for example when one has publicly to challenge an argument on the grounds that it has been constructed in unfair terms. On the other hand, such questioning of the views on the past reveals the necessity and the justification for the historical profession.

In general, it is important to register the real risk that arguing for one's alternative interpretation can easily lead one into imposing one's own ready-made view. The dividing line between clarifying one's argument and forcing one's own view upon the audience is certainly vague and identifying when one has crossed the line difficult. Two things help the historian to stay on the safe side. One is taking the time to examine the audience's reasons for cherishing their own histories and the other is ensuring that one's presentation of the findings allows readers to reach their own conclusions independently.

Observing the limits of the historian's participation in the politics of history is important, since the specialist's unavoidable involvement in the ongoing social process of history-writing gives him or her a societal role. Whether one sets out to meet lay expectations or starts the research purely on one's own inclination makes no difference here. In this respect, the traditional schism between 'objectivists' and 'representatives of partisanships' is off the mark since it is about an option the historian does not have: non-involvement in society is an impossibility. The heart of the matter is the historian's way of tackling their position in society.

The historian's position

A consensus of opinion that studies cannot be non-partisan emerged among academics in the various fields studying society and culture at the end of the twentieth century.[40] This led to it being recognized that scholars had an obligation to spell out their own position, regarding both their research practice and communication of their findings. Thorough awareness of one's own position is essential, first, in order to conduct an investigation according to the rules of the field concerned, and, secondly, because the audience must know the scholar's position in order to be able properly to evaluate the results produced.

Some historians are sceptical about the discourse on the scholar's position since they fear, and not without evidence, that it leads to demands to reveal one's various allegiances for its own sake. Their view is supported by the experiences of many colleagues in cultural studies who have tired of works in which actual research is buried beneath long explanations of the scholar's disciplinary identity and profound discussion of their positions. The situation in sociology seems to be somewhat more balanced, while historians have hardly acknowledged the necessity of reflecting on their position in the current politics of history. True, there are no longer many historians who support the 'unrealistic and undesirable extreme of extinguishing the self' (Thomas L. Haskell), but the repercussions of this nineteenth-century legacy still exert a strong influence on the profession.[41]

Elaborating one's position requires different things at the beginning of the research project and at the end of it. This is most obvious when the tasks needed are thought of in terms of texts. An explicit, detailed elucidation is called for when the aim is to identify one's intentions and work towards an awareness of one's relation to the current politics of history at the start of the project, whereas the logic of unfolding same position is different when preparing the final account. Then the context is the reception of the study and, ideally, the exposition should be as clear and concise with as few words as possible. This challenge will be discussed, together with the other aspects of the effort to convince the audience, below ('*Composing the final account*', in Chapter 5).

Reflecting on one's position is no independent task in the research process. During the planning stage thinking about it is embedded in assessing the many aspects of the chosen topic, and defining it takes place when the scholar decides on which of these features he or she will concentrate. Since the scholar's position is not separated from the other aspects of research work, the historian has several divergent positions in the politics of history because the subjects he or she studies vary. Yet, these positions are not occasional since historians tend to be consistent in their selections; each of them has his or her 'own thing'. This regularity is a dimension that will be discussed in the next chapter (section '*The historian's professional self*)'.

Together, the positions taken in the politics of history and the professional self provide the foundation for the historian's reasonable alternative to an 'objective' stance. With their awareness of these two aspects of their involvement in society, historians are able to control intellectually the circumstances in which they will perform their research and in which their findings will be received. For this control to succeed, they must be able to discipline their own thinking, not to forget the historian's basic predicament. They are responding to current concerns, but this must not lead to compromising the demand to present a fair description of the people they are studying.

Distancing oneself from one's own objectives means working towards an awareness of what one is actually doing in relation both to the people studied and to the audience. A second routine action is to anticipate where one might be accused of bias and to counter such arguments in advance. This presupposes that one has an accurate awareness of the substance of one's message and of the ways it is related to the interests, groups, ideologies, patterns of thought, and so on, referred to in the likely accusations. Doing this helps one to keep in mind the third and basic requirement in assessing one's objectives: to remember that it is the audience who decides the fate of one's message. It is those receiving the study who will decide whether or not the historian's findings are fruitful and if they are going to take note of the lesson or moral the study conveys.

Closely connected to the historian's position in the politics of history is the ethical dimension of his or her work. This has also been given increased attention in the wake of the dethroning of objectivity but the approach has been superficial as is shown by the scant attention paid to the crucial ethical aspects of the historian's work. The first was mentioned already in the beginning of this section, and is about providing the people addressed with a realistic opportunity of evaluating the results achieved. The ethical content of this requirement is not lessened by its epistemological part (that will be dealt in the section '*Arguing for the findings*' in Chapter 5). The second indication of a narrow understanding of scholarly ethics is shown by the way in which reconstruction has been treated. Fairness as the crucial aspect of plausibility has been overshadowed, almost even marginalized, by epistemological criteria.

The most widely discussed ethical issue of recent decades has been the problems connected with source material: provisions on privacy, data protection, confidentiality and intellectual property rules. Mention of the extensive literature dealing with this 'internal' side of research ethics must suffice here, although it is worth pointing out that the 'external' side has been relegated to the background.[42] The field of societal morals will be discussed in the Chapter 5 as one dimension of the historian's professional self, but here it is necessary to refer to the repercussions of the traditional 'objectivist' orthodoxy.

Indifference to the context of one's research can easily bring one close to misleading the audience, as Mary Fulbrook aptly puts it, under the guise of a 'partisan pretence of neutrality'. There is no sense in not taking a stand since the very idea of studying the chosen topic entails uncovering its role in prevalent debates in the field. In addition, the conditions of one's work as an historian are an inescapable influence and this must be reflected upon. Otherwise the historian might even become a mouthpiece for prevailing biased interpretations, or 'blindly conforms to whatever varied contemporary pressures may be', as Fulbrook formulates the risk.[43]

Probably the gravest challenge confronting historians, analysing their own thinking in order to identify prejudices, also has an ethical dimension. Its difficulty notwithstanding, coping with one's biases is among the most important tasks the historian has. A precondition for contributing to others' knowledge in an acceptable way is that one does not let oneself confirm one's own foregone conclusions. There are cases where one wonders whether objectivity has served as a pretext for intellectual laziness, with the historian failing even to attempt to scrutinize his or her own line of thought.

The requirement of neutrality is an aspect of the historian's work that is also related to ethics. This demand makes perfect sense as far as the people studied are concerned: it is not the historian's business to take part in past controversies but to expound them.[44] The opposite, however, is true when the question is of the historian's relation to his or her own culture. The stipulation of objectivity understood as neutrality is meaningless here, since the very idea of the historian's work, as has been elaborated from different perspectives above, is to have an influence on the audience. Consequently, it is unethical to deny the specialists on the uses of the past the right to take advantage of their motivation – it is after all their key asset.

The draft of the message

The planning stage of the research process comes to an end when the historian has transformed the initial idea, 'that is not how it was', into an alternative interpretation whose validity he or she sets out to test with the use of primary sources. The topic chosen has been developed into the subject of the study, and knowledge of where its significance lies turned into a draft of the message to be conveyed. The sensible historian performs these tasks with the second stage of the research process in mind, with a view to tapping the primary sources in two ways. The first aim is to find maximum support for the research assumptions, and the second to ensure fairness towards the people studied. Preparing for the reception of the study, anticipating critical questions and answering them in advance, is also an integral part of the planning stage. As John Tosh puts it, the author should be 'the first to pick holes in his or her interpretation'.[45]

The historian's draft of the alternative interpretation reflects the position of the chosen topic among existing claims to be the 'right' or 'proper' interpretation. The initial idea of the study will have been evaluated from many angles with the aim of finding the point of view best fit for purpose: conveying relevant new knowledge to the intended audience in a way that ensures fairness to the people studied. This effort to devise a hypothesis to be tested against the primary sources is in fact a research-like endeavour in itself, since the chosen topic has many diverse connections and uncovering them is hard work. On the other hand, as indicated in this and the previous chapters, it is at his or her peril that the historian neglects eliciting the grounds for making his or her particular choices in refining the subject of study.

Nevertheless, the exercise suggested for the planning stage is one that most historians do only cursorily. There are also many colleagues who are simply intellectually lazy and cover up their attitude with either of two (in fact, contradictory) arguments. Some say that it is futile to perform the suggested tasks, while others claim that it is too early a stage to conduct them. The single argument against my suggestion that has some justification refers to the inevitability of trial and error.

My point is that it pays to look before one leaps – regardless of the risk that one makes mistakes along the way. Examining the reasons for one's dissatisfaction with existing histories and accumulating knowledge as one creates the subject is worthwhile. The central idea of the study emerges from the choices made between the original topic's many aspects, and arguments for the selections are useful as material elements on which to gradually build up one's message. Still, it is not only the rationale of the planned project that is reached in this way: conducted carefully, the exercise also leads to increased knowledge of one's position in contemporary society and of one's view on history.

In addition, proceeding systematically is the main way to minimize possible errors and, especially, save time. With the subject clarified, the historian can plan the order in which to visit the numerous archives and other collections of sources, the spread of which otherwise slows down the progress of the research work markedly.

When the historian examines the conflicting interpretations, the politics of history, there are four useful perspectives with the help of which one can look at the current situation. *Shared space* is the first of these, since there must be common ground on which the different explanations meet and clash. Religion, the labour market, foreign policy and gender relations (both in general and in the context of particular societies) are examples of fields of life which also have a relatively autonomous politics of history. In any one study, it is useful to identify the relevant field/s in which the topic chosen is situated and/or to question the site proposed by prevailing interpretations.

What is also worth uncovering in the politics of history is the *perspective* from which the topic chosen has been discussed. Here it is important to realize that the matter one is elaborating has usually been dealt with from numerous points of view: theoretical, institutional, cultural, political, autobiographical and so on. A policy decision may appear in a quite different light depending on whether it has been assessed in the context of economy or democracy, for instance. As a result, analysing the politics of history inevitably leads one to discover that there are many, often contradictory, dimensions to be taken into account while specifying the central idea of the intended study. The basic point to be made, in other words, is that no topic can be interpreted only from a single, not to speak of a given, point of view.

Thirdly, the rivalry between various interpretations of the past for the dominant perspective is inherent in their *interaction*. With their different points of view, these explanations wrestle against each other for the hegemonic position in the field in question. At stake is the 'correct' way of thinking about history: is it international competitiveness or employees' rights that is the 'proper' context for an economic matter? The various positions are also often connected to certain communities and their shared histories. In these cases the rival positions are predetermined by definition, but the historian is under no obligation to accept any one of them. The rationale of the project to be launched may well be the attempt to demonstrate the misplaced foundations of the interpretations criticized.

The fourth perspective on the politics of history is that the *normative systems* connected to the rival interpretations are not stable but undergo constant transformation, and one source of changes are evolving views of the past. There is always the possibility that changes in the interpretation of particular past matters, or the emergence of a different explanation for something in the past may affect existing canons. This is why the historian must consider their responsibilities. Will the alternative interpretation offered have consequences in normative terms?

These four perspectives on the rivalry between different interpretations help to make sense of the context in which the research work will be performed. The conditions of the clash are social: different groups attempt to present the past in their own, distinct, ways in order to legitimize their current power or aspirations. The historian may wish to remain neutral in these struggles, but one's basic rationale, the endeavour to argue 'that's not how it was', is unavoidably connected to the various aspirations, which aim to exploit history for expedient purposes. Accounts of the ethnic and religious conflicts in the Balkans at the turn of the twenty-first century provide a good example of this, even if a somewhat extreme one.

The key decision in developing the subject is choosing the point of view, opting for the particular perspective from which one will analyse the topic. True, sometimes the historian will deploy more than one context for analysis, but the rationale remains the same as it is when he or she chooses only one point of view: the subject emerges from assessing the audience's views on the original topic. The key element is thinking about the relevance of the knowledge to be produced for the people addressed; it is this reflection that creates the historian's message, the meanings he or she aims to convey. In other words, the point/s of view constituting the subject is/are selected by the historian. Or to put the same point in more general terms: the meanings of past matters are always based on the choices made in the present by history-makers.

The historian approaches the past matters he or she studies with a view to their connection to the present in mind. The aim, as was argued in Chapter 2, is to convince the audience of the significance of the research results, that is, both to make a persuasive argument for the fruitfulness of the findings and to convey the lesson or moral embedded in the study as a whole. In other words, the meanings contained in the message have two sides and both of them are present in the research work from the very beginning of the project. The choices delineating the subject play a crucial role, since they direct the historian's work and set the parameters for the eventual findings. The arguments that support these choices are equally critical because they lay the groundwork for the message.

Anticipating the reception is also an aspect of the research project from its inception. The significance of one's results is a conclusion arrived at while critiquing the prevailing interpretations; uncovering the purposes for which these histories have been employed, both the obvious and the imperceptible roles, is especially useful here. Discovering how rival interpretations have been used helps in identifying the potential uses and misuses to which one's own findings may be put. This should enable the historian also to anticipate areas of possible criticism in his or her work, and to consider how to influence its reception.

On the other hand, preparing for the reception is not an uncomplicated task. The study has, for example, quite often unintended consequences – meaning that it is not possible to foresee the reception of one's study. Nor does the historian always have the possibility of choosing between the debates to which he or she contributes and those avoided. Still, there are ways of minimising the unexpectedness of the reception and of fending off unpleasant surprises – if one only aims at it. It is also good to bear in mind that criticism often focuses on secondary results in order to divert attention from the important ones.

5
Cultural Critics

The historian's job is to comment on existing histories in a way that opens up new perspectives for the audience and gives them fresh insights into their culture by comparing it with past ones. Historians have, however, viewed their role in far narrower terms, as that of scholarship. They have not, as George G. Iggers and Q. Edward Wang argue, fully recognized that their work is 'very much a part of a broader historical culture'. One result of this has been allowing 'research techniques to support national myths', but the weightiest part of the point Iggers and Wang make is broader: 'the interconnectedness of historical writing with other aspects of society' has been forgotten.[1]

The profession of historians is sited in two locations: one among academic disciplines and the other among cultural institutions. It is the use of scholarly methods that distinguishes the historian's craft from, for example, that of the playwright or journalist; judging the knowledge produced using epistemological criteria is an inseparable element of historical enquiry. The second part of their role means turning conventional priorities upside down: the work of the historian needs to be thought of first in cultural, instead of disciplinary, terms. This way of thinking points to a seemingly novel self-awareness but actually only reflects what historians have been doing all the time – despite their claim of having had a different rationale. Historians are cultural critics, and essential aspects of their research have been marginalized, or even lost, because reflection on their work has predominantly been in disciplinary terms.

What is needed is to unravel the meanings of the profession's cultural role. There is no need to reassess the identity of historical research among disciplines; the historian's distinctive function remains that of producing sound and fair knowledge of people of the past. This continues to be the absolutely essential element in research and the historian's role as a cultural critic does not undermine this fundamental obligation. What is called for is candidness: the historian acknowledges that it is the significance of the findings that carries historical enquiry forward. As specialists on the uses of the past, historians meet the demand for knowledge in their field and seek to awaken the audience's interest in their subject.

An early inspiration for the central idea of the present book was Australian historian Hugh Stretton's *The Political Sciences* (1969), with its emphasis on what historians 'actually do, rather than what their…manuals urge them to do'. His work expanded in a young scholar's mind on the analyses of E. H. Carr (*What is History?*; 1961) and the American sociologist C. Wright Mills (*The Sociological Imagination*; 1959). Stretton, among other things, lent support to my criticism of colleagues who through their works participated in current societal debates while at the same time as professing their impartiality.

His book also demonstrated that a great many excellent works on history had sunk into scholarly oblivion simply because of their authors' lack of argumentative rigour. This encouraged me as a teacher of research practices in historical enquiry to emphasize the usefulness and fruitfulness of secondary reflection on one's work. Stretton's ideas also helped to defend the weight of the historical profession during 'the golden age of sociology' (as I have grown accustomed to describing my professional experiences from the 1960s). The sub-title of Stretton's book, '*General Principles of Selection in Social Science and History*', was as positively provocative as his view that scholars who 'attempt "value-freedom" do not merely trade good politics for bad, but also damage their technical equipment and discover less'.[2]

My view on history-making as a basic social practice, the origins of which lie in Raphael Samuel's work, fits in with the pattern of thinking emanating from Carr, Mills, and Stretton. Nevertheless, it is paramount to underline that this connection was only latent during the days of the Paperiliitto history-project. It was actually only while writing the present book that I realised, as was noted above (see p. 7), that making histories as an everyday social phenomenon was not a current concern of academic historians in the sixties. Even so, it is in the creation of the subject for the study that the ideas of my early inspirers meet the central idea of this book: specifying the questions that the study will seek to answer is the most important site where the disciplinary and cultural roles of the profession have to be thought about as one.

The relative weight carried by the disciplinary and cultural aspects depends on the historian's judgement on the nature of the prospective findings. Nonetheless, both are present, and this justifies some comment. First, it is always worth hunting out potentially useful scholarly approaches, both from one's own field and from those close to it. It is also good to keep in mind that even findings of studies whose aims are strictly academic contribute, even if not immediately, to the general making sense of the past. Thirdly, it is important to emphasize here again that it is at the historian's peril that he or she compromises producing a fair account in order to make the message more convincing.

The significance given here to the outcome of research is connected to the most fundamental contention of this book, the general under-valuation of the issue 'why history?'. Historians' work would have been greatly enhanced had there been proper discussion about their social role. Yet, the sociology of history-making is lacking, as is demonstrated most clearly by the failure to recognize and analyse the capacity of those addressed to create their own histories. In any case, the progress of the research process is, at its every stage, connected to the historian's growing cognition of why the findings are significant for the audience.

Whether conscious of it or not, historians answer the question 'why this study?' during the planning stage of the research project. The second phase, working with the primary sources, and the third phase, the writing of the final account, only make real sense if the historian is able to create a convincing argument for his or her interpretation. This chapter deals with these two stages in the context of the recent paradigmatic change in historical research. It is not the intention, however, to give the second and third stages comprehensive coverage; rather, the aim is to concentrate on those issues that need reconsideration in the light of the new, more correct self-awareness.

The responsibilities of cultural critics

Historians cannot, in John Tosh's view, 'affirm the importance of their work without taking steps to secure its dissemination'. Argument among historians alone about their ideas is insufficient since, 'the readership of history and the extent of public support for its study will depend on the impact which historians make on the wider public'. Despite this, the number of academics who bring major historical issues before a general audience is small.[3] While agreeing with Tosh's analysis, I want to emphasize that as cultural critics history specialists have a duty to take their contribution to people's sense of the past seriously. They should think carefully about the significance of that understanding for the audience, that is, ask themselves why they should do more than merely act as referees of everyday history.

What kind of knowledge is the audience in need of? What justifies scholarly intervention in the debate on the topic chosen to be studied? How, exactly, can the historian as a specialist on the past, contribute? Are there responsibilities the scholar has, and what are the limits within which such an intervention must remain? In what way are scholars' works different from other histories? What exactly is the historian's role in transforming the pasts into histories? Answering these kinds of questions adequately is a useful way of exploring the central idea of the study to be launched – and, eventually, of enhancing the status of historical knowledge in society.

However, every historian needs to work towards an attainable and defensible definition of their function in society individually since the profession has not conducted systematic discussion about the historian's role. No clear guidelines on historical studies as cultural contributions are given to historians during their training. Instead, there are often heated arguments – but only on particular cases – on the historian's position in society since general agreement on the specialist's role in social history-making is very narrow.

At present, the profession is, as a result of the paradigmatic change, at something of a halfway house in building up the significance of the scholarly historian's cultural contribution. True, legitimizing the one-time 'new histories' has enlarged the scope of historical research, but it has not changed the nature of the profession, as such. Despite a successful insurgence against the traditional elitism, the idea of upholding everyday history-making has only gained, at best, a secondary position as an aspect of the historian's professional work. There is no obligation on the historian to discuss the relation of his or her subject to non-academic interpretations; it is not considered a weakness not to discuss one's position in relation to everyday history. Every historian makes choices that bear on the significance of his or her study outside the academic world, but there is no requirement to defend them.

Historians are trained neither to criticize prevailing interpretations outside the academic world, nor to think about the probable consequences of their findings. It remains up to the individual historian to determine whether and in what respect he or she should make a contribution to current debates. The decisions he or she arrives at regarding everyday history are personal ones, and he or she is under no obligation even to present them, much less to subject them to scrutiny outside academia. In other words, the historian's relation to society remains not merely a one-way affair, where influence is exerted only by the scholar, but also his or her private concern.

The challenge academics have to accept as necessary is to eliminate patronizing attitudes, that is, to take the trouble to discover what makes people engage with the past. My American colleagues Roy Rosenzweig and David Thelen point out here that there is little academic interest in 'experiences', a term 'dismissed by many professionals as random, private, shallow, and even self-deceptive'.[4] Yet, getting one's message effectively across to people means finding out their connection to their past, or to accounts of the past they share. Identifying the relevant shared histories of one's audience is an appropriate objective; analysing them may lead the historian to the opinions and values of those they seek to address.

The conventional phobia about societal influences, so strong until the late twentieth century, helps one to comprehend historians' continuing difficulty in acknowledging that their profession is an integral part of history-in-society. Their reluctance to leave their ivory tower, in turn, is partly to blame for the persisting tendency outside the academia to think that history is a dead subject with little relevance to contemporary issues. It is also doubtful whether historians have seriously taken issue with another wrong idea about history prevalent among laypeople. Have scholars tried to demonstrate and convince those outside the profession that historical knowledge is of a 'different order than that of fiction, myth, and ideology'?[5]

As regards the profession's attitude towards those who have transformed the everyday custom of calling attention to the past into deliberate creation of histories, professionals have every reason to stop labelling these efforts as amateurish and focusing on formalities, for example, making disdainful remarks about poor footnotes. Instead, they should demonstrate sustainable ways of referring to the past in studies dealing with a social evil or criticizing patronising policies, for instance.

However, even if historians have failed to discuss adequately their cultural responsibilities they have, in various parts of the world, inaugurated new kinds of research practices. These initiatives serve as incentives to historians to question the hitherto cultural profile of the profession and to recreate their individual professional identity. These two issues, dealt with in the following sections, are essential elements of the recent paradigmatic change.

Thinking about one's study as a cultural contribution is one way of meeting the demand for double detachment made necessary by the politics of history; the aim is to achieve intellectual control over one's involvement with the present. Assessing the cultural role is also helps in drawing the line between the soundness and meaningfulness of the work, and of differentiating acting as a referee from commenting on the meanings, opinions and moral judgments attached to the subject studied.

The profiles of cultural critics

At the beginning of the twenty-first century the practice of historians has changed in ways that raise a question that would not have been a current concern for mainstream history before the paradigmatic change at the end of the twentieth century: 'what is scholarly history for?' As regards the answer (in addition to the advancement of scholarly knowledge), a loose consensus about the historian's cultural responsibilities is gradually emerging, and remains, one hopes, the most that will be aimed at. The point is that progressing further would create a situation in which historians would lose their cultural freedom and become proponents of ready-made ethical and moral judgements. Recent developments and debates do not either suggest that the still ongoing changeover within the discipline will lead to other than a number of divergent profiles.

In any case, the current situation is characterized by the emergence of novel approaches to historical enquiry within the profession. These build on the epistemological foundations of research into the past, and advocate ways of thinking in which the historian's disciplinary capacity no longer subordinates their cultural role. In English-speaking countries the umbrella phrase for these new initiatives is the ambiguous term 'public history' (in the singular).

English Heritage, the National Trust and the BBC, for instance, are British institutions that have, at the present turn of century, increased their activities to encourage an interest in the past. The reaction of professional historians has been mixed, and there is criticism of the political aims embedded in public history in general, as well as in the commercial aspects of heritage. But these criticisms 'fall wide of the mark', as John Tosh remarks with good reason, since they 'overstate the ability of guardians of public history to determine popular response to their products'. The 'current craze for historical material' is there regardless of the various institutional schemes.[6]

LIVERPOOL JOHN MOORES UNIVERSITY
LEARNING SERVICES

A quite different perspective on the activities heaped under the cover of 'public history' comes from the labour market. Efforts to present the past for public consumption offer trained historians a badly needed way out of the situation created by the decreasing academic opportunities (in relation to people trained) and stand, thus, for job-creation. Historians have also taken many initiatives to broaden the use of their skills, and this provides a fruitful incentive to discuss the cultural functions of the specialists on the uses of the past – in spite of the ambiguity of the concept 'public history' in the singular.

In the terms of this book, any historian, their intentions notwithstanding, produces public histories in the sense of presenting interpretations of the past for all to see. In contrast, public history in singular denotes various activities the breadth of which is vast. As for example Ludmilla Jordanova has demonstrated, they extend from advising members of the Cabinet to supporting people engaged in building a village museum.[7] Because of this enormous variety, the customary way of using public history in singular is moot: it implies a shared characteristic stronger than is the case. The activities denoted hardly share common beliefs or morals, nor are they united by the kind of historical account produced or by the specific field of research investigated. Rather, the definition supported by empirical evidence refers to various history-related, frequent occupations of professionals outside academia.

A comprehensive analysis of the activities covered by public history in singular, with their own complex histories and the many disputes relating to them, is beyond the scope of the present book.[8] Discussing three ways in which historians have delineated their cultural profile and have attempted to increase their impact must suffice. The most ubiquitous of the three, prevalent for example in the United States, Australia and New Zealand, is the effort to demonstrate the importance of historical expertise in various parts of society.[9]

Many universities in the 'New World' offer MA programmes that give students the opportunity to explore non-teaching careers in history-related work outside academia. There is a quest for 'alternative careers' to that of the academic or classroom teacher of history and an almost unlimited number of occupations. Trained historians can work in archives and museums, on historic preservation projects, at historic sites, at state and local historical institutions, and in libraries. They may also be employed by newspapers, businesses, political parties, trade and labour organizations, as consultants, and at various levels of government. They work as editors, archivists, oral historians, administrators, curators, writers, public policy analysts and – as historians.

Connected to the efforts of increasing the supply of historical expertise has been a greater stress to communication skills, as discussed in
Chapter 3 (see pp. 71–2). Historians have also been trained to reduce the
distance between themselves and those outside academic life. An important side-effect within the profession has been enhanced self-respect and
increased esteem of professional historians working outside academia.
These changes in attitude reflect the growing awareness, also outside the
historical profession, that history is not taught solely in the classroom,
but is learned in a multitude of places, and in a variety of ways.

A more specific kind of response to the contemporary challenges is
the History & Policy initiative in the UK started in 2004: the united
effort of quite a few professional historians to make the specialists' competence count. The aim is to influence systematically both government
decision-making and current public debates, and also to demonstrate,
using the findings of historical research, that although history has significant consequences it cannot be utilized in a random way. There is,
in other words, strong emphasis on the requirement for soundness of
historical knowledge.

Criticism aroused, for example, by making superficial historical
analogies is an old chestnut, but for the historians active in History
& Policy there is a novel worrying aspect in the practice of government: employees are too busy to be able to give sufficient thought
and reflection to their work. The result is, as Pat Thane puts it, 'little
or no genuine historical knowledge and, at best, a radically fore-
shortened historical perspective'.[10] To counter this, History & Policy
provides policymakers and the media with clear and crisp communication, short, lucid briefing papers through its internet site www.
historyandpolicy.org. A recent exposition of the way in which History & Policy has transformed its initiators' disappointment over the
public sphere into a positive programme is John Tosh's *Why History
Matters*.[11]

The activities just described are not only connected to the position of
historians in the labour market or to their relation to the public sphere,
however. They reflect also an ongoing process of particular relevance
to this book: a renegotiation of the relationship between scholarly and
public histories (in plural). Characteristic of this process is that historians have devoted only scant attention to their relationship with popular
histories. This omission in delineating the cultural dimensions of the
historian's craft reveals the burden of heritage: 'there is little place for
reconsidering the scope and legitimacy of (professional) authority', to
use Michael Frisch's words.[12] The vast majority of laypeople remain, in

the historians' rethinking, passive consumers of scholarly findings, they have no active role in the making of history.

The third direction in which professional historians have developed their cultural role is a kind of antipode to the other two: the idea is to start 'from below' instead of 'from above'. These activities are informed by a 'commitment to a concern with audience and an awareness of the complex relationship between audience, historical practice and institutional context', as Ann Curthoys and Paula Hamilton have it.[13] This is a perspective that is supported by the findings of the often-mentioned Roy Rosenzweig and David Thelen's project on the popular uses of history in American life.[14]

A kind of predecessor to the recent from-below initiatives was the History Workshop – a movement that 'began life at a time when the cultural revolution of the 1960s was seemingly carrying all before it'. With adult education as its 'homeland', it was informed, 'in the first place', by 'an attempt to replace the hierarchical relationship of tutor and pupil by one of comradeship in which each became, in some sort, co-learners'. Today this tradition, which is important in upholding history-making as a basic social practice and is manifestly connected to Raphael Samuel, is maintained by the MA programme in public history at Ruskin College, Oxford.[15]

In Scandinavia studies 'from below', or rather literally in the sphere of popular histories, emerged during the late 1970s. The initiators were, as explained in Chapter 3 (pp. 58–9), the strong national organizations of adult education and for the preservation of local arts and crafts, trade unions and national popular archives, while professional historians' involvement was limited. In this sense, the Paperiliitto history project was an exception. The principal aim of these activities was to take seriously and highlight themes important to the laypersons involved. At the beginning of the twenty-first century, at least in Finland but probably also in other Scandinavian countries, these kind of pursuits have become so commonplace that they do not attract public attention any more. Professionals, not only historians but also scholars in the various fields of cultural studies, are engaged with these projects in different ways.[16]

As regards their individual identity, their *professional self*, historians would be wise to observe two things. First, the question is not of inventing anything new but actually only of becoming aware of the profile one already has. The point is that every historian is characterized by the studies worked on, as will be examined in detail in the next section. That there was no room for the notion of the historian's professional self during the time of the traditional schism between 'objectivists' and 'representatives of partisanships' is easy to understand, but the continued failure to tackle the reference of this during or after the recent paradigmatic change is an enigma.

The historian's professional self

'Every historian is entitled to ethical and political commitments which colour his or her perception of history, but these do not free her or him to fabricate a past for which there is no evidential basis.' This statement of George G. Iggers and Q. Edward Wang, history professors active in the United States, documents a telling consequence of the recent paradigmatic change in the discipline of history. Quite a few historians, perhaps even the majority, recognize today that the scholar's personal 'ethical and political' preferences 'colour' their findings.[17] This is really a recent change, as the fate of my first book on methodology testifies. The demand that one's personal commitments should be acknowledged overtly and that there was a need to discipline one's thinking was interpreted as an attempt to politicize historical research as late as the 1970s.

Nevertheless, an insufficient changeover is evident in this respect too. Even if the influence of the scholar's various commitments on his or her work has been recognized, these deep and long-held preferences have been talked over as an unspecified whole instead of analyzing them. Nor, for that matter, have representatives from other fields of research in society and culture tackled the issue of the scholar's professional self. The question is of the intrinsic elements of the researcher's cultural profile, his or her continuous special interests and concerns. What principles direct the scholar's activities, and how do they affect his or her integrity?

The degree to which the researcher's professional self has been neglected came as quite a surprise to me in 2004 when retiring from university life; I had chosen this issue as theme of my customary farewell lecture. The only comment I found on it was the German term '*Grundeinsicht*' used by the Slovenian philosopher Slavoj Zizek to characterize a lasting element in the works of the Argentine political theorist Ernesto Laclau; he referred to an interest that remains virtually unchanged. This does not, however, fit historical enquiry since it is durability rather than permanence that distinguishes the scholar's interests and concerns. The point is that two interconnected factors bring continuous change to the historian's professional self. There is, first, the historian's understanding of the ways in which they are inescapably involved in society, and, secondly, the impact on their views of the continuous dialogue they have with their contemporaries. Both these are in constant flux.[18]

The stances I hold illustrate durability as an aspect of the historian's profile. Looking back on the charges made against me by those representing the 'objectivist' tradition in the 1970s for having advocated the historian's political involvement as a historian, I had to take some of the blame for this myself. Like other 'representatives of partisanships' I had thought of the issue as one dimensional, failed to distinguish between the two ways the historian is involved in current debates. As was discussed in Chapter 4 (see p. 107), in case of a particular study the historian's position cannot be separated from the other aspects of research work; participation follows automatically from the choice of a topic to be studied. The second way of involvement is displayed by the historian's consistency in choosing topics, for instance, and this regularity indicates the scholar's professional self. The various dimensions of this durable profile are discussed in the present section.

The farewell lecture on the historian's professional self was opened by reference to the consensus among the scholars doing research into society and culture who have started their career after the late 1980s (see '*The historian's position*' in Chapter 4, p. 106). Their starting point is that it is not possible to acquire knowledge that is independent of the selections the scholar has made, and this entails the careful choice of exactly what information is presented to the audience. The people addressed must be provided with the possibility of assessing the soundness and meaningfulness of the findings at the same time as they are invited to examine the significance of the knowledge produced.[19]

This contention requires, first, that historians write themselves into their work. The resulting issue of how the scholar spells out his or her definition of the study's central issue is discussed below in '*Arguing for the findings*'. The second stipulation calls for the historian to tackle the subject in the context of the politics of history, an issue elaborated above in Chapter 4. The section here deals with the third requirement, that of establishing one's professional self in two phases: first, identifying one's durable interests and concerns, and secondly, specifying the principles guiding one's research. This is what I did when preparing the farewell lecture: started with a retrospective analysis of my own studies from the 1960s on and finished with a three-dimensional structure of the historian's professional self result.

The first dimension of the historian's professional self relates to his or her *ontological commitments*, that is, his or her assumptions about existence: 'what there is'. The idea that history and the movement of

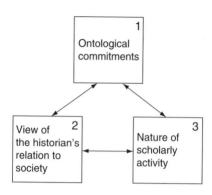

Figure 4 The three dimensions of the historian's professional self

history exist was a notion I took for granted well into the 1980s. The second thoughts were brought about by my involvement with everyday history-making; I came to the conclusion that it was untenable to claim, as the social democrats and the communists did in their different ways, that 'history is on our side'. It was, on the whole, indefensible to think about history in teleological terms, for example, as progress. Here, the historian must recall the point made above in '*Treacherous time*': passage of time and history are two different things.

Whether it is in any sense admissible to speak of 'the course of history' or, rather, the movement of history, is a philosophical issue separate from historians' concerns. Historians have, and this too is a self-critical comment, wasted plenty of time by mixing unnecessary philosophical questions with problems related to their own research practices. The question of 'what is meant by history?', a philosophical issue, should be kept disconnected from reflection on the ways in which historians do their work, historical theory and methodology. In this respect, the influence of the books by two prominent historians, E. H. Carr and G. R. Elton (*What Is History?* and *The Practice of History*) has been damaging.[20]

An ontological commitment that I removed from my way of thinking with the end of the Cold War was the notion of the contradiction between social orders based on different economic structures ('capitalism vs. socialism'). This resolution did not, however, mean giving up another concept originating in the Marxist tradition: the social nature of production. The interaction of four factors is common, for example, to both the late eighteenth- and nineteenth-century industrial revolution and to current globalization: the growth of forces of production, the increasing social division of labour, the concentration of production and capital as well as the expansion of markets. What justifies the mention of this concept is that it illuminates a common feature of the historian's ontological commitments: they are elements of his or her world view and there is seldom reason or sense in expressing them. However, they do influence the historian's work and so we had better be aware of them.

The second dimension of the historian's professional self, *view of the historian's relation to society*, is one in which the historians' standpoints obviously vary to a great degree. My own is dominated by the moral consequences of the historian's inescapable involvement, and is illustrated by the two principles emphasized repeatedly in this book. First, it is the historian's duty to make sense of the past in a way that opens new perspectives on the audience's world and gives them fresh insights into their own culture by comparing it with past ones. The second principle follows from the first and relates to one's professional responsibility to the audience.

Together, these two principles demand that the historian takes measures to control his or her inescapable involvement in society, first by maintaining personal ethics, and secondly through counteracting the misuse of history in the public sphere. On the other hand, there is always the risk that through their intervention in contemporary debates historians may compromise their integrity, and thus lose their chance to influence the audience as recognized specialists. Preparing for the reception of one's study is therefore crucial, and must, as noted (see p. 51), begin at the planning stage.

The readers' response is discussed, as the historian's challenge in the last two sections of this chapter while the historian's objectives dominate Chapter 6, which deals with the impact of the historian's work. Here, it is worth reminding ourselves of the status of Eric Hobsbawm, who presents an ideal in retaining scholarly integrity while contributing to current debates. Though a Marxist, and a member of the Communist Party, he achieved the prestige of an authority in the field of history during the Cold War in a leading western country.

Making comments on specific contemporary developments is, as was noted above (see pp. 38–9), included in my personal view of the historian's relation to society. Since the early 1960s my most important concern has been to contribute as a historian to people's right to self-determination over their lives and to their freedom from impediments to this, and in this way to increase their chances of leading good lives. Lately, this aim has focused on guaranteeing freedom from arbitrary use of economic and political power, and especially the upholding of civil rights. An alternative kind of representative democracy must be secured and the end of this book explores how, in my view, historians can contribute to this.

The third dimension of the historian's professional self relates to the *nature of scholarly activity*. In the present book it suffices to emphasize four points, since the subject has been recently discussed fairly comprehensively by both Thomas L. Haskell and Mary Fulbrook; many parts of their ideas have been presented in earlier chapters. The first of my four points refers is the requirement of double detachment that presupposes writing oneself into the text: the historian must be able to control his or her involvement in society as well as to demonstrate his or her position to the people addressed. This calls for a clear view, in general terms, of the historian's cultural role in order to be capable of singling out cases where one has an obligation to intervene and of distinguishing the limits of one's possible involvement.

My second point about the nature of scholarly activity emerges from the paradigmatic change at the end of the twentieth century. Removing the traditional notion of objectivity from its authoritative position in historical research led to awareness of the latent influence of one's socially constructed identities: gender, sexuality, religious beliefs, political commitments, nationality, and so on. The idea of reflecting on the significance of these in relation to one's research and the requirement to detach oneself from the priorities connected to them became widely accepted. What is called for is a novel kind of disciplining of one's reasoning. Contrary to the views of some scholars, the idea of this is not to exhibit one's distinctiveness, but to increase awareness of potential bias that otherwise might easily be unacknowledged. It is also important to note that the impact of these various identities changes from one study subject to another. In the case of the present book, for instance, I do not think that my gender makes a difference any more than my sexual or religious orientation, whereas being a Finnish social democrat may do.

The consequences of the linguistic turn is the third point I want to make in discussing the nature of scholarly activity: there is no acceptable excuse, at any stage of the research process, for not asking 'whose reality?' and 'whose discourse?'. The demand to give up reconstruction as an objective is not warranted, but historians must recognize that the exercise is far more complicated than is generally thought. Especially important is for the historian to remember, in reconstruction, not to take their own concept of reality and their own discourse for granted, but to regard these as part of the problem. Underlying this requirement is the traditional idea of extinguishing one's self: 'objectivity' is an active invitation to take an approach that is in fact counterproductive as far as the people studied are concerned. The tendency to produce unintended anachronisms is very real.

The fourth point to be emphasized regarding scholarly activity is its fundamentally collective nature. The need here is, on the one hand, to avoid the old tendency to attempt to emulate the natural sciences; it is wise to remember that science and art are essentially different. On the other hand, it is as untenable to claim that there is an 'historical method' owned by historians, as it is to think that there is an 'ethnological method' or a 'sociological method'. It is perfectly sensible to divide graduate training into different disciplines with reference to substance and methodology, but there is no sense in research work in refraining from using the best possible method for answering a question because it is the 'property' of another discipline. The concepts of space, site and place, together with the related concepts of borders, boundaries, centres, peripheries,margins, and so on present a good example of this: they are terms relevant to the interests of several traditional disciplines.[21]

The three-dimensional structure of the historian's professional self presented above is my own suggestion. Thomas L. Haskell gives a different kind of structure to the concept, or to the 'abiding preoccupations' informing his research; he does not use the term professional self. There are three interlocking issues that have given 'a definite centre of gravity' to his studies in spite of their topical diversity. One is 'curiosity about the *explanatory schemes*' on which we humans rely while making sense of our experiences. The second is the *history of ethics*, which covers 'collective shifts of moral sensibility' that occur over decades or centuries. Haskell's third element is his substitute for 'objectivity'. The *ethics of history* 'takes less for granted and is less weighed down by philosophical baggage'. It refers to 'the intricate network of constraints (cognitive, ethical, and institutional) that we professional historians tacitly rely on whenever we distinguish history from fiction, scholarship from propaganda, or good history from bad'.[22]

The historian's professional self also exemplifies two things. The first is a query: why have so many historians failed discuss and deal with key issues in spite of knowing that these questions are crucial to historical research. The second is the thread that runs through this whole book: embracing an alternative perspective on the historian's work rather than making radical changes in research practice is what is entailed by the self-awareness for which I argue. Thinking in terms of the cultural role of historical research instead of subordinating that role to the historian's disciplinary capacity means reflecting on the responsibilities and profile the historian as cultural critic as well as the historian's professional self. Having a different order of priorities in familiar operations and attaching new meanings to them is called for as regards the research process, too. The planning stage and composing the final account are as important stages as working with primary sources.

Designing research

It is the objective of making the points of their argument that directs, quite reasonably, the historians' research work, and this is the reason for allowing enough time, during the planning stage, to create the conditions that enable the best possible use of the researcher's key asset – his or her motivation. Selecting a topic that is currently relevant to one's contemporaries, or choosing one that the audience has either not thought of or has largely ignored, is the key task while expanding on the rationale of the study.

Once the initial idea has been clarified, the chosen topic turned into a subject, the historian enters the second stage of the research process. He or she tests now hypotheses against primary sources until the foundation of the findings has been ensured, the missing knowledge has been created and the inadequate interpretations revised. By then, what was perhaps but a dim vision at the outset of the project has also been turned into a clear message; the ensuing third and last stage is dominated by composing an account that reveals to the audience the significance of one's results. The historian aims now at convincing the people addressed that the findings are fruitful and that the lesson or moral embedded in the study is relevant to them.

The informing idea of the work changes during the second stage from controlling one's involvement in the politics of history to ensuring fairness towards the people studied. The idea of the second stage is not, as many historians state, to let the primary sources 'speak for themselves' but to allow them to challenge the historian's assumptions. Securing this, tapping the weightiest possible influence from the crucial sources requires that they have not been consulted during the planning stage – making an inventory of them suffices then.

Examining the primary sources should be thought of as a means of testing the hypotheses developed during the planning stage. The crucial task is to ensure that the point of view arrived at during the planning stage is fair, that, for instance, it is justified to analyse seventeenth-century Swedish witch-hunts in the context of contemporary gender relations. The problem dominating the second stage, as regards the people studied, is the validity of the historian's questions: what conditions must prevail for my questions to be valid to ask the questions they ask?

Focusing on the validity of the historian's questions is an approach that shows the limitation of the conventional way of thinking that proceeds in terms of anachronisms. Whether the scholar has used concepts which don't belong to the period analysed, is a question that makes sense in evaluating the completed study but does not help in planning the investigation. At that stage, the ban on anachronisms is only a reminder; resolving the dilemma calls then for using available secondary sources to assess the validity of the questions delineated.

The demand of fairness means establishing how the people studied understood their situation and what their intentions were. Unless this is done, the historian cannot advance beyond the self-awareness of these people and view their deeds from a later perspective. The point of view selected must always be assessed as being valid in two senses. It must be plausible first, when consideration is given to the circumstances in which the people studied lived, and secondly, when their subjective world is analyzed. The logic of this reconstructive work is the same as that of reading sources.

When drawing inferences from the available remnants the historian must not take these potential sources at face value but has to discover first the purpose or function the sources' creators attached to them. Only with this knowledge available can he or she determine whether the remnant in question can be used as evidence. The same is true when the question is of advancing beyond the self-awareness of the people studied: the precondition is reaching out to their beliefs and how these were expressed. This is fundamental to the historian's work, and it is what it means to approach those studied 'on their own terms'.[23] The historian really must not forget the lesson taught by the linguistic turn: it is crucial to continually ask 'whose reality?' and 'whose discourse?'

Historians must keep in mind that this requirement also applies to the discourses of their own contemporaries, the patterns of thought embedded in the various shared histories. In this respect, the present context for historians is depicted in the titles of the two-volume standard work on memory edited by Katherine Hodgkin and Susannah Radstone: '*Contested Pasts*' and '*Regimes of Memory*'. Historians must be on their guard with everyday history, because they cannot escape the constant influence of this site of power relations, the politics of history, on any analysis of the past.

The virtual dialogue of the historian with the people studied, out-lined in the introduction to Chapter 3, provides a useful metaphor for the way in which historians explore how the people studied understood their situation and defined their intentions. This method produces pos-itive results, however, only if the historian manages to avoid 'guiding' those being researched. The point is that the historian aims, firstly, to reconstruct the reality of the people studied – as they saw it. Ignoring this objective in order to depict things as the historian sees them is disallowed: it means giving up the absolutely essential element of histor-ical research, presenting a plausible and fair description of the past. The logical consequence of this way of thinking is that as part of the research project historians must also submit their own concepts and arguments to analysis. This requirement to assess one's own thinking in the light of past people's ideas is for me personally the merit and fascination of historical enquiry.

The same logic reveals the sense of the title in London historian and geographer David Lowenthal's famous book, *The Past is a Foreign Coun-try*. The past is also, as the American historian Allan Megill adds, an unvisitable and unconquerable foreign country. The past has become more and more distinct from the present since the Renaissance, 'yet at the same time increasingly manipulated by present-day aims'. It is the historians' duty to make the audience of their work realize that the past is a country 'whose customs we do not share and whose languages we do not speak'. Historical experience is the experience of 'a rift, a break, between what *we are* now and what *others were* then', as Megill compresses the point (his italics).[24]

Historical research should be thought of as a study of foreign coun-tries instead of being approached in the logic of the historicist meta-explanation, presented in the section *'The treacherous time,'* in Chapter 4. That pattern of thought, the idea that any matter is explicable in terms of its origins and recognizable through its consequences, gives an arti-ficial assignment to the historian: the aim is, in fact, not to explain the foreignness of past societies, but, rather, to reveal those aspects of them that make them inherently comprehensible. An as untenable an approach to empirical study is offered by the notion of 'historical con-tinuity', the idea of an overarching, a priori continuity; it is artificial to claim that everything in history is, in the end, bound together by the passing of time. Nor is there a place in empirical analysis for the collective singular 'history', a whole that subsumes all histories.

The idea of a foreign country also helps the historians to under-stand the limits of traditional source criticism. The conventional way of approaching primary material is an essential component that mostly allows reasonably valid inferences to be drawn – when the target is to reconstruct the intentions embedded in the source analysed. However, when historians want, as is sensible, to proceed beyond these intentions they meet what is characteristic of any source – muteness. Even the most systematic analysis of the situation in which the source has been created does not change this actuality. Historians have to accept, as was explained in the section *'The pasts present'* in Chapter 2, the nature of their sources. They are, in Paul Ricoeur's words, 'traces that signify something without making it appear', that is, it is not possible to answer unequivocally the question what they signify. Historians have to be content with, to use a legal term, circumstantial, indirect evidence. They must also 'signal to the readers' that they are moving beyond first-hand sources in their interpretation.[25]

The practices of the second stage of the research process show the pride of place reasoning takes in the historian's work – in spite of the common discourse of working in terms of sources. A more adequate common phrase is 'writing history', even if writing is assigned the key role instinctively rather than as a deliberate description. My interpretation of the phrase is that it actually refers to the context for reasoning. In any case, it is *reasoning while writing*, drawing inferences and making deductions, that is the historian's method of research – sources are just the starting point for reasoning. You advance your study when you weigh up whether to use this or that specific word or this or that order of sentences, choose between ways of structuring a paragraph or of putting in order various paragraphs, decide on how to present connections or to emphasize dissimilarities between matters studied, and so on. This idea has been aptly illustrated by E. H. Carr, according to whom 'the more I write, the more I know what I am looking for, the better I understand the significance and relevance of what I find'.[26]

It is important to bear in mind that writing functions as the context for reasoning from the very outset of the research process. Taking notes, for example, about the reasons for one's choices is likely to lead one to pay attention to aspects easily bypassed when merely thinking them through. In turn, when consulting primary sources, many students fail to realize that simply collecting material is a waste of time. In contrast, the experienced historian seizes, as the quotation from Carr testifies, this stage as an opportunity to carry forward the argument.

During the first and second stages of the research process the audience for the writing is principally the historian himself or herself, in the sense that it is he or she who attempts to sort out how things actually were. It is, however, useful, if possible, to ask peers to comment on one's work. This is especially helpful as regards the research plan, the written presentation of the subject created and the outline of the message, but it also applies to later pieces of writing. For example, the comments I received from colleagues on parts of the manuscript for the present book have been extremely useful.

However, an essential change takes place when the historian begins to compose the final account; writing at this third stage of the research process is radically different from that in earlier stages. Now that the primary sources have delivered their verdict on the historian's assumptions, and he or she has revised the draft of the message accordingly, he or she is ready to present the findings and to argue for them. Writing acquires a new rationale because the audience changes: producing the text is now dominated by the need to convince the people addressed that the message is significant.

The logic of the third stage calls for writing some new material, but first and foremost for editing existing texts. The point is that the pieces of writing produced during the earlier phases originated from clarifying particular issues whereas at the concluding stage they acquire a new context; they are now subordinated to the historian's interpretation as a whole. This work, focusing on the final account begins when historians believe that their findings rest on sound foundations and give themselves the permit to argue for the significance of what they have revealed about the people studied.

'Giving the permit to themselves' is a phrase that reminds historians of their basic predicament while working with the primary sources. The crucial decisions at the second stage are ethical by their nature: it depends on the historians' own judgement (actually, their honesty) whether the actors' views of their situation and their intentions have been adequately reconstructed. In other words, the final stage of the research project begins when the historians have convinced themselves that they are able to convince the audience that they have done justice to the people studied. To perform this task by way of writing is another hard nut to be cracked; ahead lies perhaps the most demanding part of the research process.

Arguing for the findings

When the historian sets about pulling together his or her findings he or she has an overarching purpose: the ensuing account has to demonstrate the significance of his or her message. This means, first and foremost, displaying the fruitfulness of the findings and the lesson or moral conveyed by the study, but at the same time showing the soundness of these crucial meanings. The alternative interpretation argued for must be cogent and the description of the people studied plausible. In addition, the historian's reasoning must be impeccable and observe the demand of double truthfulness. Satisfying all of these six criteria (see above pp. 44–5) calls for an arrangement in which these various aspects of the final account serve the common target. For this purpose the historian needs *composition*, a carefully constructed structure that organizes the different parts of the text into an entity.

The division Stephen Toulmin makes between the *force* and the *criteria* of an argument (see above p. 43) helps to simplify the challenge the historian faces when constructing the composition. *Force* denotes the practical implications of the argument or, in the vocabulary of this book, the historian's message. These crucial meanings also dominate the final account – but only if the foundation of the findings on which they rest is sound; it is by reference to Toulmin's *criteria* that it is ascertained whether or not the message is justified. The problem of the final account is that message (the force of the argument, as Toulmin has it) tends to subordinate its foundation (Toulmin's criteria). This instability between force and criteria appears now as the tension between the form of the final account (composition) and its content (the findings).

The meaning of the tension between content and form in the historian's final account is different from the sense of Hayden White's famous collection of essays titled by these two concepts.[27] By form I do not refer to narrative or any other literary mode discussed by the philosophers or literary critics but to composition, the structure of the historian's final account. Nor is it my argument that composition in itself gives meanings that are independent of any provided by the historian; each composition is a unique structure he or she creates freely, and is unloaded. What I want to emphasize, however, is that the constituent parts of the account are affected by their location in the composition. The meaning of an event, for instance, depends in part on the context in which it is presented. In this sense, in providing a setting that gives meanings, composition takes on a life of its own.

Creating a structure that gives every substance discussed (persons, events, matters, situations, and so on) its adequate place in the final account is the historian's challenge when constructing the composition. The way to solution, to finding a balance between Toulmin's force and criteria, is to reflect on the final account in two stages. In the first phase the historian thinks of the findings in terms of mere reasoning and, only after this, with a view to the composition. This sequence notwithstanding the resolution of the predicament is a really exacting one because, in practice, the two phases cannot be separated – it is possible *only to think of them* as different stages.

How to present one's subject is for the historian the logical point where to start thinking about the final account since it is in his or her interest to ensure that the definition of the subject, and reasoning within the frame entailed by subject, are kept apart in the reception of the study. The distinction between these two different issues gets easily blurred; it is unfortunately quite often that the historian has been accused of not discussing matters which he or she has deliberately marked outside the study. The means to prevent this is to define clearly the subject, and to argue carefully for this crucial choice; the critique of reasoning is justified only within the confines decided by the historian. To claim that the historian has opted for a too narrow frame is, of course, fully justified but it means criticizing his or her message, not his or her reasoning.

It is the historian's alternative interpretation that sets the study's parameters, and this is the reason for the crucial role presenting the subject attains in the final account: the subject crystallizes the critique of previous interpretations meaning that the more unconventional the chosen point of view is, the stronger the supporting arguments must be. The most ferocious debates among historians also focus on the appropriateness of the subject. This is true despite the recent paradigmatic change that has, thanks to the increased number of legitimate perspectival paradigms, widened the historian's room for manoeuvre in defining the frame of the study.

Deciding what is needed for presenting the subject and the arguments supporting its definition involves reflection on the way to demonstrate the message, that is, sets constructing the composition in motion. On the other hand, it is not reasonable to generalize the working practices further than this: the subjects are too different and the habits of historians too particular. Still, the criteria used by historians in evaluating the studies of their colleagues (mentioned at the outset of this section) provide one with the list of aspects of reasoning to be checked out – within the frame created by the subject.

The study will be assessed against prevailing interpretations and this requires presenting the critique of these explanations in a clear, logical and convincing way. The idea of the criterion *cogency* is that the alternative interpretation is more convincing than the existing ones, and make better sense of the past matters investigated. It is especially important to ensure that 'contrary to what is claimed or believed to have been' becomes visible because, as will be demonstrated in the next section, the reasoning cannot always be explicit in all parts.

Transparency is also necessary as regards the *fruitfulness* of the findings. True, no great trouble is normally caused by displaying the new perspectives one's study opens, but highlighting the unwarranted and unfair aspects of the interpretations criticised is a more complicated matter. Many of the stances and purposes supported by these histories are relatively obvious but the role they play in certain contexts may be even sensitive. Careful arguing is also needed in cases where the functions sustained by the interpretations criticized are not manifest: explicit pointing at these imperceptible effects is not always the most successful way of conveying one's findings to the people addressed.

Cogency and fruitfulness as criteria of evaluating the historian's critique of prevailing interpretations demonstrates, as does debates on assessing the study's subject, the close connection between the two sides of an interpretation, its soundness and meaningfulness. This link has been accentuated by the recent paradigmatic change, and has enhanced the vision of a rejuvenating historical research that was mentioned above in section *'The pasts present'* in Chapter 2 (p. 30). The greater importance attached to fruitfulness and innovativeness as attributes of the historian's work also characterizes the present situation. Both of these refer to research practices which other historians can take advantage of and which reviewers often find 'original and/or surprising'. When what is characterized in this way refers to an empirical issue, it relates to its fruitfulness, and when it refers to methodology, it describes its innovativeness. What one especially hopes for is increased appreciation for innovativeness since in line with their dislike of 'theories' historians have hitherto failed to value new approaches to making inferences, drawing conclusions and arguing.

The absolutely essential element of the historian's findings is that they are based on a *plausible description*, and it is the other specialists who are here the crucial part of the audience. The critics must not have any misgivings about the researcher's capability to master the key features in the world of the people studied. The historian has to convince the colleagues that he or she has a thorough grasp of the ideas held by the people studied and of the logic of action entailed by these views. That the task is not trivial is shown by the virtual dialogue that the historian has to construct with the people studied: he or she must both represent them and, simultaneously, defend his or her assumptions; and 'guiding' the interlocutors invalidates the whole exercise.

Meeting the criterion of plausibility is not just a matter of convincing specialists in the field, however, since they are only part of the people addressed. Other readers of the study must also accept the findings, even if the subject is unfamiliar to them. Returning to the dialogue with the people studied is useful here. In the second stage of the research process that exchange of views was a necessary means of understanding those studied while preparing the final account it helps in making the actors' deeds comprehensible to the audience. This serves an introduction to the criterion of *double truthfulness* as a perspective for judging the soundness of the knowledge produced – and to the basic rationale of historical research.

Virtual exchange of views between the people studied and the people addressed is, as was stated in the introductory chapter, the ultimate goal of historical research. The idea is, in this way, to stimulate the audience to evaluate their own views. Success in creating this kind of dialogue presupposes that the historian masters two different belief systems, that of the people studied and that of the audience, as well as the two discourses in which their views are expressed. If not, the historian can neither be fair to the people studied nor provoke (in a sustainable way) new ideas in the audience. This is where making one's reasoning transparent and demonstrating the fairness of the knowledge produced meet.

Meeting the criterion of double truthfulness is of paramount importance with an eye on the status and justification of the historical profession: the requirement shows off the exacting nature of the specialist's effort. For an individual historian it gives the opportunity to demonstrate that reconstructing life and actions in a foreign country that cannot be visited is not straightforward. In fact, it is his or her duty too, to display concretely why professional skills are needed in making sense of the past.

Reasoning within the framework created by the subject thus demands many things and satisfying them leads to a complex web of arguments with several intersecting chains of arguments, often with common elements. Frequently the chains cannot be presented as continuous wholes but have to be broken into several parts; nor is it always possible to display the supporting arguments in one place but they must be drawn from many disparate parts of the account. One must also beware creating unintended links. Slackness in structuring the account may lead one, for instance, to make causal connections between elements when such links have not actually been revealed by the research and may not exist. One must also take care to avoid contradictions within the account and unnecessary repetition. In summary, *impeccable reasoning* is no inconsiderable requirement, especially given the need, as mentioned above, for the argument to proceed logically and be easy to follow.

Nevertheless, many historians take impeccability of reasoning almost for granted. This tendency to regard it as commonplace seems to result from two characteristics of the profession. First, to exaggerate a little, reasoning is not thought of as reasoning but as the usage of sources. The other trait refers to a problem in prioritization: some historians short-cut the process and solve the basic tension between the content and form of the final account by treating it as more important to produce a lucid and aesthetically successful account than one based on impeccable reasoning.

A final remark on arguing for one's findings relates to the part of the final account where the historian introduces his or her subject. There is an unfortunate tendency to confuse this 'introductory' part of the account with the design of the research that concludes the planning stage. There is a strong sense among experienced historians, however, that the introductory part of the text should in fact be the very last bit written; it is, as everything else in the final account, subordinate to the composition. This was the case in the present book too: the Preface and Chapter 1 were written only in the spring of 2011. Looking at this part of the account through the eyes of the people addressed reveals its true nature: it is, really, the introduction to a study that has now been finished. It serves, too, as a reminder of the purpose of preparing the final account: the object is to make the audience aware of the connection between the knowledge produced and matters of relevant to them.

Composing the final account

When historians set out to compose their final account the rationale of their work changes: they move from reasoning to arguing. Writing is no longer a mode of drawing inferences and making deductions, a means of delineating assumptions and testing them against primary sources, as it was during the planning stage and while working with the primary sources. The prime objective of writing is now to convince the audience of the significance of the message and the soundness of its foundation. The main problem to be confronted is the tension between rhetoric and reasoning, the imbalance between verbal effectiveness and presenting a well-argued thesis. The temptation to compromise reasoning in order to make the message more convincing, the historian's basic predicament, is continuously present when writing the final account too.

Composing the final account has not been paid the attention it deserves, either within or outside the profession. In the heyday of postmodernism and the linguistic turn of the 1980s and 1990s, 'narrative' was the ambiguous emblem of debates about the historian's craft. The focus on this issue was however wrong-headed, the approach unreasonable. The historian's work was virtually reduced to the nature of the final account; the preceding research process, for historians the bulk of their work, was given only marginal attention. No wonder the majority of the profession remained unaffected by the discussions.

The historical profession has in the main adopted a traditional consensus, recently formulated by George G. Iggers and Q. Edward Wang as follows:

> Historical writing has many of the characteristics of literature but at the same time differs from imaginative literature, although the two overlap. Historical writing involves imagination, and serious literature always has a reference to reality. But the latter is not bound by the same standards of inquiry which govern the community of scholars. Without this distinction history would be indistinguishable from propaganda.[28]

However, given the task confronting the historian at the final stage of the research process, this description is far too loose. The standards of enquiry with regard to communicating one's findings have been taken for granted. In fact, trainee historians have been forced to find the techniques for communicating their results, here too, without instruction, by trial and error.

Composing the final account requires the historian to perform numerous tasks and it is only right that he or she should look to the profession for support and guidance. However, debate on this aspect of the historian's work is lacking. Of course, every historian's work is individual in context and the resulting account unique, but writing the final account is an integral and a key part of the historian's work and there is no excuse for not having discussed the issues concerned. Stating that each historian has their own personal style, anyway, is a lamentable defence for what is actually intellectual laziness, because the general features and problems of composition clearly outnumber those elements that are particular to a specific account.[29]

The historian's basic problem in composing the final account is to reconcile the different logics of arguing for the findings and of presenting their significance convincingly. The former objective calls for presenting a complex web of arguments that is already in itself a challenge: displaying the chains of arguments as continuous wholes or showing the supporting arguments in one place is not always possible. These difficulties notwithstanding the audience must not have any misgivings about the soundness of the findings, and to ensure this the arguments must be concise and clear. In contrast, the ideal of convincing the audience calls for a transparent exposition with as few words as possible; in the most suitable case readers draw the 'right' conclusions themselves.

This basic dilemma has been described, in very different terms, as 'the art of history' by the British historian Ian Mortimer. Specialists on the past answer the 'same fundamental questions about life, existence, ambition, love, power, desire, companionship, and suffering that move all great art'. Historians have their own ways of being 'sensitive to public perceptions and assumptions', while 'painters and poets' have theirs. The implication is that historians must look 'beyond the academic horizon', while remembering the foundation of their art: the historian 'ignores the discipline at [his or her] peril'.[30]

The fairly widely held stance within the profession is actually, without stating it directly, that every historian has the literary skills needed. It is taken for granted that they know how to write a laudable account, a text that is good read, in addition to being fluent and easy to understand. As a result, it has not been considered a neglect that trainee historians have not been provided with training in this field. A grave particular failure is missing guidance for creating a framework for the final account that makes it possible to resolve the difficulties in constructing the text. My suggestion is that this structuring of the final account is performed by composition.

It is the role and use of literary techniques that the history profession has neglected. When Hayden White's *Metahistory* was published in 1973 this might have spurred the badly needed discussion of the issue – if only those responding to his work had not been misled by White implying that the historian's room for manoeuvre was narrow. It is perfectly reasonable to employ various cultural conventions and literary devices, for example modes of emplotment or different kinds of tropes, but a history text cannot be reduced to them as White suggests. For him the most important aspect of composition is the historian's use of the four basic figures of speech – metaphor, metonymy, synecdoche, and irony – since any historical account is fundamentally a combination of these.[31]

White's contribution, as regards philosophical reflection on historiography, was to change the focus from looking at individual statements to considering the interpretation as an entity, from details to the whole account. This was a step forward: there had not been much sense in concentrating on the nature of the 'proper' historical explanation since historians are in principle eclectics as regards modes of inferring and concluding. According to the narrativist philosophers (for example F. R. Ankersmit in addition to White), the core of historians' accounts consists of narrative theses (for example 'Renaissance' or 'Cold War') which bring historical data together but do not emerge from it. In White's view, there is no point in evaluating these constructions epistemologically, while in Ankersmit's opinion such assessment is made impossible by the opaqueness of the accounts.

In the section '*The enigmatic truth*' in Chapter 2 above I argued for a view that comes close to the narrativist position as regards truth, but deviates from it as regards evaluation. The past is a terrain that does not allow for discussions in terms of truth, but this does not exclude epistemological evaluation of historians' arguments. What is called for, and is reasonable, is 'historiographical epistemology without truth' as Jouni-Matti Kuukkanen, a philosopher from the University of Leiden, suggests.[32] Regarding their practical work, historians should, in my opinion, avail themselves of Aristotle's rhetoric in composing their final account. It is helpful to approach one's interpretation in the *rhetorical context* created by the three different perspectives: *ethos, pathos* and *logos*. The first of these, *ethos*, refers to the historian, *pathos* to the audience and *logos* to the content of the study.

Ethos or 'self-presentation' invites historians to check all the elements in the text that may influence their credibility. The idea is to make sure that the historian will be taken seriously. Approaching the text from the perspective of *pathos*, in turn, tries to ensure that the text will be understood in the way the historian intends it to be. The focus is on the audience's knowledge and patterns of thinking. As to *logos*, it is paramount to acknowledge that it refers to the abstract structure of the study; as an account, in the form of a concrete web of arguments, *logos* is always subordinated by *ethos* and *pathos*. This means that the researcher and the audience are inevitably present in anything the historian says about history. The rationale of *logos* is to emphasize the role of epistemology and logic in composing the final account.

Logos refers to the historian's account from the perspective of mere reasoning, that is, is about those aspects of the final account which were discussed in the previous section. A further manifestation of *logos* is provided by the undisclosed elements of reasoning, those parts of the historian's arguments that are implicit. Every experienced historian remembers cases where he or she has avoided saying too much in order not to underestimate the audience. There are also places where to have presented an explicit argument would have undermined the force of the argument. However, the relationship between *pathos* and *logos* may also be the other way round: epistemological aspects are easily forgotten, for instance, when the historian is devising a plot that excites the audience.

Approaching the historian's account in rhetorical terms challenges the traditional orthodoxy since attention now focuses on the historian's message. Adopting Aristotle's method means eradicating the influence that nineteenth-century thinking has had on presenting the findings of an historical enquiry. The key role the historian's objectives play in shaping his or her interpretation must be recognized, just as his or her various commitments are acknowledged as elements of the historian's professional self. What follows is the need to give up the traditional ideal of a neutral, academic text devoid of the scholar's personality. The presence of the historian in the text must be thought of in a new way, in relation to his or her objectives, instead of with the hitherto silent counsel that all traces of the historian are suppressed in a good history. The idea of *ethos* is to approach the text from the perspective of the historian's credibility.

The historians' key way of strengthening their credibility is to display how they have responded to the current politics of history, that is, to demonstrate the way in which they have met the requirement for double detachment. The idea of criticizing prevailing interpretations explicitly includes distancing oneself from the positions that are sustained by them, not only showing their weaknesses as explanations. Doing this gives the historian the opportunity to argue for the meanings and implications of his or her alternative interpretation, an exercise that is also their duty. The two sides of double detachment really do condition each other.

The choices entailed by double detachment are made during the planning stage and while working with the primary sources, whereas the idea of the concluding phase is to detail the arguments that support these. In a sense, it is a question of writing the research process into the account. However, there is no point in describing all the inevitable dead-ends of research that every historian experiences; describing these is justified only if they add to the interpretation argued for. This kind of writing is not easy, which is why literary techniques are helpful – and why these skills should be included in the curriculum of researcher training.

The reason for exposing the choices made during the research process is to make the audience aware of the positions sustained by the relevant interpretations, both those criticized and those one argues for. This detaching of oneself from current views and positions involves careful consideration of the interpretations criticized and anticipating the probable consequences of the alternative one proposed. This two-fold task during the planning stage leads to the historian's most crucial decision, selecting the study's point of view, the fairness of which is tested while working with the primary sources. In other words, when composing the final account, the sensible historian reaps the benefits of his or her meticulous work during the two earlier stages of the research process. Furthermore this way of proceeding encourages self-discipline; it is a way of making sure that accountability to the audience is not forgotten.

The approach suggested also gives historians the possibility of demonstrating in concrete terms, beginning with the original topic and the initial idea, the usefulness of historical enquiry for current concerns. In the tasks that follow, the historian shows how the chosen topic has been developed into the particular subject, thus allowing those addressed to understand the reasons behind the message of the study. In this way the historian not only gives his or her reasons as to why the point of view chosen is fruitful, but also explains why alternative perspectives, which in the opinion of others might be just as important and impactful, are dismissed. Still more important is the fact that the historian's choices, the position taken in the current politics of history, appear in this approach as a valid part of the knowledge produced.

As important as it is to approach the text from the perspective of the historian's credibility is to pay attention to *pathos*, to make sure that the text is able to be understood in the way the author intends. As indicated in the previous pages, the historian can influence the reception of his or her work to a far greater extent than conventionally thought; minimizing possible unexpected responses, and looking for expedient ways of presenting the findings. Nevertheless, such efforts do not undo the point made by the writer Joseph Conrad on novel-writing, which holds equally well for historians: the author writes only half of the book, the other half is written by the readers.[33]

Taking Conrad's point seriously is a means of avoiding disappointment at the reception of one's study; the thing is not to take too much for granted about the audience. It is also good to look at the text from the audience's perspective – but bear in mind that one must still be prepared for surprises. The undisclosed elements of the account discussed above (see pp. 140–1), are a reminder of this. The American historian J. H. Hexter's aptly makes the same point: the historian always gambles with the audience's knowledge and ways of thinking.[34]

A different basic perspective on the historian's relation to the audience is opened up by the linguistic turn: it is crucial to remember that one's own concept of reality and one's expressions are integral to the study. This lesson was taught to me in concrete terms while working at Paperiliitto. Those whose research work I was directing were native Finns of my own generation, yet it took almost three years full-time work to feel I could express my points with no misgivings.

Studies on rhetoric suggest that the researcher's disposition to the audience is a further point from the perspective of *pathos* to which attention should be paid. My own experiences from the 1980s suggest that it is in the professional historians' interest to take seriously the risk of being regarded as patronizing, and sometimes even arrogant. The shared histories of the audience might come to their rescue since taking them seriously builds up the historian's trustworthiness, encouraging a positive reaction to the eventual reception of one's own work. It is also important for the historian to inspire confidence since part of the job is to criticize these histories. A third point of shared histories is that they provide the historian with ideas for how to build the bridge between the people in the past studied and the people addressed.

A fourth basic feature of the historian's relation to the audience is that one always needs to pay attention to the make-up of the audience, since this will influence one in deciding, for example, what should be made explicit and where to count on the readers' own inferences. The point is illustrated by the difference between a scholarly and lay readership. Writing for one's peers and writing for non-specialists are two very different registers for the scholar, and it is important to take note especially of the knowledge of the people addressed. However, one must also remember that neither of these audiences is homogenous.

Ricca Edmondson has nicely characterized the approach needed in relation to the people addressed, even if she writes about sociologists. The historian, too, has to find a balance 'between agreeing with (the) hypothetical reader and – since there would be little point in writing at all if (one) were *only* to agree – assaulting and altering his or her views'. She suggests thinking about the findings dialogically, in a way 'which complements, and is complemented by, the (audience's) knowledge and dispositions'.[35]

The key aspect of *ethos*, showing how the subject has been created and explaining the reasons for one's choices, is important from the perspective of *pathos* too since it works as an instrument for approaching the people addressed. To use Edmondson's concept, it is a step in 'sensitising the audience', putting the audience 'into a certain frame of mind'.[36] This is, again, a context where literary techniques would undoubtedly help but, as stated, skills for making the historian's findings easily accessible and stimulating to the audience have been grossly underrated by the profession.

Using the logic of dialogue enables the historians to achieve their ultimate goal, creating a virtually reciprocal relationship between the people of the past studied and the people addressed. The idea is to connect the past matters studied with the audience's present concerns. By exploring how the people of the past thought about themselves and their circumstances and what their intentions were the historian specifies in his or her message the present fruitfulness of this knowledge and draws out the moral/lesson therein. This can enable one to open up new perspectives on the world for the people addressed and prompt them to ponder their own values.

'I want my audience to understand how different they are from their forebears, and yet how similar they are to them, too.' This is Ian Mortimer's way of presenting what I called above the historian's ultimate goal. According to him, one should build on 'the historical correlative', in which readers automatically juxtapose historical facts with their own circumstances, leading them to rethink the world beyond 'their own experience and expectations'. People are aware that they and the society they live in have a past and they seek explanations of that past. Given the trust they have in historians, this 'amounts to a social mandate for historians' which enables 'society to gain a view of itself over time'.[37]

The basic requirement is to create an active connection between the historian's message and the audience's present situation, that is, the historian has to establish common ground between the audience and the people studied. The ideal is an account that makes it possible, as pointed out above (see p. 72) for the people addressed to 're-experience' a past situation. Historians then act, in Mary Fulbrook's words, as creative intermediaries between the two sides of the dialogue, while their accounts also work as products of a participatory historical culture.[38] This perspective, in which historians invite those addressed to make their own contribution to history-making, is explored further in the last section of this book.

The rhetoric of the final account is the last phase in the historian's dialogue with the audience, and comparing this exchange of views with that with the people studied is useful. When reconstructing the past, the researcher remains essentially one party in a debate with the actors, the people studied, and, in addition, has to adopt mostly the role of a listener. The historian's position in the dialogue with the audience is very different, since here arguing for the results makes him or her a kind of authority. On the other hand, the interchange with the audience is tricky because it is not just a question of arguing for one's findings. The historian also has to think about the influence of his or her interpretation from the perspective of upholding history-making as a basic social practice.

6
The Impact of Historical Research

The current outlook on history-in-society dominates the final chapter of this book. From the professional's angle, two challenges predominate. One is to formulate an adequate response to the proliferating attempts by different funders of historical research to steer the study of the past, and the second is to make sure that ready-made interpretations of the past are not imposed on citizens and substituted for histories created by the people themselves. Historians have to ensure that questions about the past originating in the public sphere are critically evaluated, and they must find new ways of upholding history-making as a basic social practice.

A successful response to the contemporary challenges means turning existing priorities upside down. The overshadowing of the fundamental issue 'why history?' by preoccupation with presenting the past 'as it once was' is questionable already as such and especially unsuitable in contemporary circumstances. Substantiating this claim on the level of the profession as a whole is the aim of this chapter. As regards thinking about the impact of research at the level of the individual study, it suffices to summarize the view that has informed discussion in the previous chapters.

While planning the research project, sensible historians reflect on how they have arrived at that particular subject. What are my reasons for selecting this topic and developing it into a subject to be studied? The next step is to elaborate this starting point in terms of double detachment. Are the prevailing interpretations just weak explanations or do they, in addition, sustain problematic stances? What do I want to say with my alternative and what are its probable consequences? The more carefully these questions are answered, the sounder the eventual findings are likely to be and the smoother the work will proceed.

In the second stage of the research project historians test their assumptions against the primary sources and revise them accordingly. When they are convinced that the message is substantiated, they enter the third and final phase. The task now is to prove to others that the results of the research done are sustainable, that the findings are significant and rest on a sound foundation. The final account is considered in two stages: first, with a view to constructing a well-reasoned web of chains of argument and only after that, as a composition with a rhetoric function. Here, as during the two first stages of the research project, historians must bear in mind their basic predicament: the temptation to compromise soundness in order to make the message more convincing.

The functions of the historical profession

As the battleground of divergent interpretations and explanations of past events and matters, history amounts to a reservoir of political arguments. The stock is continuously renewed, with, for example, governments twisting history to suit their own agendas. However, the ends which interpretations of the past sustain are by no means only political; they can be of innumerable kinds. History has become central to cultural battles, too, for instance. It is the usefulness of the past in the present that is the core of history.

Claims that events and matters in the past are relevant to a situation in the present are quite rightly regarded as lending support to the justification of the historical profession: experts are there to evaluate whether the grounds for the historical arguments used are adequate and sufficient. This view leads, however, from time to time, to the grossly exaggerated claim that the results of historical research offer the 'only standard to be applied' in overturning and rectifying the false beliefs flooding 'popular historical consciousness'.[1] This way of thinking is based on a conclusive division between scholarly and other histories. There certainly is a distinction, as has been demonstrated in previous chapters, but it is restricted to epistemological soundness. As regards the vastly broader field of the meanings attached to the past, the skills of professionals do not give their interpretations a privileged position.

Margaret MacMillan's *The Uses and Abuses of History*, referred to in Chapter 1, summarizes the prevailing current view of academic historians of the role of history in society: 'History is useful when it is used properly, to understand why we think and react in certain ways. But it is also susceptible to manipulation and distortion.'[2] Commenting on the expedient uses of history outside academia, by dictators, nationalists, political leaders and so on, is a self-evident part of the historian's job – and so is 'setting the record straight' in the sense of correcting mistakes and inaccurate information. Just as essential are the far more difficult interventions to correct unfair interpretations. However, these tasks do not comprehensively cover the profession's social function.

This book has sought to demonstrate that even an historian working without an agenda in current debates is inescapably involved in his or her society, and that they should take the implications of this seriously. It is also in the historian's own interest, in order to work effectively, to think about the origins of the project – what are the reasons for initiating it? Furthermore, every historian expects the completed study to be received as a specialist's contribution. However, one can easily lose this status with careless presentation of the message, or even by denying that one's research results have wider implications. Ensuring that one cannot be accused of bias, or of political naivety, is a test of the historian's craftsmanship in composing the final account and is something that the profession has not given the attention it deserves.

The requirement to 'abandon the present' has lost most of its force with the virtual end of the traditional schism within the discipline. There are, however, repercussions from the previous 'objectivist' stance. Participation in public debates is no longer disapproved of, but historians receive no training in how to get their points across. The insufficient rethinking often results in situations where historians, instead of controlling intellectually the conditions of their work, are pieces of driftwood floating on the current circumstances. A more indirect, but more profound effect of the traditional schism is that historians have hardly paid any attention to what follows from letting the ideal of 'as true and as impartial a picture of the past as possible' still take pride of place.

In fact, the profession has failed to notice that thinking about the historian's work primarily in epistemological terms means relegating the fundamental issue 'why history?' to a secondary position. The scholarly credentials of the discipline have been regarded as more essential than making sense of the past. Prioritizing sound knowledge over the demand for historical knowledge has led to missing the core of history-making. Historians have not discussed systematically the implications of *the usefulness of the past as the driver to create histories*, a rationale shared by both scholarly and other historians.

It is no surprise, in fact it is only to be expected, that indifference to the uses of the past by 'ordinary people' follows on from the poor appreciation professionals have of the task of making sense of the past. Admittedly, there are slight signs of rethinking as regards non-academic engagement with history, and patronizing attitudes towards the value of history for laypeople have begun to change. Even so, the idea that it is the historian's duty to uphold everyday history-making remains close to wishful thinking.

In their professional discussions, as has been repeatedly shown in the previous chapters, historians have a tendency to concentrate on the obvious aspects of a given issue and to keep away from its more awkward dimensions. It is quite common practice to focus only on the epistemological weakness of the prevailing interpretations, and to ignore their function in sustaining particular stances in the present. When it comes to making the point of the study conducted, historians have largely recoiled from what is entailed by the core purpose of history, the responsibility to demonstrate the relevance of their findings. That attention to this is lacking in the training of historians is the most unfortunate failure of the profession.

Neglecting the more exacting side of double detachment, revealing to the audience one's reasons for showing the relevance of some past event or matter to the present, and the implications of this, leads easily, to repeat Mary Fulbrook's fitting formulation, to a partisan pretence of neutrality. There have been cases where such a stance has been calculated, but most often the failure to examine deeply enough one's alternative interpretation is unintentional: active attempts to steer clear of contemporary disputes can result in an uncontrolled involvement in current debates. In the worst cases this strengthens prejudices about history in the audience. Often, historians have virtually given others a licence for the uninhibited use of their interpretations, to the extent that what is then presented may even contradict their own research findings.

In addition to circumventing awkward questions, as the previous chapters have demonstrated, historians also have an unfortunate tendency to overlook the multiple uses the past. Here the specialist's real challenge are the almost imperceptible positions sustained by the various interpretations of the past; the obvious meanings conveyed by various histories are less of a problem. A good example of this is provided by gender-related aspects of inequality in the organization of labour within a company or in the defence of workers' rights.

Professional historians often approach the key elements of their study without adequate consideration, disregarding their complex nature. The questions the study seeks to answer are often connected not to just one, but to many debates, for instance, and likewise, there are many different meanings that can be attached to the research results. It is rare that either the sources studied or the research findings are without ambiguity, and it is therefore essential to explore the ramifications of one's study rigorously. Failure to do so is epistemologically self-defeating, since it may result in meanings being given to one's work that do not actually represent its argument.

Becoming aware of the societal context of one's subject, and especially of the current stances attached to it, is also a means of making sure that one retains one's professional integrity, of attempting to ensure that the study will be received as the non-partisan outcome of historical expertise. The point is not that it is possible to predict the work's reception, since it never is, but that it is in the historian's own interests to try to avoid becoming a pawn used for some group's agenda or to fulfil somebody else's aspirations. In other words, it is worth the historian's while to do everything in their power to anticipate the response to their studies. Which means, for instance, guarding against the audience mistaking the issue discussed for those the historian has gone to some lengths to avoid being involved in.

Working towards preventing the uninhibited use of our findings is perfectly possible – provided we make it a conscious aim. I am not suggesting that we have power over the ways in which our findings are used, only that we must systematically try to direct their usage. It is not reasonable to blame the media and politicians for unjustified and irresponsible use of our results if we have, in effect, given them a free hand.

The role of history in society

The connection between professional historians and history-in-society is dominated by the openness of history, the relative lack of stable, definite knowledge of the past. History is prone to being put to various purposes with the ensuing risk of false interpretations and strengthened prejudices. While striving to reveal these pitfalls, and in anticipating the impact of their findings, historians can employ Figure 5 that delineates the role of history in society. The figure visualizes, given the scholar's inescapable involvement in society, the context in which the tasks of the historian should be discussed. The idea of the four fields in the figure was originally presented by my Finnish colleague Kimmo Katajala as a response to the basic ideas of the present book.[3]

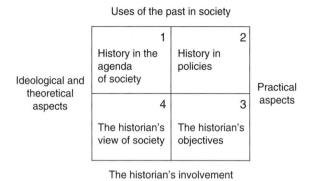

Figure 5   The role of history in society

The horizontal axis of the figure separates two ways of looking at the uses of the past: the perspective in the upper half opens from the society and in the lower half from the historian's involvement in society. The interests involved in the uses of the past, in turn, are kept apart by the vertical axis: the left area refers to ideological and theoretical and the right to practical concerns. These two divisions help us first to visualize the historians' traditional schism.

For the 'objectivists', there was no room for discussion of the relationship between historical research and society on the level of an individual historian: personal views of society had to be (to paraphrase Ranke) 'extinguished', and social objectives excluded while 'abandoning the present' (in Elton's words). Secondly, field 2 (*History and policies*) was considered a prohibited area; historians should not have, in their capacity as historians, anything to do with the government's or any organization's policies since they were not the agents of the state or any other institution. To sum up: fields 2, 3, and 4 were, in 'objectivist' thinking, classified as territories of 'the representatives of partisanships'.

The impact of historical research, for the 'objectivists', is guaranteed by the very existence of the profession. The only theme able to be discussed is that of field 1 (*History in the agenda of society*), and here they have diverse opinions. In G. R. Elton's view what counts is intellectual training rather than the immediate applicability of the research. 'The usefulness' of historical studies lies hardly at all in 'the knowledge they purvey and in the understanding of specific present problems from their prehistory'. Instead, the historical profession produces 'standards of judgement and powers of reasoning'.[4] If Elton's position character-izes the logic of 'history for its own sake', the other end of the scale within the same faction is displayed by those underlining the function of historians as referees of everyday history and those emphasizing the historian's role as the keeper of public memory.

As regards the 'representatives of partisanships', all four fields were relevant: 'history is contested terrain in which [historians] are not inno-cent bystanders' as, for example, Howard Zinn puts it. This 'simple truth' is bamboozled by expressions like 'disinterested scholarship', 'objective study', 'dispassionate learning' and 'balanced judgement'.[5] The weak-ness of this approach is the failure to differentiate between fields 3 (*The historian's objectives*) and 4 (*The historian's view of society*). As noted in the section '*The historian's professional self*' (Chapter 5, p. 123), the posi-tions in the politics of history mediated by the topics studied need to be distinguished from the historian's durable commitments.

The disruption within the discipline at the end of the twentieth cen-tury ended, among other things, the dominance of the old orthodoxy: in the present world of historical enquiry none of the four fields is pro-hibited. There is a consensus among historians, at least in principle, that all of them must be taken into account. Similarly, the profession has not been divided into rival factions that somehow resemble those of the traditional schism. True, as mentioned in the section '*History as 'an argument without end'* (Chapter 2), the variety of orientations among historians has probably never been as wide as it is today, but the ten-dency to guard territories jealously (above, p. 76) cannot be compared to the traditional schism and these new preserves have nothing like its influence.

With regard to present-day debates among historians, the vertical axis of Figure 5 draws our attention to an essential feature of these. It is the practical side that dominates, while the ideological and theoretical aspects of historical research play a secondary role. Field 3 (*The historian's objectives*) is the least controversial of the four, while field 2 (*History in policies*) points to issues raised by the attempts of funders of historical research to steer historical enquiry (to be discussed in the next section). Field 1 (*History in the agenda of society*) seems to be the most difficult one to tackle positively, and field 4 (*The historian's view of society*) attracts the least amount of attention even if (or, perhaps because) it refers to the fundamental question 'why history?'.

Francis Fukuyama's well-known phrase 'the end of history' sym-bolizes, as regards field 1, an important feature of the societal role of history in the early twenty-first century. The public sphere is no longer dominated either by teleological views about the course of history or preoccupation with the different social orders ('capitalism vs. socialism'). Since the end of the Cold War, these concerns have been replaced by globalization and climate change. Another influential political novelty is the simultaneous existence of both a strong historical continuity and a sharp break in relation to the nation-state. On the one hand, historians are expected to contribute to building a high and alluring profile (or 'brand') for competitive businesses, whether supranational, national, regional or local. On the other hand, historians are urged to adopt a global approach to history. It has been convincingly argued for example by C.A. Bayly that the current responsibility of historians is 'to rescue history from the nation'. In a world of evident interconnectedness, multiculturalism and near-instant communication, national histories no longer suffice.[6]

In globalized circumstances, the political and economic elites think of their domain as 'the competitive us', as Pauli Kettunen has characterized it. Defining the historical situation in this way derives from the rhetoric of market- managerialism which seems to be identical in Britain and Finland, for instance. This rhetoric is very strict, but it gives rise to an almost all-encompassing discourse that describes what 'our' circumstances are, defines the problems to be solved and so on – with international competitiveness as the crucial criterion. With regard to its application to history, the danger is that historians are transformed into salesmen of the 'right' history and citizens cast in the passive role of consumers of predetermined narratives.[7]

In the case of field 3 (*The historian's objectives*), scholars were assigned a new societal role by the disruption within the discipline, but also confronted with a dilemma. As mentioned above, historians are now allowed to participate in public debates but they receive no training for this. The old hegemony has been toppled but the implications of the new position created for the historian have not been systematically dealt with. The ensuing challenge is shown in field 2 (*History in policies*) and calls for the implications of making a contribution to current debates to be discussed. Have historians actually been invited to assume the role of political actors? Obviously, it is possible to claim that such a conclusion goes too far, but even granting this does not absolve the profession from finding answers to such novel issues.

The second contemporary challenge facing historians concerns field 4 (*The historian's view of society*) and is connected to the distrust of the institutions of representative democracy that so many citizens (a majority?) seem to harbour in all Western countries. Thinking about the role of the profession here, the question is no longer about practical objectives but about the status and production of historical knowledge in society in general. The way the past is researched must be reconsidered from both epistemological and political angles. At bottom, this issue is about specifying the historian's self-awareness in relation to the society in which they work.

Impact assessment by funders

When the relationship between history and public policies is discussed, it is good to keep in mind what took place when the discipline emerged: historians gained freedom from producing models, for example, for political and rhetorical purposes. It is hard to imagine an argument that would justify, in the case of the historical profession, giving up this autonomy. Yet, independent research has been put in jeopardy in the early twenty-first century and one wonders whether historians have taken the threat to their freedom seriously enough. The risk is connected to 'impact', with its roots in 'the corporate, not the academic, world', as an informing idea in higher education policies in probably all western countries.[8]

Impact has been, in a very different sense, an essential element of discussion in the previous chapters of this book. Part of my contention has been that specialists on the past, irrespective of their intentions, have an impact on society, while I also maintain that the circumstances in which historians do their work have an impact on them. As a result, the historian must discipline his or her thoughts in order to avoid playing an unconscious part in current debates.

The central idea of the present book is that asserting intellectual control over one's unavoidable present-mindedness calls for double detachment: distancing oneself both from prevailing interpretations in the current politics of history and from one's alternative explanation, in the sense of trying to become aware of its impact. Failure to discipline one's thoughts leaves historians at the mercy of their context in society, and it is this very possibility, the uninhibited impact of the surrounding circumstances on historians, that has put independent research in jeopardy today.

The *impact* of historical enquiry, in the sense in which it is used in this book, is an inevitable aspect of any historian's work. The nature of that impact depends on the choices made when the parameters of the study are defined, and this calls for careful planning of the project in the initial stages. True, reception of the work is always unpredictable, but that is no excuse for not thinking about the consequences of one's study. The historian must be prepared to defend his or her final account against professional criticism and in the wider public context. It is the historian in the capacity of citizen who is responsible for the impact of the study.

As to impact at the level of the profession as a whole, it is useful to remember that scholarly historians have generally taken it for granted that their work has an effect beyond their own scholarly circles – although this is assumed to be very diffuse and impossible to measure. The results of historical enquiry, or of research projects in the humanities in general, have been thought of by scholars from two perspectives. The achievements represent both 'public good', something which does not benefit individuals in a measurable way, and 'merit good', something which is valued by individuals for more than its immediate, measurable benefits.[9]

In contrast, as it has been defined by the British Arts and Humanities Research Council (AHRC), impact can, and should, be measured, while its substance has nothing to do with any democratic assessment.[10] What makes the AHRC's Impact Strategy, and British higher education policies in general, significant is the probability that the way of thinking implemented in the UK, the pioneer in research assessment, will be followed in other countries. This pattern has been clear-cut at least in Scandinavia.[11]

The policy of the AHRC is to 'provide mechanisms to support and encourage the arts and humanities academic community to achieve *optimum* impact and value'. In the same vein the AHRC promises to 'develop the *right* methodologies and resources to provide a confident and effective assessment of the impact and value of... research'. Both the 'optimum' impact and the 'right' methodologies are terms taken for granted, their meanings have not emerged from collective deliberation by the parties concerned. As abstract qualities, they are viewed as kind of 'objective' starting points, based on the presumption that they will be accepted by everybody involved.[12]

As an 'advocate for the arts and humanities', the AHRC aims at articulating 'the full range of economic, social and cultural impacts and benefits' derived from research in these fields that can be promoted and disseminated. There is 'an enormous contribution to the economic prosperity and social fabric of the UK' to be made. In addition to developing a framework for displaying these, the AHRC's 'impact strategy' aims to 'provide broad principles and mechanisms for identifying and capturing those impacts'.[13]

The AHRC's starting point is that there are, in addition to 'direct instrumental impacts', also 'intrinsic effects' to be taken into account – although these are 'hard to measure and value'. This is why it is important to avoid being driven only by what can be measured and valued. 'It is vital to identify and describe impact first and then only measure and value where this is possible.' The third element in the AHRC strategy is the task of 'embedding a "culture of impact" across research, postgraduate and knowledge transfer "activities"'. The AHRC 'will take the lead in cultivating a shared understanding of the impacts of arts and humanities research and the importance of being able to demonstrate such impacts'.[14]

The view that scholars have not embraced the 'culture of impact' conveys the basic tone of the AHRC document: distrust of the academic community. People doing arts and humanities research have not realized their own interests: the 'receipt of public money' calls for the AHRC to demonstrate 'that the market would not otherwise fund its activities and that the overall benefits exceed the costs'. In other words, of particular concern is the need to provide 'an account of the activities and achievements of the research unit of assessment'. In similar vein, academics must prove that 'the benefits arising from the research are commensurate with its cost'. Following these principles will make it easier for arts and humanities research to show 'greater responsiveness' to the needs of 'the economy and public services'.[15]

The views of the AHRC correspond with the proposals for the new Research Excellence Framework (REF)[16] set out in September 2009 by the Higher Education Funding Council for England (HEFCE) in partnership with other UK higher education funding bodies. The quality ratings, undertaken every four to five years since the mid-1980s, were to be continued with the aim of awarding universities and other higher education institutions units of assessment within a framework which gave them a position on a five-point scale, the criterion for allocation of funding.

The new system will continue to 'incentivise research excellence', but in addition to that 'reflect the quality of researchers' contribution to public policy making and to public engagement'; it will make sure that 'disincentives to researchers moving between academia and the private sector' are not created. From the angle of historical enquiry, a change that took place during the drafting of the HEFCE proposals is interesting. The original idea was to rely on a 'metrics-driven approach for the science-based disciplines', while in the case of assessing arts, humanities and social sciences the method would be 'light-touch expert review'.

This division was given up, in the end, in favour of 'a unified approach across all disciplines' – perhaps as a part of the general aim of the HEFCE to make the new 'mechanisms ... simpler and less burdensome'.[17]

It is the dependence on public authorities for funding that makes academic institutions vulnerable to administrative decisions which follow the kind of reasoning represented by AHRC and HEFCE. As regards research itself, the question is, in banal terms, of money. What to fund and what not to fund from the perspective of the authorities; how to beat competitors in the case of scholars. But at stake are also many fundamental matters, first among them the issue presented in the previous section, '*The role of history in society*', the profession's relation to history in various policies. The autonomy of the discipline has hitherto been well-grounded and sufficient, but there are two recent phenomena that appear to justify my concerns about the continuing freedom of academics to make their own choices regarding questions asked about the past. One is the vast expansion in the administration of higher education, both at national and institutional level, and the other the apparent readiness of the profession to acquiesce to the authorities' way of thinking – without tackling the awkward aspects of impact.

The effect of the enlarging of higher education bureaucracy, ranging from ministries to university faculties, is an issue which needs to be discussed in the light of the *Impact Strategy* of the AHRC. The question here is really about the autonomy of academic institutions. Do their governing bodies and their administrators have the freedom to make independent decisions or are their roles limited to applying agendas of the various research councils? Has their task become to redesign the curriculum and to direct the staff according to guidelines coming 'from above' and in this way to implement ready-made policies? In other words, there is now a risk that higher education administration has been turned into a mechanism that makes it possible for the government to ensure that universities align their activities with its key policies. This is the first context in which scholars in the fields of research into society and culture have been linked with the market-managerialism mentioned in the previous section ('*The role of history in society*').

As regards researchers, defending the autonomy, for example, of historical enquiry calls for proper discussion about whether funding conditions which stipulate the obligation to make an impact, as defined by the AHRC, can be embraced. That there should be a critical stance on any policy is self-evident, irrespective of whether the historian is in favour or against the policy in question. But where must the line be drawn, or are there no limits? To repeat the important question asked a few pages earlier, is the historian actually being invited to assume the role of a political actor? This issue must also be considered from another angle, scholarly policy. What kind of research is to be rewarded, individual studies or collaborative schemes?

These are questions for which the profession has barely begun the vital discussion needed. There is a real risk that because of their dependence on public funding for research, historians will have to compete against each other in terms of 'impact', and that in this way they may lose their intellectual freedom. The nightmare vision one dreads is that trained historians come to act as kinds of spin-doctors for the government rather than, their professional integrity intact, having their studies received as the contributions of independent specialists on the past.

A more indirect, but as influential an impact on research is exerted by the methodology of assessment. It is at a young academic's peril that he or she ignores the AHRC's criteria for excellence in research, secured by 'a rigorous process of peer review', as the AHRC puts it. One should participate in 'world-class postgraduate training' and aim at achieving skills 'to disseminate and transfer knowledge to ... contexts where it makes a difference'. The prescribed way of thinking applies to the AHRC itself too, since its vision is 'to be a recognised world leader in advancing arts and humanities research'.[18]

What 'world-class' entails is well known to, for example, Scandinavian scholars: Danes have successfully assessed the 'impact' of Finns or vice versa. True, there have been a few problems with the language used with the language used – though not with the substance of the work – since only a few scholars outside Finland read Finnish, but this difficulty will in any case decrease since 'written in English' is on its way to becoming a yardstick for excellence. The basic point I am making here is that the criteria of being 'world-class' are not national but supranational. And they are not only unchanging across boundaries, but also tightly implemented, as anyone who has put in an application for an academic post in Scandinavia knows.

The consequences of this are illuminated by the experiences of a young Finnish scholar attempting to secure a decent academic career in the spring of 2010. She told me: 'It is outdated to speak of doing research, what counts is publishing'. In her view it was also outdated to think in terms of monographs, since what is now merited is an article in a renowned international peer-reviewed journal.[19] The illogical nature of this supranational process of assessment, details of which are beyond the scope of this book, is shown by the frequent appearance of books that bring together groups of essays and articles that are valuable from a research perspective. The authors of the papers insist on and are provided with peer-reviewing, while inspiring these publications (the editing of which is normally a burdensome job) counts for nothing. That this is so will undoubtedly influence future historical enquiry.

The starting points for the AHRC's *Impact Strategy*, which are now driving its development, alongside the methodology of assessment, provide the second context in which historians and their colleagues doing research into society and culture now have to tackle 'market-managerialism'. Like professionals outside the academic world, they live today in an 'impact society' where the outcome has become more important than both the contents and the objectives of the work done.[20] Ignoring the pressures created by public evaluation is not now an option.

Obviously, the profession needs an in-depth discussion about higher education policies in general and the conditions of research in particular. It is the incentives and disincentives to scholarly work together with the ways of deciding over the guidelines for research that need special consideration. Conducted properly, such a debate would lead eventually to the fundamental question 'why history?'. If one takes this seriously, it also raises the question of whether there are particular kinds of policies or issues in society that trained historians should comment on. In my own case, a clue to the most pertinent of such issues, the future of democracy, is provided by a question not asked when guidelines for research have been discussed. Shouldn't the people addressed by historians, especially those in the community, region or country dealt with, have a say in selecting the issues to be researched?

The potentials of a participatory historical culture

Confusing the need for self-criticism with the obligation to conform to academic forms is quite a common trait among lay history enthusiasts. This was certainly my experience when directing historical enquiries outside the scholarly world in the 1980s. The tangle was, to a great extent, the result of scholars' manner of speaking, for example making disparaging comments about footnotes. Still, the emphasis academics put on formalities does not excuse non-professionals failing to take note of an essential aspect of history-making: getting rid of biased thinking and identifying one's own prejudices. Anyone moving from passing everyday remarks on the past to the practice of deliberate creation of histories faces the same problems that have given rise to the profession of historians. Historical enquiry calls for critical evaluation of the sources of information and impeccable reasoning when writing and interpreting the results of research.

One of the contentions of this book is that it is difficult to perceive anything other than arrogance and privilege as grounds for reserving 'research of the past' to academics. Contributing to the social process of history-making is not the prerogative of professionals. On the other hand, one can question the demands to democratize scholarship because it leads easily to subordinating the activities of historians who work outside universities to academic conventions. Would it not be more reasonable to take the aspirations of the people involved, rather than scholarly requirements, as the starting point for thinking about the non-professional study of history? Is this not, rather, the place to democratize the existing social division of labour in history-making, that is, to concretize the professionals' duty to uphold history-making as a basic social practice? To ask in which ways they can support people's efforts to make more sense of the world and one's place in it or their endeavours to fill gaps in family history, for instance?

What emerges is the idea of a participatory historical culture, a concept invented by David Thelen as a result of the often mentioned project on popular uses of history in America. He is convinced that the foundations for a collaborative practice already exist meaning that the challenge is to realize the nature of the past 'as a shared human experience' and 'history's capacity to bring [professionals and laypeople] together in dialogue and respect'.[21] This vision makes the academic to wonder, as an anonymous reader for Palgrave Macmillan had it, 'how exactly can [people] share in determining the research agenda of historians?'

The very query brings to light the normal way of thinking about knowledge of the past that is based on one-way communication: results of historical research being always disseminated to 'the public' from academics. The idea is ill-founded on two counts. First, the insights and perspectives brought about by an analysis of the past result by no means solely from the efforts of professionals, and secondly, it is not any longer only historians with academic training who do research in and produce knowledge of the past. In addition, one should keep in mind that it is the significance of the prospective findings that carries research forward, the requirement of epistemological soundness only places restrictions on the way the work is done.

Participatory historical culture is a vision that should be thought of in the context of history-in-society: there are numerous genres of history and they do serve a multitude of purposes. A grandmother's tale of some past event, for instance, is not a priori inferior to an academic study of it – these are simply two alternative perspectives. The habitual way in which people retain vivid memories of public events as intensely personal experiences exemplifies a topic of conversation that can be mutually fruitful both for laypeople and professionals.

Contained in the current popularity of history is the widespread practice of deliberate creation of histories, but academics have not been interested in these activities. This is largely due to lack of knowledge that results, as mentioned in the section *'Not just readers'* (Chapter 2; p. 59; see also p. 121), from the nature of these pieces of research: most of them are intimately connected to their regional, local and familial contexts, and there is seldom an ambition to reach beyond these confines. In part, the obscurity of non-professional studies is connected to the unorthodox ways in which the findings are disseminated; those involved in the projects do not necessarily think, as the circles in Paperiliitto demonstrated (see p. 71), in terms of written texts. Whatever the reasons for the oblivion of these activities are, the point is that professional historians are missing a golden opportunity here in ignoring the potential for collaboration with these lay initiatives for studying the past.[22]

It is on the division, repeatedly emphasized in the previous chapters, between the soundness and meaning of knowledge that the idea of a more egalitarian history-making is based. What is needed is to keep in mind that these are two different, albeit inseparable, elements of historical research. It is the present concerns that lead the research to be initiated, but the end-result is worthless if it does not rest on sound foundations. It is the professional's' duty to keep an eye on the epistemology, but this does not entitle him or her to decide what past events or matters should be researched.

Of course, specialists take part in discussion of the significance of the particular aspect of the past studied, but their prime role is to act as consultants who provide expert advice. Trained historians have useful skills in, among other things, deciding what it is possible to achieve and the best way of doing the research. Their role resembles that of a university teacher instructing postgraduate students, but the form the guidance takes depends on the nature of the support needed. The Paperiliitto history project shows that this kind of collaboration works in practice.

It is important, however, to identify the nature and expanse of the epistemological skills needed, since it is easy for the professional giving expertise to begin unintentionally foisting on others his or her own opinion of what is historically important. This risk is more serious if the expert forgets the unequal nature of cooperation in history-making:

university training endows the specialist with a position of authority. I myself was several times criticized by close colleagues in the 1980s of unconscious patronage.

A participatory historical culture suggests dynamic and reciprocal cooperation between professional historians and others, a collaboration in which both sides learn from each other, but it also demands an attitudinal change among scholars: in giving respect and creating trust. Respect means taking seriously the possibility that aspects of the past that are important to 'ordinary citizens' may be also in the perspective of advancing historiography, as significant as those discussed within the profession. The starting point is to realize that the people addressed are in the middle of the same struggle between rival historical interpretations as the specialist, and the next step is, when creating the subject, to analyse the topic also from the point of view that is currently important for the audience.. Doing this is to take a large step towards a situation where the subject to be researched and its significance are being decided collaboratively.

As to trust, it was quite an experience for an academic to learn in Paperiliitto that sly and wily are epithets often assigned to professional historians. Rosenzweig and Thelen have found the same thing in the United States. One of the greatest obstacles to their efforts turned out to be people's fear of 'being manipulated by people who distort the past to meet their own needs – whether commercial greed, political ambition, or cultural prejudice'. These American colleagues (Rosenzweig and Thelen) also underline the importance of mutual trust: the reception of our academic work depends crucially on the view the users of history have of our intentions.[23]

The emergence of the specialist's professional self also opens up a fruitful perspective on a participatory historical culture. This, again, is a context in which E.H. Carr's insights are worth taking seriously: 'Man's capacity to rise above his social and historical situation seems to be conditioned by the sensitivity with which he recognises the extent of his involvement in it.'[24] The historian's long-term commitments and special interests have been created by the shared histories under the influence of which he or she has grown up and lived, and he or she must aim to gain intellectual control over these. This is necessary in order to achieve the distance needed to be able to assess one's personal preferences: to find those shared histories in which one's preconceived ideas originated and which function to direct one's selection of research topics.

The point is that the context in which the historian's research project emerges and in which the findings will be received is created in the same way as his or her professional self. When people 'prefer to make their own histories' instead of interesting themselves in classroom history,[25] they are actually analyzing the shared histories that are relevant for them. This is the practical perspective on the historian's view of society, discussed in the previous section, *'The role of history in society'* (Field 4 in Figure 5.)

The way to tackle people's engagement with the past is to reflect on the role shared histories play in their lives. What is called for is not only to examine the nature of the opinions and values held by the people one is addressing but also the emergence of those ideas. It is with these mutually constructed accounts of the past that the historian connects the past thoughts and actions which have been yielded by different circumstances – both when defining the subject to be studied and when composing the final account which conveys the findings arrived at.

Taking the trouble to find out the reasons for and functions of prevalent views on the past outside academia is how one learns to treat other genres of history with consideration and respect. Alistair Thomson's point, expressed in the context of oral history, comes close to my thinking on this: historical research must not 'retreat into an arcane intellectual world of rarefied debate'. His idea is that scholars should take their cue for research from their 'relationship with the men and women who tell (them) their memories and by (their) efforts to engage memory in political debate for social change'.[26] The key to a participatory historical culture lies, from the professional's angle, in taking seriously the views of those who constitute the audience. And this is what a socially responsible historian does, in any case.

The risk that ready-made interpretations of the past are imposed on citizens in place of histories created by the people themselves is, in my opinion, the most pressing factor for an effective participatory historical culture. As regards history professionals, Roy Rosenzweig's contention is pertinent: he emphasizes that history professionals 'need to work harder at listening to and respecting the many ways popular history-makers traverse the terrain of the past that is so present for all of us'. For those outside the academic world, a participatory historical culture must, in David Thelen's words, provide a site for 'using the past on their own terms', in order to 'reshape the civic forum to better hear their voices and meet their needs'.[27]

The idea of a participatory historical culture opens up two closely related perspectives that are especially important in the beginning of the twenty-first century. Collective analysis of the past, with professional historians taking care of the soundness of the knowledge produced, offers the participants the possibility of tackling their own present concerns and thinking over how to make a better future for themselves. At the same time, by this way of using the past the participants not only empower themselves to come into grips with the conditions of their living but also learn that the implied strings attached to the social and political engagement offered 'from above' are not inevitable.[28]

Notes

Preface

1. 'A Participatory Historical Culture', in Roy Rosenzweig and David Thelen, *The Presence of the Past: Popular Uses of History in American Life* (New York: Columbia University Press, 1998), 190.
2. More about this in Chapter 3, pp. 53–8, 63–5, 70–1, 79.
3. 'No Thanks for the Memories', *The New York Review*, 13 January 2011.
4. *Historiantutkimus ja historia* ('*Historical Research and History*') (Helsinki: Gaudeamus/Hanki ja jää, 2000).
5. History as the citizens' resource is the idea running through John Tosh's *Why History Matters* (Basingstoke: Palgrave Macmillan, 2008).
6. David Carr, *Time, Narrative and History* (Bloomington and Indianapolis: Indiana University Press, 1986), 2–3.
7. The Canadian specialist on Punjabi culture Anne Murphy's 'History in the Sikh past' (*History and Theory*, vol. 46, no. 3 (2007), quotation at 365), actually illustrates my point here. Her aim is to 'understand multiplicity of the imagination of history, in the past as well as in the present, as a way to approach a vision of the alternative histories and social formations born of this multiplicity'. It was, unfortunately, only at a very late stage of my project that I learned about the American specialists in historiography George G. Iggers and Q. Edward Wang's (with contributions from Supriya Mukherjee) *A Global History of Modern Historiography* (Harlow: Pearson Education Limited, 2008).

Chapter 1: Introduction: Second Thoughts about History

1. E. H. Carr: *What is History?* (Basingstoke and London: Macmillan, 1986 [1961]), 29–30. Sharing Carr's view of the historian's social involvement does not entail agreeing with his stance on 'the course of history', or history as a 'procession' as he put it in that book.
2. Linda Colley on David Lowenthal's *The Heritage Crusade and the Spoils of History*, *Times Literary Supplement*, 25 November 2005. In Gordon S. Wood's view the inclination to disclaim other genres of history has taken two forms: one is paying virtually no attention to them, and the other is to 'demolish, repress' them. Wood, *No Thanks for the Memories*.
3. History-making as a basic social practice runs right through Samuel's *Theatres of Memory*, Vol. 1: *Past and Present in Contemporary Culture* (London and New York: Verso, 1994) quotation at 17. The title of Paju's book in

translation is 'Memories Repressed' (*Torjutut muistot*, Helsinki: Like, 2008), quotation at 209.

4. See the Introduction in Ilmjärv's book that was published in 2004 as *Acta Universitatis Stocholmiensis, Studia Baltica Stocholmiensia*, 24.

5. As to their substance, *public histories* and *popular histories* refer to a host of diverse accounts originating, in metaphorical terms, respectively 'from above' and 'from below'. Another distinction between them refers to public and private, or rather the social, spheres. Both concepts are vague since they are indicative of miscellaneous entities; the terms are actually shorthand for quite heterogeneous categories. Neither public nor popular histories define separate compartments and they are by no means mutually exclusive but overlapping. For the origins of Figure 1, see note 46 in Chapter 3.

6. Tosh, *Why History Matters*, passim. The quotation from the interview with Tosh is in *Historically Speaking*, Vol. X, No. 5 (November 2009).

7. London: Profile Books.

8. *Metahistory: The Historical Imagination in Nineteenth-Century Europe* (Baltimore and London: The Johns Hopkins University Press, 1973). The reason for preferring 'linguistic' to 'narrativist' to describe the change is that it was, with regard to historiography (as will be evident in several contexts below), more profound than is suggested by the terms narrative or narration. Irrespective of the status of 'narrativist' in philosophical discourse, the concept is misleading in the debates of historians, because of the connotation with 'telling stories', as was demonstrated by a lot of unnecessary confusion in the 1980s and 1990s.

9. See, e.g., Richard J. Evans, *In Defence of History* (London: Granta Books, 1997), quotation at 3. 'Postmodernism' is a catch-all label that has, one is tempted to claim at the beginning of the twenty-first century, only created confusion due to its ambiguity.

10. When Peter Burke (ed.), *New Perspectives on Historical Writing* (Cambridge: Polity Press) was published in 1991, the legitimacy of 'new histories' was about to become stabilized, whereas these orientations were discussed in 1981 by Scandinavian historians at their yearly methodological conference, revealingly, under the heading 'Invisible history': B. Wåhlin and B. Qviller (eds.) *Unsynlig historie: Studier I historisk metode XVII* (Oslo et al.: Universitetsforlaget, 1983).

11. The revolutionary nature of the changes in scholarly history at the end of the twentieth century is also illuminated by the many different perspectives on them. See, e.g., Keith Thomas, 'New Ways Revisited', *Times Literary Supplement* (TLS), 13 October 2006 and Mary Fulbrook, *Historical Theory* (London and New York: Routledge, 2002), 31–50. There are also different periodzations; see, e.g., Gordon S. Wood, *The Purpose of History: Reflections on the Uses of History* (Penguin Press, USA, 2008), 1–6.

12. The situation is aptly illustrated by abstracts from the conference *Memory from Transdisciplinary Perspectives: Agency, Practices and Mediation*, organized

by the Research Centre of Culture and Communication, University of Tartu, Estonia, 11–14 January, 2007, and published by the Centre for conference participants. See also J. McDonald (ed.), *The Historic Turn in the Human Sciences* (Ann Arbor: University of Michigan Press, 1996).

13.   'The History Craze' is the title of the first chapter in her 2009 book *The Uses and Abuses of History*. By contrast, according to Raphael Samuel, this enthusiasm is not short-lived: everyday history-making is no mere novelty but a long-lasting practice, and his two books on *Theatres of Memory* warrant this claim. For Samuel's first volume, see Chapter 1, note 3; for the second volume (published posthumously and edited by Alison Light with Sally Alexander and Gareth Stedman Jones), *Theatres of Memory*, Vol. 2: *Island Stories: Unravelling Britain* (London and New York: Verso, 1998).

14.   *Historian tutkimusprosessi: Metodinen opas oman ajan historia tutkiville* ('The *research process in history. A methodological guide for students of contemporary* history') (Helsinki: Gaudeamus, 1972).

15.   Paul Smith's review of Owen Chadwick's *Acton and History* in *London Review of Books* (LRB), 10 June 1999.

16.   Edvard Bull: *Retten til en fortid, Sosialhistoriske artikler* (Oslo: , Universitetsforlaget, 1981), 97.

17.   *Historical Theory* (London and New York: Routledge, 2002), passim.

18.   According Peter Novick (*That Noble Dream: The 'Objectivity Question' and the American Historical Profession* [Cambridge, Mass.: Cambridge University Press, 1988], 573–629), this was the situation already at the end of the 1980s. See also Allan Megill, *Historical Knowledge, Historical Error: A Contemporary Guide to Practice* (Chicago and London: The University of Chicago Press, 2007), 159–164. A useful, much broader perspective on the disruption of the late twentieth century is opened by Iggers and Wang, *A Global History*, 364–94.

19.   Quotations from John Tosh, *The Pursuit of History. Aims, Methods and New Directions in the Study of Modern History* (Harlow: Pearson, fourth edition, 2006), p.xiii.

20.   Quotations in this and the following paragraph from the interview with MacMillan in *Historically Speaking*, Vol. X, No. 5 (November 2009).

21.   Both quotations from Paul Ricoeur, *Time and Narrative*, Vol. 3 (Chicago and London: University of Chicago Press, 1990 [1988]), 150.

22.   Quoted in Jenny Uglow's review (*New York Review*, 24 June 2010) of Steven Shapin's *Never Pure: Historical Studies of Science as if It Was Produced by People with Bodies, Situated in Time, Space, Culture, and Society, and Struggling for Credibility and Authority* (Baltimore: Johns Hopkins University Press, 2010).

23.   See especially the opening page (11) of my 1972 book, *Historian tutkimusprosessi*.

24.   On the historians' relation to common sense (and for the following quotations), see Thomas L. Haskell, *Objectivity Is Not Neutrality: Explanatory*

Schemes in History (Baltimore and London: The Johns Hopkins University Press, 1998), 1–24.

25. Haskell, *Objectivity Is Not Neutrality*, 5–6.
26. Reinhart Koselleck, *Futures Past: On the Semantics of Historical Time* (Cambridge, Mass.: MIT Press, 1985), 151. In the German original (*Vergangene Zukunft: Zur Semantik Geschichtlicher Zeiten* [Frankfurt am Main: Suhrkamp Verlag, 1979], 202) the terms are '*Objektivisten*' and '*Vertretern der Parteilichkeit*'.
27. G. R. Elton, according to John Tosh, *Historians on History: An Anthology Edited and Introduced by Johan Tosh* (Harlow et al.: Longman 2000), 20.
28. 'Ich wünschte mein selbst gleichsam auszulöschen...'; according to Kolleck 1979, 180. See also Paul Ricoeur, *Time and Narrative*, Vol. 3, 310.
29. G. R. Elton, *The Practice of History* (London: Fontana Press, 1989 [1967]), 66.
30. For current ideas of objectivity, see Megill, *Historical Knowledge, Historical*, Chapter 5.
31. In his review of Raphael Samuel, *Theatres of Memory*, Vol. 1, in *The Times Literary Supplement*, 10 March 1995.
32. Hugh Stretton, *The Political Sciences. General principles of selection in social science and history* (London: Routledge & Kegan Paul, 1969) abounds with examples of historians' failure in this respect.
33. Haskell, *Objectivity Is Not Neutrality,* 7, 6.
34. Quotations from Fulbrook, *Historical Theory*, ix and Haskell, *Objectivity Is Not Neutrality*, 7–8.
35. Carr, *What is History?*, 38. The quotation at the end of the next paragraph is from the same page.
36. A comprehensive approach to the issue as such would presuppose many more works like *Participating in the Knowledge Society. Researchers Beyond the University Walls* which emerged 2005 within the British Open University, was edited by Ruth Finnegan, and published by Palgrave Macmillan. The quotation is from Finnegan's 'Should We Notice Researchers Outside the University?', *British Academy Review*, Issue 10, 2007.
37. The idea of a participatory historical culture originates in Thelen, 'A Participatory Historical Culture' (1998). See also the introductory chapter by Paul Ashton and Hilda Kean to the collection edited by them, *People and their Pasts: Public History Today* (Basingstoke: Palgrave Macmillan, 2009).
38. For Bailyn, see Wood, *No Thanks for the Memories*; Roy Rosenzweig, 'Everyone a Historian', in Rosenzweig and Thelen, *The Presence of the Past*, 181.

Chapter 2: Historical Research

1. Peter Mandler, *History and National Life* (London: Profile Books, 2002), 143–63; quotations at 149, 162–3. See also Mandler's 'What is History For?', *History Today* (July 2002).
2. For Huizinga, see *Im Bann der Geschichte* (Nijmegen: Pantheon, 1942); the quotation has been translated by the author from the Finnish edition,

Historian olemus (Helsinki and Porvoo: WSOY, 1967), 64. The quotation from Evans is from his 'The Wonderfulness of Us (the Tory Interpretation of History)', *London Review of Books*, 17 March 2011.

3. Daniel Snowman, 'The Historian as VIP', *Historically Speaking* (March/April 2007), quotatitions at 42 and 41. The article is an edited version of the introduction to Snowman's *Historians* (Basingstoke: Palgrave Macmillan, 2006). See also Pilvi Torsti, *Divergent Stories, Convergent Attitudes: A Study of the Presence of History, History Textbooks and the Thinking of Youth in Post-War Bosnia and Herzegovina* (Helsinki: Taifuuni, 2003).

4. Rosenzweig, 'Everyone a Historian', 178; Allan Megill, 'What role should theory play in historical research and writing?', paper presented at the 2010 conference of the Finnish Historical Society in Jyväskylä, 22 October (he refers to Peter Laslett, *The World We Have Lost* [New York: Scribner's, 1965]).

5. Glimpses into the various ways in which the past affects our actions and thinking are provided for instance by Jonathan Potter, *Representing Reality: Discourse, Rhetoric and Social Construction* (London: Sage Publications, 2000 (1996)). One of the secondary aims of the present study is to encourage research in the sociology of everyday historical practices.

6. Rosenzweig, 'Everyone a Historian' paraphrases, of course, the famous essay of Carl Becker from 1931 'Everyman His Own Historian', *American Historical Review,* Vol. 37, No. 2, 221–36.

7. Thelen, 'A Pariticipatory Historical Culture', 205.

8. The term 'usable past' was attributed to Sussman in Ronald J. Greele's email to the author, 2 August 2008; Rosenzweig 'Everyone a historian', 178.

9. *Using History* (London: Hodder Arnold, 2005), 9–10, 13–26.

10. *London Stories: Personal Lives, Public Histories. (Creating Personal and Public Histories of Working-class London)* (London, Sydney, Chicago: Rivers Oram Press, 2004).

11. Ricoeur, *Time and Narrative*, Vol. 3, 124–5. The idea of the muteness of remnants should not be confused with the postmodernist notion that there is no independent reality outside the text. The argument about the references of a remnant has nothing to do with artistic representation, it is epistemological by its nature.

12. The University of Chicago Press has published to date (since 1999, by 2010) four volumes of Nora's most famous work *(Les Lieux de mémoire)* under the title *Realms of Memory*.

13. Oral history has turned out to be an extremely fruitful vantage point from which to reflect on the methodology of historical enquiry. See, e.g., Jorma Kalela, 'The Challenge of Oral History – The Need To Rethink Source Criticism', in Anne Ollila (ed.), *Historical Perspectives on Memory*, (Helsinki: Suomen Historiallinen Seura, 1999).

14. Quotation from Hobsbawm's review of Richard Overy, *Britain between the Wars*, in *London Review of Books*, 6 August 2009.

15. For the case of Troy (and quotations) see, Strauss, 'Why is Troy still burning?', *Historically Speaking* (September/October 2006), 18–20.

16. If the historians 'do not make what they are doing intelligible to the public, then others will rush to fill the void', is Margaret MacMillan's way of formulating the same argument: *The Uses and Abuses of History*, 36.

17. Iggers and Wang, *A Global History*, 24–9.

18. Ricoeur, *Time and Narrative*, Vol. 3, 142–3, 152.

19. See especially, Frank Ankersmit, *The Reality Effect in the Writing of History: the Dynamics of Historiographical Topology* (Amsterdam: Elsevier Science & Technology, 1989).

20. Ricoeur, *Time and Narrative*, Vol. 3, 152, 142.

21. Koselleck, *Futures Past*, 21–38.

22. Tosh, *The Pursuit of History*, 2, 343, 341.

23. 'Objectivity is Not Neutrality: Rhetoric vs Practice', in Peter Novick, *That Noble Dream'*, *History and Theory*, Vol. 29 (1990), 134. This article is one of the essays republished in Haskell, *Objectivity is not Neutrality* (1998).

24. Blair Worden on Jeffrey R. Collins, *The Allegiance of Thomas Hobbes*, in *Times Literary Supplement*, 4 August 2006.

25. The discussion took place during the conference 'Memory and Narration', in Helsinki, 15 November 2006. For Grele's paper, see 'Reflections on the Practice of Oral History: Retrieving what we can from an earlier critique', *Suomen Antropologi, Journal of the Finnish Anthropological Society,* Special Issue: *Memory and Narration – Oral History Research in the Northern European Context*, Vol. 32, No. 4 (Winter 2007), 11–23.

26. Fulbrook, *Historical Theory* 145, 162.

27. Cf. Thomas L. Haskell, 'Objectivity is Not Neutrality', *History and Theory* (1990), 134.

28. Rolf Torstendahl: *Introduktion till historieforskningen. Historia om vetenskap.* Natur och kultur; Stockholm 1966, 20–49. See also Carr, *What is History?*, 2, and Tosh 2006, 48–50.

29. Fulbrook (37–40) argues that 'what basically distinguishes the perspectival paradigms is their choice of what to look at'. See also Jorma Kalela: 'The 'Fragmentation' of Historiography and the Work of Historians as a Collective Undertaking', *Suomen Antropologi,*Vol. 20, No. 1 (March 1995).

30. The 'new cultural history' in the United States is perhaps an exception; see Wood, *The Purpose of The Past, 4.*

31. The first quotation, Tosh, *The Pursuit of History* 2006, p. x; others, Carr, *What is History?*, 60–2, 37–8.

32. Pieter Geyl, *Debates with Historians* (London: Collins, 1955), 278. The same point has been nicely put by Antony Beevor in *La Guerra Civil Española*: '... history, which is never tidy, must always end with questions. Conclusions are much too convenient.' See Felipe Fernandez-Armesto's review of Beevor, in *Times Literary Supplement*, 2 June 2006.

33. 'Anything goes' is associated with Paul Feyerabend, *Against Method: Outline of an Anarchistic Theory of Knowledge* (London: New Left Books,1975). History as a social form of knowledge is the thread running through Samuel, *Theatres of Memory, Volume 1*.

34. Arthur Schlesinger Jr., 'History and National Stupidity', *New York Review of Books* (27 April 2006), 14.

35. Carr, *What is History?*, 10.

36. 'Hybrids' is the concluding chapter of Samuel's *Theatres of Memory*, Vol. 1, 429–47; quotations at 430–1, 443.

37. For Carl Hempel's Covering Law Model, see, e.g., Megill, *Historical Knowledge, Historial error,* 68–9. An example of contemporary criticism of discussions within the profession in those days is Kalela, *Historian tutkimusprosessi,* 44–7.

38. The many aspects of truth demanded a whole chapter in my previous book (Kalela, *Historiantutkimus ja historia*); the title of that chapter could be translated as 'The burdensome truth'.

39. The distinction results from an analysis of reviews written by historians; see Jorma Kalela, 'Argumentaatio ja rekonstruktio tutkimusprosessissa' *(Turun yliopisto: Poliittinen historia,* Julkaisuja C:43, 1993), 51–60. It was only afterwards I learned of Toulmin's distinction. His *The Uses of Argument* (Cambridge: Cambridge University Press, 1990 [1958]), 30–5, is a work unfortunately neglected by historians during the years they debated the Covering Law Model. What follows here is an abridged version of Kalela, *Historiantutkimus ja historia,* 161–216.

40. For more on impeccability and the undisclosed elements of the historian's account, see the sections '*Arguing for the findings*' and '*Composing the final account*' in Chapter 5.

41. *New York Review of Books,* 17 December 2009.

42. Here I owe a great deal to Antoon Van den Braembussche's ideas in his 'The Silenced Past: On the Nature of Historical Taboos', in Wojciecha, W. (ed.): *Swiat historii: Festschrift in honour of Jerzy Topolski.* Poznan: Instytut Historii UAM 1998. Another important source has been John Tosh: *Thinking with History: A Resource for Citizens*; Kathleen Fitzpatrick Lecture at the University of Melbourne, 18 May 2006. University of Melbourne History Occasional Papers no. 18.

43. Discussions with the philosopher Jouni-Matti Kuukkanen (see, e.g., his 'Kuhn, the Correspondence Theory of Truth and Coherentist Epistemology', *Studies in History and Philosophy of Science,* Vol. 38 (2007)), have been fruitful in clarifying my position concerning truth. For the term field-dependent, see Toulmin *The Uses of Argument*, ch. 1 ('Fields of argument and modals').

44. The argument is that it is not reasonable to discuss 'truth' in the field of history, in the sense of correspondence theory truth. I share the stance of Haskell, according to whom 'what truth requires is not unassailable

foundations but self-correcting social processes': Haskell, *Objectivity is not Neutrality*, 10–11.

45. The characterizations are from Eric Arnesen, 'The recent historiography of British abolitionism: academic scholarship, popular history, and the broader reading public', *Historically Speaking* (July/August 2006). For Hochschild, *Bury the Chains: Prophets and Rebels in the Fight to Free an Empire's Slaves*, (Basingstoke: Macmillan, 2005) and Schma, *Rough Crossings: Britain, the Slaves and the American Revolution* (London: BBC Books, 2005).

46. Jorma Kalela, *Grannar på skilda vägar. Det finländsk–svenska samarbetet i den finländska och svenska utrikespolitiken 1921–1923*, Helsingfors: Söderströms 1971.

Chapter 3: The People Addressed

1. For more on this, see Tosh, *Why History Matters*, 106–10.

2. It is worth repeating that 'to whom' is general by nature; it is still relevant, for example, in cases where the audience is made up only of the two people marking an undergraduate's work.

3. J. H. Hexter, 'The Rhetoric of History', *History and Theory*, Vol. 18 (1967), 1–13.

4. Fulbrook, *Historical Theory*, 162.

5. See especially the collection of my essays at the turn of 1990s, *Aika, historia ja yleisö: Kirjoituksia historiantutkimuksen lähtökohdista*, (Turun yliopisto: Poliittinen historia, Julkaisuja C:44, 1993). For the metaphor of vortex see Gareth Stedman Jones: 'Faith in history', *History Workshop Journal* 30 (1990).

6. For more on this, see Jorma Kalela, 'Paperiliitto history project', *Adult Education in Finland*, Vol. 1–2 (1987), 33–7. The most comprehensive presentation of the project and its background is Jorma Kalela, *Näkökulmia tulevaisuuteen. Paperiliiton historia 1944–1986* (Helsinki: Paperiliitto1986), 11–47.

7. A comprehensive presentation of the revision of my plan is Jorma Kalela, *Näkökulmia tulevaisuuteen*, 11–15. For an English presentation, see Jorma Kalela, *Paperiliitto history project*.

8. See Kalela, *Näkökulmia tulevaisuuteen,* 8–37 for the research circles, and 37–47 for some of the first steps made towards the concepts outlined in this book.

9. Quotation from Thelen, 'A Participatory Historical Culture', 192.

10. Rosenzweig, Everyone a historian, 184.

11. Unfortunately, I never found time to reflect systematically on my 'participant observation'.

12. See, e.g., Raphael Samuel (ed.), 'History Workshop A Collectanea 1967–1991', *History Workshop*, Vol. 25 (1991), and Jorma Kalela, 'Politics of

History and History Politics: Some Conceptual Suggestions as to Political Aspects of History', in Johanna Valenius (ed.), *Ajankohta: Poliittisen historian vuosikirja 2004* (Turku: Poliittinen historia Helsingin ja Turun yliopistot, 2004).

13. Sven Lindqvist: *Gräv där su står: Hur man utforskar ett jobb* (Stockholm: Bonniers, 1979); Gunnar Sillén, *Stiga vi mot ljuset: Om dokumentation av industri-och arbetarminnen* (Stockholm: Raben and Sjögren, 1977).

14. Sillén, Stiga vi mot ljuset, passim and Raphael Samuel, 'Editorial introduction' in Samuel (ed.), 'History Workshop'.

15. Since the 1990s I have met a great number of colleagues in Finland, Sweden, Norway and the UK involved in these kinds of projects, but no studies of their proliferation. On the other hand, the relationship between place and belonging as an issue has been discussed by several scholars. See, e.g., Paula Hamilton and Linda Shopes (eds.), *Oral History and Public Memories* (Philadelphia: Temple University Press, 2008), passim.

16. 'Quelle histoire pour quel avenir? Whose History for Whose Future?', Sixth Biennial Conference on the Teaching, Learning and Communicating of History, Quebec, Canada, 24–26 October 2008. Information from Pilvi Torsti who took part in the conference.

17. David Thelen, 'A Participatory Historical Culture', 190; Roy Rosenzweig and David Thelen: 'Introduction: Scenes form a Survey', in Rosenzweig and Thelen (eds.), *The Presence of the Past*, 12–13.

18. Rosenzweig and Thelen, *Introduction: Scenes form a Survey*, 12–13.

19. Tosh, *Why History Matters*, 10–11.

20. The starting point for what follows is Jay Winter's review of several works dealing with the First World War: 'P vs C. The still burning anger when the Frenc talk of the First World War' (*Times Literary Supplement*, 16 June 2006). The comment on the bestselling books was made, according to him, by Antoine Prost.

21. In addition to Black, *Using History*; MacMillan, *The Uses and Abuses of History*; and Tosh, *Why History Matters*; see also Peter Aronson, *Historiebruk – att använda det förflutna* (Lund: Studentlitteratur, 2004).

22. Tosh, Why History Matters, especially 120–43.

23. Thelen, *A Participatory Historical Culture*, 195–202.

24. Hilda Kean, *London Stories*, 12–15. See also Paul Ashton and Paula Hamilton, 'At Home with the Past: Background and Initial Findings from the National Survey' (Australians and the Past, Special issue of *Australian Cultural History*, 22 (2003), pp. 5–30).

25. Paul Ashton and Hilda Kean, 'Introduction' to ibid., *People and their Pasts*, 1–20.

26. The quotations from Hilda Kean, ' "Public history" and Raphael Samuel. A forgotten radical pedagogy?', *Public History Review*. Vol. 11 (2004), 52–3.

27. The 1991 paper in Oxford has not been published; the 2009 article appeared in S. Tiitinen et al. (eds.), *Challenges for Finland and Democracy: Parliament of Finland Centennial 12* (Helsinki: Edita 2009).

28. The quotations on Sen's *Identity and Violence: The Illusion of Destiny* are from the back cover of the Penguin Books edition, 2007.

29. This state of affairs began to come into sight towards the end of my assignment in Paperiliitto and analysing its political consequences has been a central theme in my research since. See, e.g., ch. 5 in Kalela, *Näkökulmia tulevaisuuteen* and Jorma Kalela, 'Kansalaiset, poliittinen järjestelmä ja yhteiskuntamoraali', *Tiedepolitiikka*, Vol. 2 (1990), 5–16.

30. Mandler, *History and National Life*, 147–8.

31. For Gilroy, *After Empire: Melancholia or Convivial Culture* (London: Routledge, 2005), see Bhikhu Parekh's review in the *Times Literary Suppplement*, 9 September 2005; Hall, according to Tosh, *Why History Matters*, 15.

32. Derek Fewster, *Visions of Past Glory: Nationalism and the Construction of Early Finnish History* (Helsinki: Finnish Literature Society, 2006), Tuula Karjalainen, *Kantakuvat – yhteinen muistimme* (Helsinki: Maahenki, 2009), Maunu Häyrynen, *Kuvitettu maa: Suomen kansallisen maisemakuvaston rakentuminen* (Helsinki: Suomalaisen Kirjallisuuden Seura, 2009).

33. Quotation Mandler, *History and National Life*, 147. Connected to the problem of identity is discussion of the histories of various minorities from the angle 'who owns history'; this multifaceted issue is, however, beyond the scope of this book. About its various dimensions, see, for e.g., Grele, 'Reflections on the practice of oral history', 19–21.

34. Arnesen, 'The recent historiography', 22–4.

35. Richard Overy, 'The historical present', *Times Higher Education Supplement*, 29 April 2010.

36. The latter quotation from Bruce L. Berger, 'Narrative and Popular History', *Historically Speaking*, May/June 2006, 42.

37. See, e.g., Gerda Lerner, 'The Necessity of History and Professional Historian', *Journal of American History*, Vol. 69, No 1 (1982), quoted in and discussed by Pertti Haapala,'Sosiaalihistorian lupaus', in Pekka Ahtiainen et al. (eds.), *Historia nyt: Näkemyksiä suomalaisesta historiantutkimuksesta* (Helsinki: WSOY, 1990), 82–3.

38. The expression has been used by Katharine Hodgkin and Susannah Radstone in 'Introduction. Contested pasts', to Hodgkin and Radstone (eds.), *Memory, History, Nation: Contested Memories, Studies in Memory and Narrative* (New Brunswick: Transaction Publishers, 2006).

39. The commonplace nature of history was the theme of a book titled (in translation) *Everyday History*, which succeeded, at the beginning of the 2000s, in drawing attention to this aspect of history in Finland. See Jorma Kalela and Ilari Lindroos (eds.), *Jokapäiväinen historia* (Helsinki: Tietolipas 177, Suomalaisen Kirjallisuuden Seura, 2001, and Google entry: *Jokapäiväinen historia*:

40. G. R. Elton, *The Practice of History* (London: Fontana Press, 1989 [1967]), 66.

41. In the article referred to in note 11 in this chapter, I used the misleading term 'social memories' to refer to this analytical category.

42. For more on popular histories (albeit not using this term) see, e.g., R. Samuel and P. Thompson (eds.), *The Myths We Live By* (London and New York: Routledge, 1990).

43. For more on this perspective (and for the quotation) see, e.g., Joseph Mali, *Mythistory: The Making of a Modern Historiography* (Chicago and London: University of Chicago Press, 2003); quotation at 4–6.

44. Examples of recent works include Black, *Using History* and Peter Aronsson, *Historiebruk: Att använda det förflutna*. An older, more or less standard treatise is M.I. Finley, *The Use and Abuse of History: From the Myths of the Greeks to Lévi-Strauss, The Past Alive and the Present Illumined* (London: Chatto and Windus, 1972; reprint London: Penguin Books, 1990).

45. Recent works are the two volumes edited by Katharine Hodgkin and Susannah Radstone: Hodgkin and Radstone, *Memory, History, Nation* and Radstone and Hodgkin (eds.), *Regimes of Memory: Studies in Memory and Narrative* (New Brunswick: Transcation Publishers, 2006). These books also display the wide interdisciplinary interest in 'memory' with various attributes (e.g. 'collective memory') since the 1970s.

46. Popular Memory Group, 'Popular Memory: Theory, Politics, Method', in R. Johnson, G. McLennan, B. Schwartz and D. Sutton (eds.), *Making Histories: Studies in History-writing and Politics* (London: Hutchinson, 1982), 205–52. The terms used by the Group were 'public representations' and 'private memory'. Comments on this article abound in the literature on the study of memory; see, e.g., Hodgkin and Radstone, *Memory, History, Nation* and Radstone and Hodgkin, *Regimes of Memory*. I have myself referred constantly to the Group's work since 1984 (see my 'Minnesforskning, oral history och historierörelsen', *Sociologisk Forskning*, Vols 3–4 (1984), 47–67).

47. In his article on the subject, 'The historical present', referred to in note 35 in this chapter Richard Overy writes of the popular 'misperception that popular history and popular history writers are doing in some sense *real* history' (my italics).

48. In the yearly conference for the historians of the labour movement in Linz 1981 I underlined that it was not for nothing that the historical profession had developed their methodological tools: *Internationale Tagung der Historiker der Arbeiterbewegung, 17: Linzer Konferenz 1981* (Vienna: Europaverlag,1983, 581–2. See also Kalela, *Minnesforskning, oral history och historierörelsen*.

49. Finnegan, *Should We Notice Researchers Outside the University?*, 60.

50. The quotation is from an anonymous review (in January 2011) of the draft for this book requested by Palgrave Macmillan.

51. For sources, see Chapter 5, note 9.

52. The articles of Sillén and myself appeared in *Meddelande från Arbetarrörelsens arkiv och bibliotek*, Vol. 23, Nos. 2 and 3 (1982). For the relationship between history and art, see Ian Mortimer, 'The Art of History', *Historically Speaking*, (June 2010); the points he raises are discussed in the section *'Composing the final account'* in Chapter 5, p. 144.

53. Markku Hyrkkänen, 'All History is, More or Less, Intellectual History: R.G. Collingwood's Contribution to the Theory and Methodology of Intellectual History', *Intellectual History Review*, Vol. 19, No. 2 (2009); quotations at 263. See also Thelen, 'A participatory historical culture', 191. About Collingwood himself, see his *The Idea of History* (London: Oxford University Press, 1961 [1946]), Part V, § 4, 'History as Re-enactment of Past Experiences'.

54. See also Mandler, *History and National Life*, 146–7. I was reminded about the importance of the distinction between empathy and sympathy by Sofie Strandén when giving an expert opinion on her PhD thesis to Åbo Akademi University in July 2010.

55. Himmerlfarb, according to Tosh, *Historians on History*, 290–1.

56. The review was published by the *London Review of Books*, 19 February 2004.

57. In his review of Raphael Samuel, *Theatres of Memory, Volume 1* in *The Times Literary Supplement*, 10 March 1995; Pauli Kettunen, *Globalisaatio ja kansallinen me: Kansallisen katseen historiallinen kritiikki* (Tampere: Vastapaino, 2008), 24.

58. London: Macmillan Press, 1984; quotation at 157.

59. Questioning conventional thinking about authorship in historical writing is the focus of *A Shared Authority. Essays on the Craft and Meaning of Oral and Public History*, by Michael Frisch (State University of New York Press; Albany 1990, xx–xxiii), but he doesn't use the concept of shared histories, the use and role of which is the theme of the next two subchapters. Still, see below the end of the last section in this chapter, '*The liquid social fabric*'.

60. Samuel, *Theatres of Memory*, Vol. 1, 8.

61. In *The Lessons of History* (London: Oxford University Press, 1989),quoted in Tosh, *Historians on History*, 180.

62. According to Anderson nations are 'imagined communities' which do not merely invent but actually consist in myths of historical unity and continuity: *Imagined Communities: Reflections on the Origin and Spread of Nationalism* (London: Verso, 1983), 19.

63. Anne Heimo, *Kapina Sammatissa. Vuoden 1918 paikalliset tulkinnat osana historian yhteiskunnallisen rakentamisen prosessia* (Helsinki: Suomalaisen Kirjallisuuden Seura, 2010); with an English summary: *Rebellion in Sammatti: Local Interpretations of the 1918 Finnish Civil War as Part of the Social Process of History Making*.

64. The fruitfulness of Rosenzweig and Thelen's work is not essentially weakened by their survey method, that is, a method in which the interviewees' world (in this case their past) has been virtually defined by the scholars in advance.

65. Frisch, *A Shared Authority*, pp. xv–xx; Alessandro Portelli, *The Battle of Valle Giulia: Oral History and the Art of Dialogue* (Madison, The University of Wisconsin Press, 1997), 12; Hamilton and Shopes (eds.), *Oral History and Public Memories* (Philadelphia; Temple University Press, 2008), p. x.

66. A standard presentation of this field of study is the two-part collection edited by Katharine Hodgkin and Susannah Radstone, *Memory, History, Nation* and *Regimes of Memory*. According to David Berliner, 'The Abuses of Memory: 'Reflections on the Memory Boom in Anthropology', (*Anthropological Quarterly*, Vol. 78, No.1 [Winter 2005]), the reference of memory has been lost because of the inflation of (scholarly) attributes to memory.

67. The quotation at p. xi.

68. Mali, *Mythistory*; James V. Wertsch, *Voices of Collective Remembering* (Cambridge: Cambridge University Press, 2002).

69. Quotation from Ashton and Kean, *People and Their Pasts*, 5.

70. Tosh, *Why History* Matters, 99–139. The Dutch philosopher of history Chris Lorenz, in turn, underlines that the rise of the 'new histories' testifies to 'the declining significance of the nation state as the 'natural' framework of academic history'. Chris Lorenz, 'Unstuck in Time. On the sudden presence of the past', in K. Tilmans, F. van Vree and J. Winter (eds.), *Performing the Past. Memory, History, and Identity in Modern Europe* (Amsterdam: Amsterdan University Press, 2010), 81–6.

71. Thelen, '*A Paricipatory Historical Culture*', 199–200.

72. Marina Warner, 'In the Time of Not Yet: Marina Warner on the imaginary of Edward Said', *London Review of Books*, 16 December 2010.

73. Elina Makkonen, *Muistitiedon etnografiaa tuottamassa* (Joensuu; Joensuun yliopiston humanistisia julkaisuja, Vol. 58 [2009]), passim; with an English summary: *Producing an ethnography of oral history.*

74. The historian would be wise to take seriously what for scholars in folkloristics is commonplace: 'Memory need not be dramatic or well told to be a key narrative: the tale can just as well deal with a moment of joy or it can be scant and fumbling in its methods when narrating a trauma.': Annikki Kaivola-Bregenhöj, 'History bursts into story: women's tales of war', *Folklore Fellows' Network*, No. 37 (December 2009), 13.

75. Rosenzweig, 'Everyyone a Historian', quotation at 189; Thelen, 'A Participatory Historical Culture', 190.

76. Frisch, *A Shared Authority*, p. xx.

Chapter 4: The Politics of History

1. Jasper Griffin on Paul Cartridge's *Thermopylae: The Battle That Changed the World*, (New York: Vintage books, 2006), *New York Review of Books*, 6 December 2007.

2. Victor Davis Hanson on Tom Holland's *Persian Fire* (New York: DoubleDay, 2005), *The Times Literary Supplement*, 7 October 2005.

3. Quotations from the review by James J. Sheehan of Christopher Clark's *Iron Kingdom: The Rise and Downfall of Prussia, 1600–1947* (London: Allen Lane, 2006), *The Times Literary Supplement*, 17 November 2006. My point does not imply denying Clark the right to state his position in the way he has done:

'...I am happily dispensed from the obligation (or temptation) either to lament or to celebrate the Prussian record'. What I mean is that, irrespective of the scholar's primary objective, his or her results are a comment on previous interpretations. In addition, it is hard to avoid existing interpretations. This is true of Clark as well, as Sheehan notes: 'there are plenty of lamentations and a few celebrations in this book'.

4. Giles Milton's review of James Reston, *Dogs of God: Columbus, the Inquisition and the Defeat of the Moors* (New York: Barnes & Noble, 2005), *Guardian Weekly*, 21 October 2005.

5. Pauli Kettunen, 'Kirkuvan harmaa 70-luku', *Työväentutkimus* (2006), 4–11; Jorma Kalela, 'Miksi ei pidä ajatella, että historiantutkija tuottaa kertomuksia?', in S. Hägg, M. Lehtimäki and L. Steinby (toim.), *Näkökulmia kertomuksen tutkimukseen* (Helsinki: Suomalaisen Kirjallisuuden Seura, 2009).

6. Irwin's book was published in 2006 by Allen Lane (London) and Said's in 1978 by Vintage Books (New York). The first and second quotations are from Christopher de Bellaigue's review in *The Times Literary Supplement*, 19 May 2006, the third from Maya Jasanoff's article in the *London Review of Books*, 8 June 2006 (later references to de Bellaigue and Jasanoff are to these articles). See also Philip Hensher's evaluation in *The Spectator*, 29 January 2006 and David Tresilian's assesment in *Al-Ahram*, 23 February 2006.

7. See also Fulbrook, *Historical Theory*, 185–8.

8. Fulbrook, *Historical Theory*, 196.

9. Amit Chaudhuri's review of Ramachandra Guha's *India After Gandhi: The History of the World's Largest Democracy* (New York: Ecco, 2007), in *Guardian Weekly*, 11 May 2007.

10. London: Allen Lane, 2007. The following quotations are from Ferguson's review in *The Times Literary Supplement*, 21 September 2007. Ferguson has been a central figure in the discussion about 'virtual history'; see Megill, *Historical Knowledge, Historical Error*, Chapter 7.

11. Fulbrook, *Historical Theory*, 195–6.

12. Fulbrook, *Historical Theory*, 196.

13. The interview was conducted by J.-P. Rantanen on Finnish TV 1, 25 February 2010.

14. Tyerman, 'Some modern myths about the medieval crusades', *Historically Speaking*, (September/October 2006), 22. See also Robert Irwin's review of Tyerman's *God's War* (London: Penguin, 2005), *The Times Literary Supplement*, 8 September 2006.

15. Quotations from Malise Ruthven's review of Phillips's *Holy Warriors: A Modern History of the Crusades* (London:The Bodley Head, 2010), and of Asbridge's *The Crusades: The War for the Holy Land* (London: Simon & Schuster, 2010), *Guardian Weekly*, 22 January 2010.

16. Tosh,'In defence of applied history: the History and Policy website', *History & Policy*, Policy Papers 37 (2006), <www.historyandpolicy.org> (20.4.2006). See also Tosh, *The Pursuit of History*, 2006, 38–40.

17. Anu Suoranta, *Halvennettu työ. Pätkätyö ja sukupuoli sopimusyhteiskuntaa edletävissä työmarkkinakäytännöissä* (Tampere: Vastapaino, 2009) (title in translation: 'Unvalued Work: Gender and fragmented labour before the national collective bargaining').

18. For these works see Chapter 3, note 44 above.

19. For more about the difference between the two concepts, see Jorma Kalela, *'Politics of history and history politics'*; in this article I used 'history politics' as a translation of the German *'Geschichtspolitik'*.

20. For more on taboos and traumas see, e.g., Antoon Van den Braembussche, *The Silence of Belgium: Taboo and Trauma in Belgian Memory*, Yale French Studies, No. 102 (New Haven, CT: Yale University Press, 2002). About silences in general, see, e.g., Ludmilla Jordanova, *History in Practice* (London: Arnold, 2000), 142–5.

21. *New York Reviewof Books* 22 November 2007. Lal's book was published by Cambridge University Press, in 2005.

22. Mortimer, 'Beyond the Facts', *The Times Literary Supplement,* 26 September 2008.

23. Quotations from Daniel Blackie's review of Thane, *Old Age in English History* (Oxford: Oxford University Press, 2000), *Ennen & nyt* (April 2001).

24. David Coward's review of Crossley's *Consumable Metaphors* (Bern: Peter Lang, 2005), *The Times Literary Supplement*, 9 June 2006.

25. A more comprehensive examination of these themes is presented in Kalela, *Historiantutkimus ja historia*, Chapter 5, the title of which can be translated as 'The prison of time'. A key source of inspiration was the review by Peter Munz of Donald J. Wilcox's 'The Measures of Times Past' (Chicago and London: University of Chicago Press, 1987), *History and Theory*, Vol. 2, No. 28 (1989).

26. In the mid-1990s I argued that the historicist meta-explanation continued to unite the historical profession in spite of the fragmentation following the disruption within the discipline: Jorma Kalela, 'The "Fragmentation' of Historiography and the Work of Historians as a Collective Undertaking', *Suomen Antropologi,* Vol. 20, No. 1 (March 1995), 12–17.

27. Review of Elizabeth Roberts, *Realm of the Black Mountain: A History of Montenegro* (Ithaca: Cornell University Press, 2007), *New York Review of Books,* 6 December 2007. Malcolm also emphasizes that this tendency led to the author underplaying the recent achievement of Montenegro to create a society where minorities feel more at ease than those in many other states in the region.

28. The trap of hindsight lies in favouring the retrospective half of Danish philosopher Sören Kierkegaard's famous dictum, 'life … can only be understood backwards' and forgetting the other half, 'but it must be lived forwards' . According to Jane Kamensky, 'Novelties: A Historian's Field Notes from Fiction', *Historically Speaking* (April 2011), 5.

29. Tosh, *Why History Matters*, 49; Tosh, *The Pursuit of History*, 190.

30. Mandler, *History and National Life*, 145.

31. Koselleck, *Futures Past;* German original *Vergangene Zukunft.*
32. Nilsson, 'Historia som humaniora', *Historisk Tidskrift*, No. 1 (1989), 1–15.
33. Clifford S.L. Davies, 'A rose by another name: why we are wrong to talk about' 'the Tudors' ', *The Times Literary Supplement,* 13 June 2008.
34. Alex Burghart's review of Veronica Ortenberg, *In Search of the Holy Grail: The Quest for the Middle Ages* (New York: Barnes & Noble, 2007), *The Times Literary Supplement,* 16 February 2007.
35. J.L. Nelson's review of Christopher Tyerman, *God's War: A New History of the Crusades* (Cambridge: Harvard University Press, 2006), *London Review of Books*, 29 November 2007.
36. Useful short presentations of Braudel's ideas are Tosh, *The Pursuit of History*, 163 and Tosh, *Why History Matters*, 51. See also John R. Hall, 'The Time of History and the History of Times', *History and Theory*, Vol. 19 (1980), 113–131.
37. Barbara Adam, *Time and Social Theory* (Cambridge: Polity Press, 1990), 1–3.
38. Susan Pedersen on Chris Wrigley, *A.J.P. Taylor: Radical Historian of Europe* (London: I.B. Tauris, 2006), *The Times Literary Supplement*, 10 May 2007; Gordon S. Wood on the biographies written by Barnet Schecter ('George Washington's America' [New York: Barnes & Noble, 2010]) and Ron Chernow ('Washington: A Life' [New York: Penguin Press, 2010]) *New York Review of Books*, 9 December 2010.
39. Peter Mandler, 'The Responsibility of the Historian', in H. Jones, K. Ostberg and N. Randeraad (eds.), *History on Trial: The Public Use of Contemporary History in Europe since 1989* (Manchester: Manchester University Press, 2007), 12–26.
40. The beginning of this section is based on discussions during an interdisciplinary national seminar titled 'The scholar in his or her study' in Turku in November 2004. See my comment 26.
41. Haskell, 'Objectivity is not neutrality', 147.
42. Haskell's intriguing discussion on the connection between causal reasoning and ethical judgement, or causal attribution and moral responsibility, can be seen as criticism of of the narrowness of the conventional understanding of scholarly ethics; see Haskell, *Objectivity Is Not Neutrality*, 11–24 and Part 3.
43. Fulbrook, *Historical Theory*, 196. Her examples include the tendency 'towards repeated exemplification of particular traditions or innovative proclamation of 'new approaches' ', or 'towards explicit partisanship'.
44. See also the way of dealing with moral judgements, discussed on p. xx.
45. Tosh, *The Pursuit of History*, 207.

Chapter 5: Cultural Critics

1. Iggers and Wang, *A Global History*, 4–5.
2. Quotations from the dust jacket of Stretton's book. The influence of Carr, Mills and Stretton (together with the works the Finnish historian Pentti

Renvall and the Finnish sociologist Antti Eskola) dominate my *Historian tutkimusprosessi* from 1972.

3. Tosh, *Historians on History*, 14. See also MacMillan, *The Uses and Abuses of History*.
4. Quotation from Thelen, 'A Participatory Historical Culture', 191.
5. Fulbrook, *Historical Theory*, 196; see also 188.
6. Tosh, *The Pursuit of History 2006*, pp. xii–xiv.
7. Drawing attention to activities relevant to the discipline of history, but too rarely discussed in undergraduate courses, is what in Ludmilla Jordanova's opinion makes 'public history' (in the singular) a 'useful phrase'. In a way, it is the very ambiguity of the term that is the important point in her presentation. Jordanova, *History in Practice*, 141–71.
8. The history of 'public history' and the controversies involved have been introduced by, e.g., Ashton and Kean, *People and Their Pasts*, 9–14.
9. My main source for this discussion has been the internet. In addition to the home pages of several universities offering training in public history, there are those of the National Council on Public History, The Public Historian and the Public History Research Center (all in the United States), as well as Public History Review in Australia.
10. Pat Thane: 'History and Policy', *History Workshop Journal* 67 (2009) (1): 140–45.
11. See the various editorial statements on the website, <http://www.history andpolicy.org>.
12. Frisch, *A Shared Authority*, p. xxi.
13. Australian *Public History Review*, No. 1 (1992), quoted in Ashton and Kean, *People and Their Pasts*, 12–13.
14. Rosenzweig and Thelen, *Introduction: Scenes from a Survey*.
15. For more on the early phases, see Samuel (ed.), *History Workshop*; quotations from his 'Editorial Introduction', 1. See also, e.g., the website of Ruskin College (www.ruskin.ac.uk) and Ashton and Kean, *People and Their Pasts*, 'Introduction'. This book, the collection of papers presented at a conference of the same name in 2006, illustrates the basic idea of the Ruskin programme.
16. A typical recent Finnish example is Anu-Hanna Anttila, Kirsi Mäki ja Ritva Laitinen, *Kesämaja appelsiinilaatikoista. Kivinokka Stadin kupeessa.*(Helsinki: Kivinokkalaiset ry, 2011); two of the editors are professionals representing sociology and history while the third editor and most of the writers are non-scholars. See also above p. 121 and Elina Makkonen, *Muistitiedon etnografiaa tuottamassa*.
17. Iggers and Wang, *A Global History*, 16.
18. For Zizek, see Slavoj Zizek and Glyn Daly, *Conversations with Zizek* (Cambridge: Polity Press, 2004), 40–3. The characteristic I have in mind has actually been clarified by E. H. Carr when he discusses the historian 'in flux', and shows 'how closely the work of the historian mirrors

the society in which he works'. Carr, *What is History?*, 29–38, quotation at 36.

19. The farewell lecture has been published in a slightly edited form as Jorma Kalela, '*Jatkomenoinen uudistaminen*'. Politiikka historiassa ja historiantutkimuksessa' in *Historiallinen Aikakauskirja*, 3/2005, 282–297.

20. I agree with the starting point (but not with all the conclusions) of Keith Jenkins, *On 'What is History?' From Carr and Elton to Rorty and White* (London and New York: Routledge, 1995).

21. A sign of the present times is that the spatial dimension of historical enquiry has recently provoked interest in Scandinavian historical research. See the theme number of the Finnish *Historiallinen Aikakauskirja* 1/2010.

22. Haskell, *Objectivity is not Neutrality*, 1–3.

23. An intriguing novel perspective on fairness is opened up by the American history professor Jane Kamensky's reflections on writing the novel *Blindspot* with another history professor Jill Leporte; Kamensky, *Novelties*.

24. The first quotation is from the dust jacket of Lowenthal's *The Past is a Foreign Country* (Cambridge et al.: Cambridge University Press, 1985) and the others from Megill, *Historical Knowledge, Historical Error*, 213.

25. Megill, *Historical Knowledge, Historical Error*, p. xii; he writes about 'speculation in a self-aware manner', rather than circumstantial evidence. Detailed discussion of this issue in Megill's book (Part III, ch. 6) has been authored by Megill together with Steven Shepard and Phillip Honenberg.

26. Carr, *What is History?*, 22–3.

27. *The Content of the Form: Narrative Discourse and Historical Representation* (Baltimore, MD and London: Johns Hopkins University Press, 1987).

28. Iggers and Wang, *A Global History*, 16.

29. My hope is that Haskell, *Objectivity is not Neutrality* and Megill, *Historical Knowledge, Historical Error* will eventually lead the profession to the necessary discussion.

30. Mortimer, 'The Art of History'; see also his interview in the same issue of *Historically Speaking* (June 2010).

31. In recent years White has revised his original position (see, e.g., his 'Afterword: manifesto time' in K. Jenkins, S. Morgan and A. Munslow (eds.), *Manifestos for History* (London and New York:Routledge, 2007), but it was the ideas of *Metahistory* which figured in the crucial debates during the following two decades after its publication in 1974.

32. Jouni-Matti Kuukkanen, 'Narrativistinen ja jälki-narrativistinen historiografian filosofia', in J. Pulkkinen ja K. Väyrynen (toim.), *Historian filosofia ja teoria*. Helsinki: Gaudeamus, 2012.

33. See the end of section '*The draft of the message*' in Chapter 4. For Conrad, Olof Lagercrantz, *Om konsten att läsa och skriva* (Stockholm: Wahlström & Widstrand, 1997), 9. See also Haskell, *Objectivity is Not Neutrality*, 134.

34. For more on this, see the introduction to Chapter 3; for Hexter see p. 52.

35. Edmondson, *The Rhetoric of Sociology*, 150. See also the quote by Edmondson, on p. 74.

36. Edmondson, *The Rhetoric of Sociology,* 17–19.
37. For quotations, Mortimer, 'The Art of History', 15, 15, 14, 13; see also p. 96.
38. For Fulbrook, see *Historical Theory,* 162.

Chapter 6: The Impact of Historical Research

1. Quotations from the statement of an anonymous, established Finnish professor of history in an investigation by the Academy of Finland concerning the impact of historical research: *Sivistystä ei voi tuoda* (Suomen Akatemian julkaisuja 5/2006), 18–19.
2. Quotation from the back cover of her book.
3. Kimmo Katajala, 'Historiantutkimus, politiikka, vaikuttavuus ja eettiset ratkaisut', *Historiallinen Aikakauskirja* 2/2009, 228–32.
4. According to Tosh, *The Pursuit of History,* 45.
5. Quotations from the back cover of Howard Zinn, *The Politics of History,* 2nd edition with a new introduction (Urbana, IL and Chicago: University of Illinois Press, 1990 [1970]).
6. David Arnold supports this view in his review of C.A. Bayly, *The Birth of the Modern World 1780–1914. Global Connections and Comparisons* (Malden, MA et al.: Blackwell Publishing, 2004), *The Times Literary Supplement,* 20 February 2004. According to Linda Colley, professional historians have become increasingly impatient and suspicious of 'linear and unalloyed master narratives (of) national history' which 'rarely withstand detached scrutiny'. Colley's review of Boyd Hilton, *A Mad, Bad & Dangerous People? England 1783–1846* (Oxford: Clarendon Press, 2006) and James Belich, *The Settler Revolution and the Rise of Engloworld, 1980–1939,* (Oxford: Oxford University Press) *London Review of Books,* 22 July 2010.
7. Pauli Kettunen, 'The Nordic Model and Consensual Competitiveness in Finland', in A.-M. Castren, M. Lonkila and M. Peltonen (eds.), *Between Sociology and History: Essays on Microhistory, Collective Action, and Nation-Building* (Helsinki: Suomalaisen Kirjallisuuden Seura, 2004); Jorma Kalela, *Denial of Politics as Government Policy.*
8. The quotation is from Simon Head's 'The Grim Threat to British Universities', *New York Review of Books,* 13 January 2011, which appeared when this section had already been written. Head's (from the Rothermere American Institute at Oxford) analysis of the 'business school background' of the educational policies discussed in this section, with the vision of 'a 'quality control' exercise imposed on academics by politicians', points to an irreversible, and frightening, trend.
9. For comments on an earlier version of this section, I am grateful especially to Peter Mandler, and for discussions around impact, to Hilda Kean and Pat Thane – in addition to numerous Finnish colleagues. See also *Times Higher Education Supplement,* 29 April 2010 dealing with impact.
10. The outline and discussion of the *AHRC Impact Strategy* that follows is based on the AHRC website, where the *Impact Strategy* may be located: <http://www.ahrc.ac.uk/pages/default.aspx>, accessed 20 May 2010.

11. Substantiating this claim is the point of my recent article ('Historiantutkimus vaikuttavuusyhteiskunnassa') in the journal of Finnish historians: *Historiallinen Aikakauskirja* (2/2010, 232–7) It was Ross McKibbin, ('Good for Business', *London Review of Books*, 25 February 2010) who drew my attention to the similarities between Britain and Scandinavia.

12. *AHRC Impact Strategy*, 3; my italics.

13. *AHRC Impact Strategy*, 1.

14. *AHRC Impact Strategy*, 2, 3.

15. *AHRC Impact Strategy*, 2, 5.

16. The old name was the Research Assessment Exercise (RAE).

17. HEFCE, *Research Excellence Framework: Second Consultation on the Assessment and Funding of Research* (September 2009), 5, 4 (notes 1 and 2).

18. *AHRC Impact Strategy*, 5, 4.

19. An additional consequence has been highlighted by Gordon S. Wood in his review article in *New York Review of Books*, 9 December 2010; Chapter 4, note 38 above, albeit without reference to the policies criticized here: writing simultaneously for both their 'fellow academicians and educated general readers' is 'normally no longer possible'.

20. 'Impact society' is a translation of the title of Marketta Rajavaara's doctoral thesis: *Vaikuttavuusyhteiskunta: Sosiaalisten olojen arvostelusta vaikutusten todentamiseen* (Helsinki: Sosiaali-ja terveysturvan tutkimuksia 84, Kelan tutkimusosasto, 2007).

21. Thelen, 'A Participatory Historical Culture', 203.

22. Ashton and Kean, *People and their Pasts*, 12–13, view this situation from a somewhat different perspective.

23. Rosenzweig and Thelen, *Introduction: Scenes from a Survey*, 12–13.

24. Carr, *What is History?*, 38.

25. Cf. Thelen, 'A Participatory Historical Culture', 202–7; quotation at 204.

26. Alistair Thomson, 'Four Paradigm Revolutions in Oral History', *Oral History Review*, Vol. 34, No. 1 (200).

27. Rosenzweig, 'Everyone a Historian', 188–9; Thelen, 'A Participatory Historical Culture', 207. For the scholar's position in the context of rhetoric, see section 5.6 (*Composing the final account*).

28. Opera is also a field where laypeople produce cultural artefacts in collaboration with professionals: the world premier of *Opera by You: Free Will* will take place at Savonlinna Opera Festival in Finland on 21 July 2012. The basic idea is conveyed by the invitation to public. 'In Opera by You, you have the opportunity to take part in the conception of this first opera ever created by an online community. You have at your disposal opera singers, a full 80 member opera choir, a symphony orchestra and a live audience of 5000. The actual opera plot, music and visualization are up to you.' The project can be followed at http://www.operafestival.fi/In_English (accessed 22 August 2011).

Select Bibliography

Abrams, Lynn, *Oral History Theory*. London and New York: Routledge, 2010.

Abrams, Philip, *Historical Sociology*. Ithaca, NY: Cornell University Press, 1982.

Adam, Barbara, *Time and Social Theory*. Cambridge: Polity Press, 1990.

Anderson, Benedict, *Imagined Communities: Reflections on the Origin and Spread of Nationalism*. London: Verso, 1983.

Anttonen, Pertti J., *Tradition through Modernity: Postmodernism and the Nation-State in Folklore Scholarship*. Helsinki: Finnish Literature Society, 2005.

Appleby, Joyce, Hunt, Lynn and Jacob, Margaret, *Telling the Truth about History*. New York and London: W.W. Norton & Company, 1994.

Ankersmit, F. R., *The Reality Effect in the Writing of History: The Dynamics of Historiographical Topology*. Amsterdam: Elsevier, 1989.

Aronson, Peter, *Historiebruk – att använda det förflutna*. Lund: Studentlitteratur, 2004.

Ashton, Paul and Kean, Hilda (eds.), *People and their Pasts: Public History Today*. Basingstoke: Palgrave Macmillan, 2009.

Barraclough, Geoffrey, *An Introduction to Contemporary History*. Harmondsworth: Penguin Books, 1974 (C. A. Watts, 1964.)

Bayly, C. A., *The Birth of the Modern World 1780 – 1914: Global connections Connections and Comparisons*. Oxford and Carlton: Blackwell, 2004.

Bedarida, Francois (ed.), *The Social Responsibility of the Historian: Diogenes*. Oxford and Providence: Berghahn Books, 1994.

Berger, Peter L. and Luckman, Thomas, *The Social Construction of Reality: A Ttreatise in the Sociology of Knowledge*. London: Penguin Books, 1991 (1966).

Black, Jeremy, *Using History*. London: Hodder Arnold, 2005.

Bloch, Marc, *The Historian's Craft*. Manchester: Manchester University Press, 1967 (1954).

Braembussche, Antoon Van den, ' "The Silence of Belgium: Taboo and Trauma in Belgian Memory" ', in *Yale French Studies*, No. 102 (2002).

Bull, Edvard, *Retten til en fortid: Sosialhistoriske artikler*. Oslo: Universitetsforlaget, 1981.

Burke, Peter, *History & and Social Theory*. Cambridge: Polity Press, 1992.

Burke, Peter (ed.), *New Perspectives on Historical Writing*. Cambridge: Polity Press, 1991.

Carr, David, *Time, Narrative and History*. Bloomington, IN: Indiana University Press, 1986.

Carr, E. H., *What is History?* Basingstoke and London: Macmillan, 1986 (1961).

Collingwood, R. G., *The Idea of History*. Glasgow: Oxford University Press, 1961.

Dahl, Ottar, *Grunntrekk I historieforskningens metodlaere*. Oslo: Universitetsforlaget, 1967.

De Certeau, Michel, *The Writing of History*. New York: Columbia University Press, 1988 (Paris: Editions Gallimard, 1975).

Edmondson, Ricca, *The Rhetoric of Sociology*. London: Macmillan, 1984.

Elton, G. R., *The Practice of History*. London: Fontana Press, 1989 (Sydney: Sydney University Press, 1967).

Evans, Richard J., *In Defence of History*. London: Granta Books, 1997.

Finley, M. I., *The Use and Abuse of History: From the Myths of the Greeks to Lévi-Strauss, The Past Alive and the Present Illumined*. London: Penguin Books, 1990 (London: Chatto and Windus, 1972).

Finnegan, Ruth (ed.), *Participating in the Knowledge Society: Researchers Beyond the University Walls*. Basingstoke: Palgrave Macmillan, 2005.

Fisher, David Hackett, *Historians' Fallacies: Toward a Logic of Historical Thought*. New York and Evanston: Harper Torchbooks, 1970.

Frisch, Michael, *A Shared Authority: Essays on the Craft and Meaning of Oral and Public History*. Albany, NY: State University of New York Press, 1990.

Fulbrook, Mary, *Historical Theory*. London and New York: Routledge, 2002.

Geyl, Pieter, *Debates with Historians*. London: Collins, 1955.

Ginzburg, Carlo, *Checking the Evidence: The Judge and the Historian*. Chicago: The University of Chicago Press, 1991.

Ginzburg, Carlo, *Clues, Myths, and the Historical Method*. Baltimore, MD: Johns Hopkins University Press, 1992.

Goodman, Nelson, *Ways of Worldmaking*. Indianapolis, IN: Hackett, 1978.

Grele, Ronald J., *Envelopes of Sound: The Art of Oral History*, 2nd edn. New York: Praeger, 1991 (1985).

Grele, Ronald J., ' "Reflections on The Practice of Oral History: Retrieving what we can from an Earlier Critique" ', in *Suomen Antropologi – Journal of the Finnish Anthropological Society, Special Issue: Memory and Narration: Oral History Research in the Northern European Context*, Vol. 32, No. 4 (Winter 2007).

Hamilton, Paula and Shopes, Linda (eds.), *Oral History and Public Memories*. Philadelphia, PA: Temple University Press, 2008.

Haskell, Thomas L., *Objectivity Is Not Neutrality: Explanatory Schemes in History*. Baltimore, MD and London: Johns Hopkins University Press, 1998.

Hodgkin, Katherine and Radstone, Susannah (eds.), *Memory, History, Nation: Contested Memories. Studies in Memory and Narrative*. New Brunswick, NJ: Transaction Publishers, 2006.

Hodne, Bjarne, Kjeldstadli, Knut and Rosander, Göran (eds.), *Muntlige Kilder: Om bruk av interrvjuer i etnologi, folkeminnevitenskap og histories*. Oslo, Bergen and Tromso: Universitetsforlaget, 1981.

Iggers, George G. and Wang, Q. Edward (with contributions from Supriya Mukherjee), *A Global History of Modern Historiography*. Harlow: Pearson Education Limited, 2008.

James, Daniel, *Dona Maria's Story: Life History, Memory, and Political Identity*. Durham, NC and Longon: Duke University Press, 2000.

Jenkins, Keith, *Rethinking History*. London and New York: Routledge, 1991.

Jenkins, Keith, *On 'What is History': From Carr and Elton to Rorty and White*. London and New York: Routledge, 1995.

Jenkins, Keith, Morgan, Sue and Munslow, Alun (eds.), *Manifestos for History*. London and New York: Routledge, 2007.

Johnson, Richard, McLennan, Gregor, Schwarz, Bill and Sutton, David (eds.), *Making Histories: Studies in History-writing and Politics*. London et al.: Hutchinson, 1982.

Johnson, Richard, with Dawson, Graham (for '"Popular Memory Group"'), '"Popular memory: theory, politics, method."', in Johnson & et al., *Making Histories*, 1982.

Jones, Harriet, Ostberg, Kjell and Randeraad, Nico (eds.), *History on Trial: The Public Use of Contemporary History in Europe since 1989*. Manchester: Manchester University Press, 2007.

Jordanova, Ludmilla, *History in Practice*. London: Arnold, 2000.

Kalela, Jorma, *Historiantutkimus ja historia*. Helsinki: Gaudeamus/Hanki ja jää; 2000.

Kalela, Jorma, *Historian tutkimusprosessi: Metodinen opas oman ajan historia tutkiville*. Helsinki: Gaudeamus; Helsinki, 1972.

Kalela, Jorma, *Näkökulmia tulevaisuuteen: Paperiliiton historia 1944–1986*. Helsinki: Paperiliitto, 1986.

Kalela, Jorma, '"The Challenge of Oral History – The Need to Rethink Source Criticism"', in Ollila, Anne, 1999.

Kalela, Jorma, *Historiantutkimus ja historia*. Helsinki: Gaudeamus / Hanki ja jää, 2000.

Kean, Hilda, *London Stories: Personal Lives, Public Histories*. London, Sydney and Chicago: Rivers Oram Press, 2004.

Kettunen, Pauli, *Globalisaatio ja kansallinen me: Kansallisen katseen historiallinen kritiikki*. Tampere: Vastapaino, 2008.

Koselleck, Reinhart, *Futures Past: On the Semantics of Historical Time*. Cambridge, MA: MIT Press, 1985.

La Capra, Dominick, *Rethinking Intellectual History. Texts, Contexts, Language*. Ithaca, NY and London: Cornell University Press, 1983.

Lowenthal, David, *The Heritage Crusade and the Spoils of History*. Cambridge: Cambridge University Press, 1998 (1997).

Lowenthal, David, *The Past is a Foreign Country*. Cambridge: Cambridge University Press, 1985.

McDonald, J. (ed.), *The Historic Turn in the Human Sciences*. Ann Arbor: The University of Michigan Press, 1996.

MacMillan, Margaret, *The Uses and Abuses of History*. London: Profile Books, 2009.

Mali, Joseph, *Mythistory: The Making of a Modern Historiography*. Chicago and London: The University of Chicago Press, 2003.

Mandler, Peter, *History and National Life*. London: Profile Books, 2002.

Marwick, Arthur, *The Nature of History*, 3rd edn. Basingstoke: Macmillan, 1993 (1989).

Megill, Allan, *Historical Knowledge, Historical Error: A Contemporary Guide to Practice*. Chicago and London: The University of Chicago Press, 2007.

Mills, C. Wright, *The Sociological Imagination*. Harmondsworth: Penguin Books, 1970 (Oxford: Oxford University Press, 1959).

Munslow, Alun, *The Future of History*. Basingstoke: Palgrave Macmillan, 2010.

Novick, Peter, *That Noble Dream: The ' "Objectivity Question" ' and the American Historical Profession*. Cambridge, MA: Cambridge University Press, 1988.

Ollila, Anne (ed.), *Historical Perspectives on Memory*. Helsinki: SHS, 1999.

Perks, Robert and Thomson, Alistair (eds.), *The Oral History Reader*. London: Routledge, 1998.

Portelli, Alessandro, *The Battle of Valle Giulia: Oral History and the Art of Dialogue*. Madison: The University of Wisconsin Press, 1997.

Potter, Jonathan, *Representing Reality: Discourse, Rhetoric and Social Construction*. London: Sage Publications, 2000 (1996).

Ricoeur, Paul, *Memory, History, Forgetting*. Chicago and London: University of Chicago Press, 2006 (2004).

Ricoeur, Paul, *The Rule of Metaphor: Multidisciplinary Studies of the Creation of Meaning in Language*. London: Routledge and Kegan Paul, 1986 (Paris: Editions du Seuil, 1975).

Ricoeur, Paul, *Time and Narrative*, Vol. 3. Chicago and London: The University of Chicago Press, 1988 (Paris: Editions du Seuil, 1985).

Rosenzweig, Roy, ' "Everyone a Historian" ', in Rosenzweig and and Thelen, *The Presence of the Past* (1998).

Rosenzweig, Roy and Thelen, David, *The Presence of the Past: Popular Uses of History in American Life*. New York: Columbia University Press, 1998.

Samuel, Raphael, *Theatres of Memory*, Vol. 1: *Past and Present in Contemporary Culture*. London and New York: Verso, 1994.

Samuel, Raphael, *Theatres of Memory*, Vol. 2: *Island Stories: Unravelling Britain*, ed. Alison Light, Sally Alexander and Gareth Stedman Jones. London and New York: Verso, 1998.

Samuel, Raphael (ed.), *People's History and Socialist Theory*. History Workshop Series. London, Boston, MA and Henley: Routledge and Kegan Paul, 1981.

Samuel, Raphael (ed.), *History Workshop: A Collectanea 1967–1991*, History Workshop 25 (1991).

Samuel, Raphael and Thompson, Paul (eds.), *The Myths We Live By*. London and New York: Routledge, 1990.

Sen, Amartya, *Identity and and Violence: The Illusion of Destiny*. London: Penguin Books, 2007.

Sillén, Gunnar, *Stiga vi mot ljuset: Om dokumentation av industri- och arbetarminnen*. Stockholm: Raben and Sjögren, 1977.

Skinner, Quentin, *The Return of Grand Theory in the Human Sciences*. Cambridge: Cambridge University Press, 1990 (1985).

Steedman, Carolyn, *Dust*. Manchester: Manchester University Press, 2001.

Stretton, Hugh, *The Political Sciences: General Principles of Selection in Social Science and History*. London: Routledge and Kegan Paul, 1969.

Thane, Pat, 'History and Policy', *History Workshop Journal*, Vol. 67, No. 1 (2009) 67 (1).

Thelen, David, 'A Participatory Historical Culture', in Rosenzweig and Thelen, *The Presence of the Past* (1998).

Thompson, Paul, *The Voice of the Past: Oral History*. Oxford and New York: Oxford University Press, 1988 (1978).

Torstendahl, Rolf, *Introduktion till historieforskningen: Historia om vetenskap*. Stockholm: Natur och kultur, 1966.

Tosh, John, *Historians on History*. An Anthology Edited and Introduced by John Tosh. Edinburgh: Pearson Education, 2000.

Tosh, John, *The Pursuit of History: Aims, Methods and New Directions in the Study of History*. 4th edn. Harlow: Pearson, 2006.

Tosh, John, 'In Defence of Applied History: the History and Policy Website', *History & Policy*, *Policy Papers 37* <http://www.historyandpolicy.org>.

Tosh, John, *Why History Matters*. Basingstoke: Palgrave Macmillan, 2008.

Toulmin, Stephen, *The Uses of Argument*. Cambridge: Cambridge University Press, 1990 (1958).

Wertsch, James V., *Voices of Collective Remembering*. Cambridge: Cambridge University Press, 2002.

White, Hayden, *Metahistory: The Historical Imagination in Nineteenth-Century Europe*. Baltimore, MD and London: Johns Hopkins University Press, 1973.

White, Hayden, *The Content of the Form: Narrative Discourse and Historical Representation*. Baltimore, MD and London: Johns Hopkins University Press, 1987.

Wood, Gordon S., *The Purpose of the Past: Reflections on the Uses of History*. New York: Penguin Books, 2008.

Zinn, Howard, *The Politics of History* (2nd edn with a new introd). Urbana, IL and Chicago: University of Illinois Press, 1990 (1970).

Index of Topics

Idea / rationale of a historical study

'it wasn't like that' / alternative interpretation, 21, 25, 39, 41, 43, 49, 74, 82, 84, 85, 93, 109, 111, 128, 134–5, 136

give fresh insights & provoke rethinking, 16–20, 38, 45, 61, 113–14, 125, 130, 136, 144

making sense of the past, 32, 43, 44, 53, 86, 104–5, 134–5, 136, 148–9

message / the point of the undertaking, 20–2, 36–7, 49, 50–1, 84, 107, 111–12, 133, 142

dialogue with the audience, 74, 80, 135–6, 145

dialogue between the audience and the people studied, 18–19, 37, 80, 136, 143, 144

'why history', x–xii, 20, 72–3, 115, 146, 152, 159

Everyday history

concept and relevance of, 3, 16, 28, 67, 74, 124, 129

everyday accounts and their genres, x–xi, 1, 2, 25–6, 28, 30, 62, 67, 146, 160–1, 163

history-in-society, xi–xiii, 1, 7, 10, 13, 18, 25, 43, 50, 113, 117, 146, 150, 160–1

popular histories, 2–4, 18, 20, 21, 67, 88

public histories, 2–4, 19, 20, 21, 67, 88

scholarly histories, 3–4, 20, 28, 67, 88

shared histories, 9, 12–13, 27, 42, 74, 107, 117, 129, 143, 162–3

social process of history-making, 1, 12, 15, 18, 19, 28, 39, 67, 74, 116

heritage, 8–9, 60, 77, 118, 120

Historian / historical profession

basic predicament of, 23, 29, 44–5, 47, 49, 73, 107, 115, 132, 133–4, 137–8, 147

acting as a referee, 19, 32, 33, 67, 82, 103, 116, 118, 147

context of a study, 3–4, 7, 28, 33, 74

involvement in society, 4–5, 18, 39, 91, 106, 107, 122–3, 125, 154, 159

limits of intervention, 33, 90, 103–5, 105–6, 116, 125, 126, 159

social and cultural role of, 10–11, 13, 16–7, 18–20, 21–3, 25, 72, 103, 104–5, 116, 126, 127–8

self-awareness, x–xi, 2, 8–9, 16–17, 18–20, 22–3, 32, 46, 57, 72, 85, 93, 107, 114, 121, 154

ethics and morals, 24, 44, 83, 104–5, 107–9, 112, 118, 125, 127

upholding everyday history-making as a basic social practice, 18–20, 21, 57, 60, 70, 75, 80, 81, 100–1, 101, 121, 125, 145, 146, 149

Paradigmatic change of the discipline

concept and relevance of, 4–5, 6, 115, 116, 117, 118, 122, 126, 135, 146

traditional schism, 13–5, 25, 47, 106, 121–2, 148, 151

disruption within the discipline, 5–6, 60, 64–5, 152, 153

Index of Writers